英美概况

A Guide to the UK and the US

（第2版）

顾问 王九萍
主编 王燕萍 邹甜甜
编者（按拼音顺序排列）
陈韵 刘一鸣 龙湛 潘薇

西安交通大学出版社
XI'AN JIAOTONG UNIVERSITY PRESS

图书在版编目（CIP）数据

英美概况 / 王燕萍，邹甜甜主编. --2版. --西安：西安交通大学出版社，2025.1. -- ISBN 978-7-5693-1816-6

Ⅰ. H319.39

中国国家版本馆CIP数据核字第202418Y5D6号

英美概况
Yingmei Gaikuang

顾　　问	王九萍
主　　编	王燕萍　邹甜甜
编　　者	陈　韵　刘一鸣　龙　湛　潘　薇（按拼音顺序排列）
责任编辑	牛瑞鑫
数字编辑	宋庆庆
责任校对	许方怿
装帧设计	伍　胜

出版发行	西安交通大学出版社 （西安市兴庆南路1号　邮政编码710048）
网　　址	http://www.xjtupress.com
电　　话	（029）82668357　82667874（市场营销中心) （029）82668315（总编办）
传　　真	（029）82668280
印　　刷	陕西思维印务有限公司
开　　本	889mm×1194mm　1/16　印张　14　字数　436千字
版次印次	2025年1月第1版　2025年1月第1次印刷
书　　号	ISBN 978-7-5693-1816-6
定　　价	58.00元

如发现印装质量问题，请与本社市场营销中心联系。

订购热线：（029）82665248　（029）82667874

投稿热线：（029）82665371

版权所有　侵权必究

前言
Preface

进入新时代以来，我国高等教育改革稳步推进，服务国家战略和区域经济社会的能力不断增强。依据教育部发布的《普通高等学校本科外国语言文学类专业教学指南》及《高等学校课程思政建设指导纲要》，外语类专业和外语类课程应将培养学生的"家国情怀、国际视野"作为核心目标。

本书为已出版教材《英美概况》（书号为978-7-5605-3049-9）的第二版，面向英语专业及非英语专业的本科生和研究生，以培养学生的家国情怀、国际视野和跨文化交流能力为核心目标。本教材主要介绍英国和美国这两个主要英语国家的地理、历史、政治、经济、教育、文学等，同时融入了课程思政的创新元素。全书语言流畅、结构合理、知识性强，能帮助学生了解英美国家的社会文化背景，克服文化障碍，更有效地向这些国家的人们讲好中国故事，提升中国的国际话语权和国际传播能力，实现知识传授、能力培养和价值引领的有机结合。

本教材具有如下特色。

一、更新了信息，选用最新素材和统计数据，信息时效性较强。

二、参考资料权威，提供信息准确。编者参考了众多国内外出版的权威教材及相关部门的官方网站，对大量信息进行筛选，保证教材内容准确、客观、详实。

三、优化章节架构，体系编排合理。每章围绕一个主题，自成一体，又紧密联系。

四、全英文编写，语言准确地道、难易适中。对于较难词汇和专有名词，教材给出了注释；同时为一些文化信息提供脚注，便于学生了解相关背景知识，加深理解。

五、练习丰富，题型多样。每章提供四种形式的练习，能启发学生积极思考，激发学生的学习兴趣。

六、课程思政落地。本教材在编写中融入思政元素，每个单元的课后练习中，都有编者精心设计的融入思政元素的讨论题，能更好地引导学生，提升其思辨能力，帮助学生树立道路自信、理论自信、文化自信和制度自信。

本教材由西安电子科技大学王燕萍和邹甜甜担任主编，来自西安电子科技大学和西安外国语大学的多位骨干教师，承担了本书的编写工作。本教材编写团队拥有十余年"英美概况"及"英美文化"课程教学经验，团队成员深入分析课程内容及课程目标，为广大读者呈现了更为全面、更有深度的教材内容。

西安外国语大学王九萍为本教材的编写提供了指导，西安交通大学出版社对本教材的编辑出版给予了大力支持，西安电子科技大学林淳和袁璐为部分章节收集了资料，在此一并感谢。另外，本书在编写过程中借鉴了一些图书和网络资料，特此致谢！

教材慕课资源上线中国高校外语慕课平台，可供免费学习。课程链接为 https://umoocs.unipus.cn/course/4664（最后四位数字会因开课学期不同而变化，但本链接会跳转至最新课程）；或在 https://umoocs.unipus.cn/ 网址上搜索"英美概况"，开课单位为西安电子科技大学。

本教材可作为英语专业本科生、非英语专业本科生及研究生"英美文化"和"英美概况"课程的教材，也可供其他英语学习者自主学习使用。书中如有不当或纰漏之处，敬请读者批评指正。

编者

2024 年 10 月

目 录
Contents

Part I　The United Kingdom of Great Britain and Northern Ireland 1

　　Chapter 1　Geography, People and Language 3

　　Chapter 2　 History 21

　　Chapter 3　Government 43

　　Chapter 4　Economy 57

　　Chapter 5　Education, Media and Holidays 73

　　Chapter 6　Literature 91

Part II　The United States of America 111

　　Chapter 7　Geography and People 113

　　Chapter 8　History 131

　　Chapter 9　Government 147

　　Chapter 10　Economy 163

　　Chapter 11　Education, Media and Holidays 179

　　Chapter 12　Literature 195

References 213

Part I

The United Kingdom of Great Britain and Northern Ireland

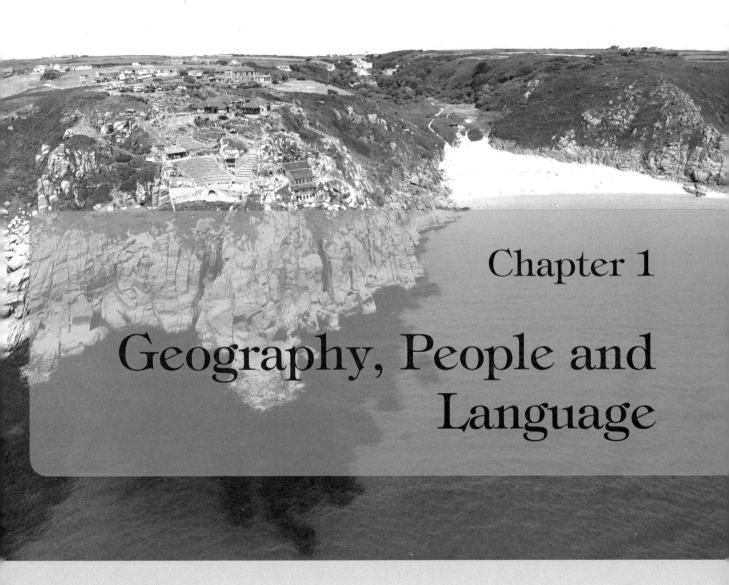

Chapter 1
Geography, People and Language

英美概况
A Guide to the UK and the US

1. Where is the UK located?
2. What are the four parts that make up the UK?
3. What do you know about major geographical features of the UK?
4. What do you know about the major cities of the UK?

Geography

1   Geographical Components and Location

The United Kingdom of Great Britain and Northern Ireland, commonly known as the UK, constitutes the greater part of the British Isles, a group of islands lying off the northwest coast of mainland Europe. Among these the largest islands are Great Britain (comprising the mainland of England, Wales and Scotland) and Ireland (comprising Northern Ireland and the Republic of Ireland). England is the largest and most populous division of the island of Great Britain, making up the south and east. Wales is on the west and Scotland is on the north. Northern Ireland is located in the northeastern corner of the island of Ireland, the second largest island in the British Isles. The capital of the United Kingdom is the city of London, situated near the southeastern tip of England.

People often confuse the names for this country, and frequently make mistakes in using them. The United Kingdom, UK and Britain are all proper terms for the entire nation, although the term Britain is also often used when talking about the island of Great Britain. The use of the term Great Britain to refer to the entire nation is now outdated; the term Great Britain, properly used, refers only to the island of Great Britain, which does not include Northern Ireland. The term England should never be used to describe Britain because England is only one part of the island. It is always correct to call people from England, Scotland, or Wales British, although people from England may also properly be called English, people from Scotland Scottish, and people from Wales Welsh.

Chapter 1   Geography, People and Language

The UK is surrounded by the Atlantic Ocean, the North Sea, the English Channel, and the Irish Sea. To the east, it faces countries such as Belgium, the Netherlands, Germany, Denmark, and Norway across the North Sea. To the west, it neighbors Ireland across the Irish Sea, with the United States and Canada across the vast expanse of the Atlantic Ocean. To the north, it extends to Iceland across the Atlantic Ocean. To the south, it is only 35 km from France and linked by tunnel under the English Channel. Covering an area of approximately 242,500 square kilometers, the UK is home to a population of over 68.3 million people as of 2023.

2 Geographical Features

Climate

The UK has a maritime climate, which is influenced by the surrounding seas and oceans. The weather in the UK is known for being mild and temperate, with relatively small temperature variations throughout the year. However, the weather can be quite changeable and unpredictable, with rapid shifts from sunshine to rain and back again.

One of the defining characteristics of the UK's climate is its abundance of rainfall, with the west generally being wetter than the east. This is due to the prevailing westerly winds that bring moist air from the Atlantic Ocean, causing it to release rain as it rises over the western regions.

The UK experiences four distinct seasons. Spring typically begins in March and lasts through May, with moderate temperatures and blooming flowers. While summer in most parts of the world means hot and dry, the UK experiences quite a temperate season with average temperatures ranging from 15°C to 27°C. Autumn typically has the most weather variability of all the seasons. September and October can still be quite warm, but November is typically quite cold and is among the wettest months of the year. Winter is the coldest season in the UK, with temperatures often dropping to freezing.

The UK is also prone to weather phenomena such as fog, mist, and drizzle, particularly in the autumn and winter months. Coastal areas can experience sea mists, while inland regions may see valley fog during calm, clear nights. These weather conditions can affect visibility and travel, so it is important for residents and visitors to stay informed about local weather forecasts.

Natural Regions and Topography

The UK is traditionally divided into a highland zone and a lowland zone. A line from the mouth of the River Exe in the southwest to that of the River Tees in the northeast roughly divides these two areas.

(1) The Highland Zone

The highlands were formed over a long time. However, they are not very high compared to mountains in

Europe. The tallest mountain, Ben Nevis, is just 1,343 meters high.

In Scotland, there are two main parts: the northern Highlands and the southern Uplands. They are divided by a lower area called the Midland Valley. This area is also known as the Central Lowlands. The Southern Uplands have less dramatic hills compared to the Highlands. They have wide, flat areas with many valleys. The Midland Valley has a steep edge where it meets the Highlands, but the border with the Southern Uplands is not very clear near the coast.

Figure 1.1 Scottish Highlands

In Northern Ireland, there are mountains that look like the Scottish Highlands, with the Sperrin Mountains being the tallest at 678 meters and covered in peat. The middle of Northern Ireland has a big flat area made by lava, and it has a large lake called Lough Neagh, which is the biggest lake with fresh water in the British Isles.

The peninsula of Wales is almost entirely covered by mountains. The Cambrian Mountains go from northeast to southeast, with high, rocky tops and open land. The highest mountain in Wales, Snowdon, is here, and it's 1,085 meters high. In the south, there are smaller mountains called the Brecon Beacons, extending in a roughly east-west direction.

(2) The Lowland Zone

Britain's lowlands are very different from the rough highlands. They cover a large part of southern and eastern England, some parts of Wales, and the Midlands. These areas have flat and gentle land, good soil, and rich cultural history. They are mostly flat with not too much rain and more sunshine. Most of this area is low, below 150 meters, and the hills are not very high, usually under 300 meters. People have lived, farmed, and raised animals here for a very long time. Most people in Britain live in these lowlands, and big cities like London are located here.

The lowland zone has very flat areas, especially in the east, like a big hump called East Anglia. There is a place called the Wash near the north coast of East Anglia. It used to be surrounded by flat, wetlands, but now most of it is dry. South of a line of hills called the Pennines is a wide area called the Midland Plain. To the west of the Pennines is another flat area, the Lancashire-Cheshire plain.

Rivers, Lakes and Coastlines

Since Britain has a moist climate with much rainfall, rivers and lakes are numerous. Rivers in central and eastern Britain tend to flow slowly and steadily all year long because they are fed by frequent rain. Many rivers have been navigable, and from the earliest times they have served people interested in either commerce or invasion. The Highlands act as a divide and determine whether rivers flow west to the Irish Sea or east to the North Sea. Rivers and streams moving westward down from the Highlands tend to be swift and turbulent; rivers flowing eastward tend to be long, graceful, and gentle, with slowly moving waters.

The Thames and the Severn are the longest rivers in Britain and are almost equal in length. The Severn flows south out of the mountains of central Wales to the Bristol Channel at Bristol. It is 354km long. The Thames, 338km long, flows eastward out of the Cotswold Hills and weaves through the metropolis of London. The Thames provides water to the city of London and is used to carry commercial freight.

Most of the large lakes in the UK are located in the upland areas of Scotland and northern England, but the largest lake, Lough Neagh, lies in Northern Ireland. Loch Lomond, on the southwestern edge of the Highlands of Scotland, is the largest lake in Scotland; and Lake Windermere is the largest of the 15 major lakes in the famous Lake District of northwestern England.

The UK's coastline is rich and varied, spanning over 7,700 miles. The coastlines of Scotland, England, Wales, and Northern Ireland all have their own unique characteristics. The eastern coast of England is characterized by long stretches of sandy beaches, coastal marshes, and iconic landmarks such as the White Cliffs of Dover. Moving north, the North Sea coast is marked by low-lying areas and mudflats, providing important habitats for wildlife. The western coastlines of England, Wales, Scotland, and Northern Ireland offer a stark contrast, featuring rugged cliffs, rocky headlands, and picturesque coves. The dramatic landscapes of the Jurassic Coast in Dorset, the remote beauty of the Scottish Highlands, and the wild charm of the Giant's Causeway in Northern Ireland showcase the diverse geological history and coastal formations of the UK.

Natural Resources

(1) Coal

Britain has large deposits of coal, mined for more than 300 years. For most of the 19th and 20th centuries, coal was Britain's richest natural resource, meeting most of the nation's requirements for energy. In 1970, the UK was the third largest producer of coal but coal production has declined rapidly since then. In 2000, only 35 million tons of coal was produced compared to 145 million in 1970. South Wales, northern England, and Scotland were once important centers of the UK's coal mining industry and made significant contributions to the country's industrial revolution. Over time, and with increasing demand for clean energy sources, the scale of the UK's coal mining industry has significantly decreased. The coal-producing regions in the UK underwent a significant economic transformation over the past few decades, with a key aspect being the shift towards service industries and technology sectors. However, these areas still retain rich coal mining heritage sites.

(2) Oil and Natural Gas

The UK's oil and gas resources, primarily located in the North Sea region, have been experiencing significant decline in recent years. According to the 2023 UK Oil & Gas Report, the country's proven and probable reserves have decreased substantially—oil reserves fell from 507 million tons in 2018 to 313 million tons in 2022, representing a compound annual decline rate of 11.4%. Similarly, gas reserves dropped from 279 billion cubic meters to 195 billion cubic meters over the same period, showing a 9.3% annual decline rate. The declining investment by offshore firms and growing focus on sustainability may lead to an even more dramatic 80% drop in the North Sea region's proven and probable oil reserves by 2030. The UK's domestic production only covered 63% of national demand in 2022, with the remaining 37% being met through imports, primarily from Norway and the USA.

(3) Wind Power

In addition to traditional oil and gas reserves, the UK is also exploring new opportunities for energy production, such as wind power. From 2009 to 2020, electricity generation from wind power in the UK increased by 715%, with turnover from wind energy reaching nearly £6 billion in 2019. The UK has the largest offshore wind farm in the world, located off the coast of Yorkshire. In 2020, the UK generated 75,610 gigawatt hours (GWh) of electricity from both offshore and onshore wind. Wind energy generation accounted for 24% of total electricity generation, with offshore wind accounting for 13% and onshore wind accounting for 11%.

(4) Minerals

The UK's metallic mineral resources are relatively scarce, with only a small amount of minerals such as iron, tin, lead, gold, and silver. The iron ore deposits in the UK are mainly sedimentary and are mainly distributed in the Northamptonshire and Fladbury areas north of Lincoln, characterized by their low iron content. Tin mines in the UK are mainly located on the Cornwall Peninsula in the southwest of the country. The Cornwall tin mining area is the world's oldest and most famous tin mining area, with mining activities dating back to 1000 BCE. Gold resources are not abundant, mainly distributed in Northern Ireland and Wales.

The UK has abundant non-metallic mineral resources, mainly including potash, gypsum, fluorspar, kaolin, sand, and gravel. Potash resources are mainly distributed in the Cheshire Basin and Cleveland County. Kaolin resources rank second globally, primarily found in Cornwall and Devon counties on the southwest Cornwall Peninsula. Gypsum deposits are mainly located in Leicestershire in central England; fluorspar is primarily found in Northern Ireland. The UK has relatively rich fluorite mineral resources, concentrated in two major fluorite-producing areas in the northern and southern parts of the Pennine Mountains.

Major Cities

(1) London

London, the capital city of the UK, is a vibrant and multicultural metropolis that blends history, modernity, and diversity. With a rich heritage stretching back over two millennia, London has evolved into a global hub of finance, commerce, culture, and innovation. London covers an area of approximately 1,572 square kilometers and has a population of around 9 million people, making it one of the most populous cities in Europe.

One of the most iconic landmarks in London is the majestic Big Ben, a clock tower situated at the north end of the Palace of Westminster. It is a symbol of the city and often represents the essence of British architecture and tradition. Nearby stands the magnificent Westminster Abbey, a UNESCO World Heritage site, where coronations, weddings, and burials of British monarchs take place. The River Thames runs through the heart of London, dividing the city into North and South. Along its banks are famous attractions such as the Tower of London, a historic

Figure 1.2　Big Ben and the Palace of Westminster

castle that has served as a royal palace, prison, and treasury. The Tower Bridge, an impressive victorian bridge with iconic towers, offers breathtaking views of the city.

Figure 1.3　The Tower Bridge on the Thames

London is also renowned for its world-class museums and art galleries. The British Museum houses a vast collection of artifacts from around the world. The National Gallery showcases masterpieces by renowned artists like Van Gogh, Monet, and Da Vinci.

London's cultural diversity is reflected in its neighborhoods. Chinatown, located in the heart of the city's West End, with its vibrant atmosphere and authentic Chinese cuisine, offers a taste of the East. Brick Lane in East London is known for its vibrant street art scene and multicultural atmosphere. Notting Hill, famous for its colorful houses and the annual Notting Hill Carnival, celebrates Caribbean culture.

Transportation within London is convenient, with an extensive network of buses, underground trains (known as the Tube), and taxis. The Tube network covers a vast area of Greater London, providing essential links to key destinations such as Heathrow Airport, Wembley Stadium, and the West End. The Jubilee Line, for instance, connects the bustling financial district of Canary Wharf with major attractions like the London Eye and the Westfield shopping center. Meanwhile, the Piccadilly Line provides direct access to Heathrow Airport, making it a crucial link for international travelers. In addition to the Underground, London's public transportation network includes the famous red double-decker buses, which offer a picturesque and convenient way to explore the city. Furthermore, the London Overground and Docklands Light Railway (DLR) complement the tube network, extending connectivity to various neighborhoods and areas not covered by traditional underground lines.

London is a global center for international finance. The city's financial district, known as the City of London or simply the "Square Mile," is a bustling hub where major financial institutions converge. It houses the headquarters of banks such as Barclays, HSBC, and Standard Chartered, as well as insurance companies like Lloyd's of London.

(2) Edinburgh

Edinburgh, the capital city of Scotland, is located in southeastern Scotland with its center near the southern shore of the Firth of Forth, an arm of the North Sea that thrusts westward into the Scottish Lowlands.

Edinburgh Castle, one of the most iconic features of Edinburgh, dominates the city's skyline and offers panoramic views of the city from this ancient fortress. The Royal Mile, a historic street that stretches from the castle to the Palace of Holyrood house, serves as the main thoroughfare connecting the Old Town and the New Town. The Old Town of Edinburgh is a UNESCO World Heritage Site, characterized by narrow winding streets, hidden alleyways, and medieval architecture. In contrast, the New Town, also a UNESCO World Heritage Site, showcases elegant Georgian architecture and wide, tree-lined streets.

Beyond its architectural splendor, Edinburgh is a hub of cultural activity. The city hosts numerous festivals throughout the year, including the renowned Edinburgh Festival Fringe, the largest arts festival in the world. Edinburgh is also home to several world-class museums and galleries, such as the National Museum of Scotland, the Scottish National Gallery, and the Royal Yacht Britannia.

Figure 1.4　Edinburgh Castle

Edinburgh's economy is diverse and thriving, with a mix of traditional industries and cutting-edge technology companies. The city is home to major financial institutions like Royal Bank of Scotland (RBS) and Standard Life Aberdeen, as well as a growing number of fintech firms.

(3) Birmingham

Birmingham is the second largest city in the UK and a metropolitan borough in the West Midlands metropolitan county. It lies near the geographic center of England, at the crossing points of the national railway and motorway systems. Birmingham is the largest city of the West Midlands conurbation—one of England's principal industrial and commercial areas—for which it acts as an administrative, recreational, and cultural center. The city lies approximately 177 km northwest of London.

Birmingham is the cultural center for a wide area. The Birmingham Repertory Theatre, opened in 1913, has acquired national renown. The Birmingham Hippodrome plays host to original theatrical productions and serves as the home for the Birmingham Royal Ballet Company. The Midlands Arts Centre for Young People, built in the 1960s, houses theaters, a concert hall, an art gallery, and workshops and studios. The Birmingham and Midland Institute also has educational and artistic facilities. The city's symphony orchestra—based at the International Convention Center's Symphony Hall—has toured the globe. Birmingham's Central Public Library is one of the largest municipal libraries in the country.

Birmingham remains the chief center of Britain's light and medium industry and is still sometimes described as "the city of 1,001 different trades." The key to its economic success was the diversity of its industrial base, though it has been principally concerned with the metal and engineering trades. The largest single

industry in terms of employment is the production of motor vehicles. The major manufacturers include the British multinational automotive company Jaguar Land Rover, the British luxury sports car manufacturer Aston Martin, and MG Motor UK which specializes in producing stylish and high-performance affordable cars. The city is also one of the main centers of the machine-tool industry. Since the 1970s, however, the city's service sector has grown to rival the manufacturing sector. Another significant driver of Birmingham's economy is the events and conferences sector. The city hosts a wide range of national and international events, conferences, and exhibitions every year. Venues such as the NEC (National Exhibition Centre) and ICC (International Convention Centre) attract business travelers and delegates, bringing in revenue for the city's hospitality and service industries.

(4) Manchester

Manchester is a vibrant and diverse city located in the northwest of England. One of the defining features of Manchester is its industrial past. During the Industrial Revolution, Manchester was a key player in the textile industry, earning it the nickname "Cottonopolis." The city's cotton mills and warehouses were once at the heart of the world's textile trade, shaping the urban landscape and economy of the region.

Today, Manchester is a thriving hub of culture and arts. The city is home to a range of museums, galleries, and theaters, including the iconic Manchester Art Gallery and the Museum of Science and Industry. The vibrant music scene in Manchester has also produced legendary bands such as Oasis, The Smiths, and Joy Division, solidifying the city's reputation as a cultural hotbed.

Manchester is also known for its lively sports scene. The city is home to two major football clubs, Manchester United and Manchester City, both of which have passionate fan bases and storied histories. Football matches at Old Trafford and the Etihad Stadium are not just sporting events but cultural experiences that bring the city together.

Manchester is also a center for education and innovation. The city is home to several universities, including the prestigious University of Manchester and Manchester Metropolitan University, attracting students and researchers from around the world. Manchester's reputation as a tech and creative hub continues to grow, with MediaCityUK serving as a focal point for digital and media companies. Manchester has a long-standing tradition of advanced manufacturing in the aerospace, automotive, and materials science sectors. British Aerospace (BAE) Systems focuses on advanced engineering and manufacturing, playing a crucial role in the development of military and commercial aircraft components and systems. Siemens, on the other hand, has its operations in Manchester primarily focused on industrial automation, digitalization, and energy management solutions, contributing to advancements in manufacturing technology.

People

1 Population

The current population of the UK is estimated to be 68.3 million. Over the 10 years between 2011 and 2021, the population of England increased by 6.5% to an estimated 56,536,000, the highest rate of the four countries of the UK; the estimated population of Northern Ireland increased by 5.0% to 1,905,000, Scotland by 3.4% to 5,480,000, and Wales by 1.4% to an estimated 3,105,000.

In the UK, both rural and urban areas have seen an increase in overall population between 2011 and 2019. The rural population increased by 5.2% and urban by 6.2%. In 2019, 56.3 million people lived in urban areas (82.9% of England's population) and 9.6 million in rural areas (17.1%).

Change in population size at the UK level has four components: births, deaths, immigration, and emigration. The difference between the number of live births and deaths is referred to as "natural change." When natural change is positive, there are more births than deaths in the timeframe. When it is negative, there are more deaths than births. In 2020, the UK experienced a natural change of negative 8,069, with 681,560 live births and 689,629 deaths. This is the first time the population has decreased through natural change since 1976 and the second time since data has been collected. The number of births in 2020 is the lowest since 2002. The difference between the number of long-term immigrants (people moving into the UK for at least 12 months) and the number of long-term emigrants (people moving out of the UK for more than 12 months) is termed "net migration." Natural change has previously been the main driver of UK population growth. However, since the 1990s, the influence of net migration has increased, becoming the main source of growth. Long-term international migration from the year ending December 2020 shows that migrants continued to add to the UK population. From the modeled estimates, an estimated 33,000 more people moved to the UK than left in the year ending December 2020.

2 Ethnic Composition

Britain has a diverse population that includes people with connections to every continent of the world. The ethnic origins of this population have been complicated by immigration, intermarriage, and the constant relocation of people in this highly developed industrial and technological society. Nevertheless, a few particulars about the historical formation of the population are noteworthy.

Early Ethnic Groups

Britain's predominant historical stock is called Anglo-Saxon. Germanic peoples from Europe—the Angles, the Saxons, and the Jutes—arrived in Britain in massive numbers between the 5th and 7th centuries AD. These people tended to be tall, blond, and blue-eyed. Their language became the foundation of the basic, short, everyday words in modern English. These groups invaded and overwhelmed Roman Britain, choosing to settle on the plains of England because of the mild climate and good soils. Native Britons fought the great flood of Germanic peoples, and many Britons who survived fled west to the hill country. These refugees and native Britons were Celts who had absorbed the earliest peoples on the island, the prehistoric people known as Iberians. Celts tended to be shorter than Anglo-Saxons and had rounder heads. Most had darker hair, but a strikingly high percentage of Celts had red hair.

After the Anglo-Saxon conquest, the Celts remained in Wales, Scotland, Ireland, and the West Country, where Celtic languages are still used to some extent and Celtic culture is still celebrated. This geographic separation between the Germanic Anglo-Saxons and the Celts has broken down over the centuries as people have migrated and intermarried. A substantial number of Scandinavians raided and settled in Great Britain and Ireland during the 9th century. By then the Anglo-Saxons had established agricultural and Christian communities, and eventually they succeeded in subduing and integrating the Scandinavians into their kingdoms. In 1066 the Normans, French-speaking invaders of Norse origin, conquered England, adding yet another ethnic component. Although the Normans were the last major group to add their stock to the British population, waves of other foreigners and refugees immigrated to Britain for religious, political, and economic reasons. Protestant French sought refuge in the 17th century, sailors of African ancestry came in the 18th century, and Jews from central and eastern Europe immigrated in the late 19th century and during the 1930s and late 1940s.

Immigration After World War II

Most British people attribute their origins to the early invaders, calling themselves English, Scottish, Irish, Welsh, or Ulsterites. The remaining share of the population consists of minorities who arrived, for the most part, in the decades following the end of World War II in 1945. These minorities—Chinese, Asian Indians, Pakistanis, Africans, and Caribbean people of African ancestry—came to Britain in substantial numbers after 1945. Immigration from the South Asian subcontinent stabilized in the 1990s, but immigration from African countries continued to rise. By the late 1990s, more than half of the people in these categories had been born in the UK. These newer ethnic groups tend to live in the more urban and industrial areas of England, especially in London, Birmingham, and Leeds. In 2004 the right to work in Britain was opened to people in central Europe and the Baltic countries, and they began to form the latest group of immigrants.

The 2021 population census for the main constituent parts of the UK—England and Wales—showed, the total population of England and Wales was 59.6 million, and 81.7% of the population was white. People from Asian ethnic groups made up the second largest percentage of the population (9.3%), followed by black (4.0%), mixed (2.9%) and other (2.1%) ethnic groups. Out of the 19 ethnic groups, white British people made up the largest percentage of the population (74.4%), followed by people in the white "other" (6.2%) and Indian (3.1%) ethnic groups.

Language

1 Old English

Old English, also termed Anglo-Saxon, is the earliest documented form of the English language, originating with the 5th-century Germanic invasions of England. The language was a diverse group of West Germanic dialects spoken by the Angles, Saxons, and Jutes, later influenced by the Old Norse of the Viking settlers. The most significant feature of Old English was its inflectional system, which indicated grammatical relationships between words through various endings. Nouns, for instance, had five different cases: nominative, accusative, genitive, dative, and instrumental. Verbs were conjugated based on tense, mood, person, and number, and there was a clear distinction between different tenses and aspects.

Old English poetry is known for its rhythmic structure, characterized by alliteration and the use of stress rather than rhyme. The most famous work from this period is *Beowulf*, an epic poem detailing the heroic deeds of the protagonist against monsters and a dragon.

The Christianization of the Anglo-Saxon kingdoms had a profound impact on Old English. As Christianity spread, the need arose to translate Latin religious texts into the vernacular, allowing the common people to understand them. This process led to a substantial adoption of Latin words into Old English, thereby enriching the language's vocabulary with a wealth of new terms related to religion, art, science, and governance.

The Old English period came to a close with the Norman Conquest of 1066, which initiated a significant shift in the language due to the influence of the Old Norman language, a dialect of Old French.

2 Middle English

Following the rich tapestry of Old English, the advent of Middle English introduced new threads into the linguistic fabric of England. The period, stretching from the late 11th to the late 15th century, was marked by the profound impact of the Norman Conquest and the subsequent influx of Old French and Latin into the English language.

The Middle English period saw an unprecedented expansion of the English lexicon. The influence of Old French was particularly evident, especially in the realms of law, governance, and the church. This led to a significant adoption of French loanwords that have since become integral to the English language, such as "justice" "government" and "religion." While Old English was characterized by a complex system of inflections, Middle English simplified this structure. The reduction in noun and adjective endings meant that word order became more rigid, and prepositions were used more frequently to indicate relationships between words.

The Middle English period is perhaps most famous for the works of Geoffrey Chaucer, particularly *The Canterbury Tales*. This work is a collection of stories told by a group of pilgrims on a journey, showcasing a variety of dialects and offering a rich insight into the social and cultural landscape of the time.

The Middle English period gradually gave way to the Early Modern English period with the onset of the Great Vowel Shift, which altered the pronunciation of long vowels. This phonetic change, along with the invention of the printing press by **Johannes Gutenberg**[1], solidified the transition.

3 Modern English

The emergence of Modern English in the late 17th century marked a new chapter in the language evolution, characterized by significant standardization and expansion. This period saw English solidifying as the language of science, literature, and international communication.

The standardization of English grammar and spelling advanced during this period with the publication of influential grammar books and dictionaries. The first comprehensive English dictionary, compiled by Samuel Johnson in 1755, played a crucial role in defining the language. Additionally, the scientific revolution brought about a surge in technical vocabulary, as new discoveries and inventions necessitated precise terminology.

The expansion of the British Empire had a profound impact on the spread of English. As English-speaking settlers and administrators spread across the globe, so too did the language. This led to the establishment of English as a first or second language in countries like the United States, Canada, Australia, and India, further diversifying the dialects and varieties of English.

---

1 Johannes Gutenberg: a German blacksmith, goldsmith, inventor, and printer who is best known for his invention of the movable-type printing press in the mid-15th century. His invention revolutionized the way information was disseminated and had profound effects on the development of the modern English language.

Chapter 1　Geography, People and Language

In the 20th and 21st centuries, English has continued to evolve rapidly with the rise of global communication, mass media, and the Internet. This has led to a more informal and flexible language use, with the creation of new slang, jargon, and the blending of dialects and languages in contact with English. The development of English as a second language in many countries has also influenced its evolution, with non-native speakers often adapting the language to fit their own cultural and linguistic needs.

Each of these periods above has left an indelible mark on the English language, shaping it into the diverse and dynamic language it is today. The historical development of English is a testament to its capacity for change and adaptation, reflecting the cultural, social, and political shifts of the societies in which it has been spoken.

Exercises

Part I. Decide whether the following statements are true (T) or false (F). Write T or F in the brackets.

1. The UK consists of the island of Great Britain and Ireland. (　　)
2. The term "Great Britain" is used to refer to the entire nation, including Northern Ireland. (　　)
3. The UK lacks extensive metallic mineral resources but possesses plentiful non-metallic mineral resources. (　　)
4. The UK has a continental climate with extreme temperature variations throughout the year. (　　)
5. The western regions of the UK tend to be drier and receive more sunshine than the eastern regions. (　　)
6. The UK is surrounded by the Pacific Ocean, the Mediterranean Sea, the English Channel, and the Irish Sea. (　　)
7. The official language of the UK is English, but Welsh, Scottish Gaelic, and Irish are also spoken in certain regions. (　　)
8. The primary reason for the adoption of Latin words into Old English was the Christianization of the Anglo-Saxon kingdoms. (　　)

Part II. Fill in the blanks with the best choice.

1. The capital of the United Kingdom is located in _____.

   A. Northern Ireland

   B. Scotland

   C. England

   D. Wales

2. One of the geographical features that contribute to the UK's maritime climate is _____.

   A. mountains and plateaus

   B. prevailing westerly winds from the Atlantic Ocean

   C. proximity to the North Sea

   D. large freshwater lakes

3. _____ is the primary source of the UK's population growth since the 1990s.

   A. Natural change

   B. Birth rate

   C. Net migration

   D. Immigration

4. The largest offshore wind farm in the world is located _____.

   A. off the coast of Wales

   B. off the coast of Northern Ireland

   C. off the coast of Scotland

   D. off the coast of Yorkshire

5. _____ became a joint official language with English in Wales in 1993.

   A. Scottish Gaelic

   B. Irish

   C. Norman

   D. Welsh

6. _____ ethnic group predominantly settled in the eastern plains of England due to the mild climate and good soils.

   A. Anglo-Saxon

   B. Celtic

   C. Scandinavian

   D. Norman

7. _____ is the most widely spoken language in Northern Ireland.

   A. English

   B. Norman

   C. Scottish Gaelic

   D. Irish

8. Which of the following is NOT a feature of Edinburgh?

   A. Edinburgh Castle is one of its most iconic features.

   B. It hosts the Edinburgh Festival Fringe.

   C. The city is known for its industrial past.

   D. The Royal Mile connects the Old Town and the New Town.

Part III. State your understanding of the following questions.

1. Over the past several decades, the UK has closed a large number of coal mines and shifted towards clean energy sources such as wind power. What lessons does this hold for economic development? Please analyze from the perspectives of environmental sustainability, innovation and technological development, and industrial diversification. Explain how China is committed to achieving economic transformation, improving environmental governance capabilities, and enhancing the quality of coal industry development in old coal industrial areas.

2. In addition to the UK, many countries around the world have numerous UNESCO World Heritage sites. With reference to relevant information, describe the efforts that China has made in protecting its heritage sites. What kinds of cooperation can countries engage in to jointly protect the heritages?

Chapter 2

History

1. Why is it said that British history has been a history of invasion?
2. How did the constitutional monarchy begin in Britain?
3. Why did the Industrial Revolution start in Britain?

Early Britain

1 Prehistoric Britain

The UK has had a long and storied history of thousands of years. At the end of the Ice Age about 8000 BCE, the rising sea level formed the English Channel and the North Sea, which separated Britain from the European continent. The archaeological evidence suggests the introduction of agriculture by Neolithic immigrants from the coasts of western Europe about 4000 BCE. The first known settlers were Iberians, who came to settle Britain around 3000 BCE. Originally from the Iberian Peninsula (nowadays Spain and Portugal), the Iberians lived in Britain during the Stone and Bronze Ages. They began the early agriculture and the use of bronze tools and weaponry. It is said that they built the mysterious and great prehistoric monument—Stonehenge, which stands on the vast Salisbury plains. After about 800 BCE, the Celts migrated from Central Europe to Britain. The word "Celt" comes from the Greek word "Keltoi," which means barbarians. It is used to collectively describe all the Celtic tribes during the Iron Age. Compared with the prior settlers, the Celts were skilled at various artistic crafts, including ironwork and pottery. The legacy of their language and culture is still prominent today.

2 Roman Britain

Despite the wide presence of Celts in Britain, the Romans had known about Britain long before they decided to invade. The first Roman invasion took place with Julius Caesar's first landing in Kent in 55 BCE. The year 55 BCE is regarded as the beginning of the recorded history of Britain. Just one year after his initial raid, in 54 BCE, Julius Caesar launched a second attack on Britain. Although these campaigns did not result in conquest, he extracted tribute from the British tribes and gained knowledge of southern Britain's natural resources and their potential value to Rome. It was not until 43 CE that Romans under Claudius I eventually mounted a successful attack against the Britons. Since then, the Romans controlled most of present-day England and Wales. By the time **Emperor Hadrian**[1] came to power in 117, the Romans no longer sought to expand their territory. Instead, they wanted to protect what they had. On the orders of Hadrian, the Roman governors of Britain began building Hadrian's Wall, which became the northern frontier.

Figure 2.1　Hadrian's Wall

In the 5th century, the Romans progressively abandoned Britain, as their Empire was falling apart and legions (古罗马军团) were needed to protect Rome. After 4 centuries of peaceful occupation, the Roman occupation of the island ended. However, the years that followed could not erase all of the empire's impact on the people and culture of the island: a superb network of roads, still in use for 1400 years; numerous forts throughout Britain, many of which became the cities and towns of today; Latin, remaining the language of education, law, and literature for over one thousand years after the end of the Roman Empire.

Figure 2.2　Julius Caesar

1　Emperor Hadrian: Emperor Hadrian was a Roman emperor from 117 to 138 CE, who was famous for his building projects, especially Hadrian's Wall in Britain.

3 Anglo-Saxon Britain

When the Roman legions left Britain, the Germanic-speaking Angles, Saxons and Jutes took over Britain, pushing back all the Celtic tribes to Wales and Cornwall. The various Anglo-Saxon tribes settled in different areas of the so-called "Angle-land," founding seven independent kingdoms known as "**Heptarchy**[1]," which included East Anglia, Essex, Kent, Mecia, Northumbria, Sussex and Wessex. With this vast invasion and settlement, the local Britons began to adopt the Anglo-Saxon way of life, gradually speaking their language and learning their customs and beliefs. Anglo-Saxons once worshipped lots of different Pagan gods, but around the 7th century many of them were converted to Christianity after the arrival of the missionary St. Augustine from Rome.

The flourishing culture developed by the Anglo-Saxons attracted the attention of the Vikings from the Scandinavian countries. In the 8th century, the Vikings launched several invasions against the Anglo-Saxon Britain, plundering and raiding towns and villages along the British coastline. In the process of resisting the Vikings, Alfred the Great, King of Wessex, defeated this Danish army in 878 and established a boundary between the Saxons and the Vikings, with the north and east part of the island under Danish control (**Danelaw**[2]). By creating an English navy, reorganizing the Anglo-Saxon militia, and building strategic forts, Alfred recaptured London from the Vikings in 886. Alfred was credited with uniting Anglo-Saxon England and laying the foundations for its future as a nation, such that he earned the title "King of the Anglo-Saxons."

Although Anglo-Saxons were not politically unified until the 9th century, their reign over England was interrupted by 26 years of Danish rule that began in 1016 with the accession of Canute, the king of Denmark and England. Soon after his death, the throne was returned to Edward the Confessor, the English King, in 1042.

In 1066, when King Edward died without an heir, a new king was chosen to rule England—King Harold II. However, Duke William of Normandy (a distant cousin of Harold) challenged Harold's succession. On September 27th, William crossed the English Channel with an army to claim the throne. On October 14th, William's army defeated the

Fig. 2.3 **William the Conqueror**

---

1 Heptarchy: Heptarchy means "rule by seven" in Greek, and it refers to the seven English kingdoms that existed during the seventh and eighth centuries.

2 Danelaw: Danelaw is the part of northern and eastern England occupied or administered by Danes from the late 9th century until after the Norman Conquest.

English army and killed Harold at the Battle of Hastings. On Christmas Day, William was crowned King of England as William I in Westminster Abbey. It is believed that the Norman Conquest of England in 1066, led by William the Conqueror, marked the establishment of feudalism in England, transforming its social, political, and cultural landscape. The Norman aristocracy replaced the Anglo-Saxon nobility, and the English language absorbed many French words, creating the foundation for modern English.

Medieval Britain

The Medieval period started in 1066 with the Norman Conquest of England. William the Conqueror of Normandy became William I and established the Norman dynasty. The first thing the Normans did was to carry out a census of the population. This document became known as the **Doomsday Book**[1], recording a land governed by feudal ties. In such a feudal society, landlords and the upper class were loyal and responsible to the king or lord in exchange for land, while farmers were demoted to the class of serfs, bound to the soil. This system of land tenure formed the basis of feudalism, which dominated Europe in the Middle Ages.

1 Reform of Henry II

William's youngest son, Henry I, managed to maintain peace and stability during his reign. But the country descended into chaos and civil war when Henry's nephew Stephen was crowned king, despite the rival claim of Henry's daughter Matilda. Order was restored by Matilda's son, Henry II, who ascended the throne in 1154 and thus began the rule of the House of Anjou in England, also known as the House of Plantagenet. Under Henry II's rule, the mighty Plantagenet Empire stretched from Scotland to the Pyrenees (比利牛斯山脉) in distant France. Henry was also regarded as "the Father of the Common Law." He institutionalized the common law by creating a unified court system applicable to the whole of England, which demonstrated the growing power of the king and resulted in revolutionary changes in the English legal system.

2 Magna Carta and the Emergence of Parliament

When Henry died in 1189, his oldest surviving son, Richard the Lionheart became King Richard I of England and Duke of Normandy. However, he had little interest in the government of the country and soon

---

1 Doomsday Book: Doomsday Book is a record of a survey of English lands and landholdings made by order of William the Conqueror about 1086.

embarked on Crusade (十字军东征). When he was killed in France, his brother John Lackland ascended the throne in 1199.

Since King John demanded more feudal taxes and army service in the wars with France, he was facing down a possible rebellion by the country's powerful barons. In order to limit the King's power and prevent arbitrary royal acts, in June 1215, the barons forced King John to sign the Magna Carta (or Great Charter) that would place him and all of England's future sovereigns within a rule of law. The Magna Carta lived on for 800 years, which provided a new framework for the relationship between the King and his subjects. It has inspired people across the centuries and is regarded as the foundation of democracy in England.

When King John died, his son Henry III was crowned in 1216, but Henry's poor leadership was resented by the English nobility. In 1258, when Henry III sought financial aid from Parliament, he was confronted by a group of barons. They drafted the Provisions of Oxford to further limit the king's power. The Provisions provided for the creation of a 15-member **Privy Council**[1] to advise the king and oversee the entire administration.

Simon de Montfort, Earl of Leicester, was the leader of the baronial rebellion against King Henry III. In 1264, he defeated Henry III in the Battle of Lewes and took control of the government, though he was still ruling in the name of the King, who was his captive. In January 1265, Montfort called a Parliament to discuss the release of Henry III. As well as the lords, he summoned knights from the shires and representatives from towns, who were known as burgesses. This was the first time that "common men" had been found in the Parliament to discuss national issues, which marked the first parliament in the modern sense.

3 Hundred Years' War

There was a bitter rivalry between England and France throughout the 14th and 15th century, and their frequent battles in this period are now known as the Hundred Years' War.

The Hundred Years' War refers to a series of connected conflicts between England and France over trade, territory, security and the throne from 1337 to 1453. The leading cause of the war was the interest of both countries to dominate Flanders, a wealthy region known to be the center of industrialization in Northern Europe through its manufacture of clothing. To add fuel to the fire was the untimely death of King Philip IV's last son that denoted the end of the direct male heir. Edward III of England, who was Philip IV's grandson by his daughter Isabella, attempted to assert his claim to the French throne. The war began when Edward III invaded Flanders in 1337, and it went exceptionally well for England in the early stages.

---

1 Privy Council: Privy Council is the group of people chosen by the British king or queen to serve as advisers.

Especially after Henry V succeeded to the throne in 1413, he claimed extensive lands in France, and his stunning victory at the Battle of Agincourt made England one of the greatest powers in Europe. However, the reign of Henry VI was marked by constant turmoil due to his political weaknesses. Therefore, the French forces regained control of French territory.

The war continued intermittently for more than 100 years with ups and downs for both sides, but it ended in victory for the French. Although England lost more of its lands in France, the war developed what became known as a special "English identity," promoted the development of the textile industry, and contributed to the decline of the feudal system in England.

4 Wars of the Roses

With the defeat in 1453, Henry VI was compelled to abandon the war in order to deal with issues in England. Two years after the ending of the Hundred Years' War with France, England was thrown into another series of civil wars, generally known as the Wars of the Roses.

The Wars of the Roses were a series of dynastic conflicts between two branches of Edward III of England's descendants, the Yorks and Lancasters. The flowery name of the wars was coined by the novelist Sir **Walter Scott**[1] (1771–1832) because of the supposed badges of the two contending houses: the white rose of York and the red rose of Lancaster.

The main causes for the outbreak were the incompetent rule and periodic insanity of the Lancastrian king Henry VI, and the ambition of Richard, Duke of York, who demanded a top role in government. Stretching on for 30 years, the Wars of the Roses ended in 1485, when Henry Tudor won the crown at Bosworth for the Lancasters. A few months later, the two Houses were united by Henry's marriage to Elizabeth of York, the daughter of Edward IV. Henry Tudor became King Henry VII, thus launching a new Tudor Dynasty that flourished until the early 17th century. To symbolize the end of the Wars of the Roses, he also adopted a new "Tudor Rose" emblem that incorporated both the white rose of the Yorks and the red rose of the Lancasters.

Fig. 2.4   **Tudor Rose**

---

1   Walter Scott: Walter Scott is a Scottish novelist and poet who is recognized as the master of the historical novel.

Tudor Britain

Henry VII succeeded in ending the Wars of the Roses and founded the highly successful Tudor house. The Tudors ruled England and Wales from 1485 to 1603, which was one of the most exciting periods in English history, featuring all sorts of political and social turmoil, intrigue in the royal court, and a variety of wars, dramas, executions, and controversies.

Henry VII was the first Tudor monarch. He used his children's marriages to make peace with France, the Netherlands, and Scotland; he strengthened the power of the monarchy by tightening royal administration and increasing revenues; he promoted English trade by making commercial treaties. Under Henry VII, England came to be more prosperous and powerful.

1 Religious Reformation

In the 16th century, the Religious Reformation spread in northern and central Europe. The greatest leaders included **Martin Luther**[1], **John Calvin**[2] and Henry VIII. Having far-reaching political, economic, and social effects, the Reformation resulted in the creation of Protestantism, one of the three major branches of Christianity.

In England, the Reformation began with Henry VIII's quest for a legitimate male heir. He pursued a divorce from his first wife Catherine of Aragon to marry Anne Boleyn. When Pope refused to grant him a marriage annulment, Henry made the decision to break with Rome. In 1534, Henry established the Anglican Church with the king as the supreme head. In spite of the political implications, it initiated the reformation of English religion. Over the next 20 years, there was religious turbulence in England as Queen Mary I restored Roman Catholicism in England while persecuting and executing

Fig. 2.5 Henry VIII

---

1 Martin Luther: Martin Luther was a German priest, monk, and theologian who became the central figure of the Protestant Reformation.

2 John Calvin: John Calvin was a French Reformer, pastor, and theologian considered among the greatest of the Protestant Reformation along with Martin Luther.

Protestants, only to have Queen Elizabeth I and her Parliament adopt a relatively moderate approach to religion, casting the Church of England as a "middle way" between the extremes of Roman Catholicism and Puritanism.

2 Elizabeth Age

Elizabeth succeeded her elder half-sister Mary I of England in 1558. Her 44-year reign was filled with so many momentous events that the second half of the 16th century is now known as the Elizabethan Era and still regarded as a "Golden Age" for England.

Elizabeth I, who inherited intelligence, determination and shrewdness from her parents, was passionately devoted to her country. Besides her establishment of a moderately Protestant Church of England and the great victory over the Spanish Armada, she ruled England and made the country grow in confidence and national pride, witnessed flowering of the English Renaissance, and saw the exploration and colonization of the New World.

Elizabeth I presided over England's rise to glory abroad and to prosperity and literary achievement at home. During this period, England developed into a major world power in every respect. Elizabeth died aged 69 in 1603, and as the Virgin Queen left no heir, she was succeeded by her closest relative James VI of Scotland, who became James I of England.

Fig. 2.6   Elizabeth I

Stuart Britain

James I, who was also James VI of Scotland, succeeded Elizabeth I in 1603, thus unifying the two long-warring nations of England and Scotland for the first time. Born a Catholic but raised a Protestant, James adopted a tolerant approach to religious conformity, yet agitating both the Catholics and Protestants. His religious policies led to the Gunpowder Plot, a failed attempt by Roman Catholic priests and Puritans to blow up King James I and the Parliament on November 5, 1605. Despite threats to his reign, he maintained peace and prosperity at home and abroad.

1 Civil War

James' son, Charles I, succeeded him on the throne of England, Scotland, and Ireland in 1625. His marriage to a Catholic princess, Henrietta Maria of France, aroused mistrust among Puritans, who were more radical Protestants. He believed strongly in his divine right, which stated that his right to rule came from God rather than any earthly authority. This brought him into direct and persistent conflict with Parliament that wanted a greater role in government.

From 1629 to 1640, King Charles I ruled without Parliament, denying its involvement in passing laws and authorizing taxes. To raise money, Charles resorted to a number of unpopular measures, such as outdated taxes such as "**ship money**[1]" and various fines, which infuriated the population and nobles. This period became known as the "personal rule of Charles I" as well as "the Eleven Years' Tyranny."

Fig. 2.7 The Beheading of King Charles I

---

1 Ship money: Ship money was a nonparliamentary tax first levied by medieval monarchs on English coastal cities and counties for naval defense in time of war.

In 1640, a Scottish army defeated Charles' forces and invaded England. Short on funds, Charles was compelled to recall Parliament to help raise the necessary money for the war. In return for their help, Parliament made several demands including prohibiting the king from dissolving Parliament without the members' consent. The relations between Parliament and Charles deteriorated when Parliament had the Earl of Strafford, one of Charles I's top advisors, tried and executed in 1641.

In 1642, Charles declared war on Parliament. The country began to splinter into two rival camps: Royalists (known as Cavaliers) and Parliamentarians (known as Roundheads). The three most significant battles during the Civil War took place at Edgehill in 1642, Marston Moor in 1644 and Naseby in 1645. In the Battle of Naseby, Oliver Cromwell, who was made General of the New Model Army, played a prominent part in the defeat of the King. The Civil War ended with Parliament victories.

Tried and found guilty of treason, Charles I was beheaded in 1649. Between 1649 and 1653, the country became a republic known as the Commonwealth. Although refusing the title of king, Cromwell agreed to become Lord Protector and ruled as a "King in all but name." England was now virtually a military dictatorship.

2 Restoration and Glorious Revolution

After the Civil War, Charles II was obliged to flee to France. Oliver Cromwell ruled the Commonwealth republic as Lord Protector from 1653 to 1659. After his death, his son Richard Cromwell was not supported for long for he had little interest in politics. This paved way for the Restoration of the Monarchy. Charles II came back to England from his French exile in 1660, but he had to rule alongside a much more powerful Parliament. Known as the "Merry Monarch," Charles was less skilled in governing than in indulging in hedonistic pleasures.

Because Charles II had no legitimate heir, when he died in 1685, his brother, the openly Catholic James, became king as James II. James' support of Catholicism and close ties with France angered many nobles and drove a dangerous political wedge between the monarchy and the Parliament. In 1687, James II issued a controversial Declaration of Indulgence to improve the status of Catholics. Later the same year, he dissolved Parliament and tried to create a new Parliament that would support him unconditionally. The final straw came when James had a male heir, who would be raised Catholic. Many prominent Protestants felt it was time to take action.

In 1688, a group of Protestant nobles wrote to the Dutch leader, William of Orange, who was the grandson of Charles I and had married James II's daughter Mary, inviting him to become king of England, Scotland, and Ireland. Responding favorably to the invitation, William planned an invasion of England to overthrow James. Meanwhile, James was left isolated, deserted by his former supporters. Therefore, James fled the country into exile, and he was succeeded by his Protestant daughter Mary II and her Dutch husband, Prince William III of Orange. This change of regime became known as the Bloodless Revolution or the Glorious Revolution because it had occurred entirely peacefully.

In 1689, William and Mary, as joint-monarchs, signed the Bill of Rights, which acknowledged several constitutional principles, including the right for regular Parliaments, free elections and freedom of speech in Parliament. The Bill of Rights reduced the powers of the monarchy and increased those of Parliament. Thus, a new form of monarchy and government was created, known as a constitutional monarchy, the system which is still seen today in the United Kingdom. The Glorious Revolution was one of the most important events leading to Britain's transformation from an absolute monarchy to a constitutional monarchy.

Fig. 2.8　Glorious Revolution

Georgian Britain

The reign of Queen Anne, younger daughter of James II, saw the end of the Stuart dynasty and laid the way for the Georgian era. When Queen Anne died in 1714, she left no male heir to the throne. The crown passed to Georg Ludwig, Elector of Hanover, her nearest Protestant relative in Northern Germany, becoming George I. George I scarcely spoke English, and he spent a fifth of his reign living in Germany. The King's trust in his government allowed men like Robert Walpole, Britain's first Prime Minister, to run the country. Since then, British monarchs ruled indirectly through appointed ministers who gathered and managed supporters in Parliament. Emerging as the leading force in government, Parliament passed laws, controlled foreign policies, and approved the taxes that allowed the monarch to pay the salaries of officials, the military, and the royal family.

1 The First British Empire

Since the establishment of the first permanent English colony in North America in 1607, English explorers ventured east and west in search of raw materials, luxury goods, and trading partners.

Over the course of the 17th and 18th centuries, an increasingly powerful Britain fought with other European nations and gained major colonies in North America and further south in the West Indies, today known as the Caribbean Islands. The British government created royal monopolies—private companies to whom the monarch granted exclusive rights to trade in a particular region or field of commerce. For example, the East India Company had a monopoly to trade in the east, the Royal African Company to enter the slave trade, and the Hudson's Bay Company to exploit the fisheries of Nova Scotia and Newfoundland. The lands that these companies claimed became possessions of the crown, and investors bought shares in successful companies on the London Stock Exchange.

The years from 1775 to 1783 were a turning point in British history as Britain lost a huge part of its empire in the American War of Independence, an armed rebellion through which 13 colonies in North America sought independence. As France, Spain and Netherland joined the colonies against Britain, the colonies won the war, and gained independence, becoming the United States of America. This marked the end of what is now called the "First British Empire."

2 Industrial Revolution

The industrial Revolution marks a major turning point in the Britain history. It refers to a period of major mechanization and innovation that began in Britain during the mid-18th century and early 19th century and later spread gradually throughout Europe and other parts of the world.

The Industrial Revolution began in Britain for a number of reasons, which can be seen from an economic, political, social and technological point of view.

From the economic point of view, the availability of capital and the need to expand trade were the most relevant causes. The rapid growth of industrial capitalism in Britain increased the need for expansion of markets. As a major colonial power, Britain competed with other European states for the global resources. The British colonies in America and India provided British industry with cheap materials and a monopoly market. From these colonies, Britain acquired enormous wealth, helping to develop its industries and fuel the Industrial Revolution.

From the political point of view, the Glorious Revolution ensured the political stability in the country and paved the way for the peaceful development of Britain. Additionally, the political system of Britain supported the growth of the new economy and encouraged entrepreneurship. A straightforward legal system allowed the formation of joint-stock companies, enforced property rights, and respected patents for inventions.

From the social point of view, the availability of labor due to the agriculture revolution was an essential element for the development of the Industrial Revolution. The enclosure movement and the rise in productivity accelerated the decline of the agricultural share of the labor force and added to the urban workforce on which industrialization depended.

Finally, from the technological point of view, the rise in scientific temperament and a society more open to ideas formed a fertile ground for innovations and newer ideas. The appearance of the steam engine and other inventions was the true trigger of this process.

The Industrial Revolution began in the textile industry and was marked by a series of inventions. Starting in the mid-18th century, inventions such as the spinning jenny, the flying shuttle, the water frame and the power loom made cloth production much easier and faster, which greatly improved the textile industry.

While textile machinery was developing, progress was made in other directions. In the 1760s, James Watt, made major improvements on the inefficient Newcomen steam engine, and received a patent for his

Fig. 2.9 Industrial Revolultion

own steam engine, which was widely utilized during the Industrial Revolution.

The use of waterpower and then the steam engine to perform mechanical work in the second half of the 18th century marked the beginning of the factory system, which entailed increased division of labor and specialization of function.

There were also many new developments in transportation. In the early 1800s, the steam-powered locomotive was invented, and the first railway was completed. By 1870, Britain had about 21,700 kilometers of railroad. By that time, steam-powered boats and ships were already in wide use, carrying goods along Britain's rivers and canals to all parts of the world.

By the middle of the 19th century, the Industrial Revolution was accomplished in Britain, which brought about sweeping changes in economic and social organization. It raised productivity dramatically, causing an unprecedented population growth, the acceleration of urbanization, and the transition of Britain from an agricultural society to an industrial one. Two new social classes were created: the proletariat and the industrial bourgeoisie. All in all, as the birthplace and leading force in the Industrial Revolution, Great Britain became the largest imperial power in Europe.

Victorian Britain

The Victorian era of the UK and its overseas Empire was the period of Queen Victoria's rule from 1837 to 1901. Her reign for 63 years made her Britain's second-longest reigning monarch (surpassed only by Queen Elizabeth II). This period brought about the unprecedented power and wealth in the Great Britain. Hence, this period was also called as a "golden age" in the British history.

Aided by the Industrial Revolution and the expanding British Empire, this period was featured by enormous developments in areas such as industry, science, technology and medicine. Apart from this, things like railways, the telephone, the radio, x-rays, sewing machines etc. were invented.

As the most progressive and prosperous nation in the world, Britain ruled one-fourth of the world's population. Due to the increasing fertility rates and declining mortality rates, the Victorian era witnessed an unprecedented population boom. Also, the demand for goods like food, clothes, and housing

Fig. 2.10   Queen Victoria

increased substantially as a consequence of the increase in population from 13.9 million in 1831 to 32.5 million in 1901. As more people became able to read, Victorian literature boomed. Many of the era's novels are still hailed as masterpieces today.

The underlying belief of Victorian society was in progress—that things were better than ever before and could be made better still. This belief was the impetus for thousands of voluntary associations that worked to improve the lives of the poor both at home and abroad. It also underlay the charitable foundations created by wealthy benefactors and the public philanthropies of some of the greatest industrialists.

The Victorian era witnessed the establishment of the Second British Empire. British naval power enabled Britain to control a far-flung empire and dominate the local people, especially after the development of steam-powered warships. Therefore, the British government adopted a very aggressive foreign policy known as New Imperialism, and the geographical emphasis shifted from the west to the east, with the most important dominions located in the South Pacific, South Asia, and Africa. In Asia, The British government waged the Opium War against China in 1839 and forced the Qing government to sign the Treaty of Nanjing in 1842. In 1876, Queen Victoria was announced as Empress of India. As "Jewel in the Crown," India not only helped enhance the British economy by virtue of its natural and human resources, but also acted as a gateway for Britain to enter into trade with other countries in Asia. On the African continent, Britain became the major shareholder in the Suez Canal Company, and strengthened its control over Egypt in 1875. After the Zulu War in 1879, Britain consolidated its power over most of the colonies of South Africa. Then the **Boer War**[1] resulted in the creation of the Union of South Africa in 1910. South Africa followed Canada, Australia and New Zealand in becoming the fourth self-governing dominion of the British Empire.

By the end of the 19th century, the British Empire extended over nearly a quarter of the world's landmass. During this period, the British Empire became the foremost superpower in the world, giving rise to the claim "The sun never sets on the British Empire."

Modern Britain

After Queen Victoria died in 1901, her son, Edward VII, succeeded the throne. Since the 19th century, while Britain was still considered a major global power, the rise of other countries and changing geopolitical dynamics gradually eroded its dominance.

---

1 Boer War: Boer War was a colonial war between Britain and the Boers in South Africa from 1899 to 1902, resulting in British victory.

1 Britain in World Wars

As the Industrial Revolution emerged in other countries such as Germany and the United States, these countries gained economic strength and were eager to compete with Britain in overseas markets. They began to exert their influence on the global stage. The tension relations and colonial rivalry involved two camps—the Allies and the Central Powers. The Allies consisted of primarily the British Empire, France, and Russia, while the Central Powers were mainly Germany, Austria-Hungary, and Turkey. The conflict eventually escalated into a world war.

The spark that ignited World War I was struck in Sarajevo, where the Austrian Archduke Franz Ferdinand was assassinated by a Serbian nationalist on June 28, 1914. Austria-Hungary blamed the Serbian government for the attack and hoped to use the incident as justification for settling the issue of Serbian nationalism once and for all. Both sides pledged support from their respective allies, Germany and Russia. On July 28, World War I began when Austria-Hungary declared war on Serbia. Britain wavered until German armies marched through neutral Belgium to attack France. The tenuous peace between Europe's great powers quickly collapsed.

The destruction of the war was immense. The war inflicted significant economic and human costs on Britain, which accelerated the decline of British hegemony. Moreover, new powers, such as the United States, emerged, further undermining Britain's position as the world's leading superpower.

A decade later, the worldwide economic depression of 1929 struck Britain hard. The number of unemployed people rose to 2.5 million within a year and reached an all-time record of 3 million at the beginning of 1933. Business was slack, many factories were closed down and taxes soared. This economic instability and the rise of Nazi Party in Germany led to the start of another war in Europe.

When Hitler became Chancellor of Germany in 1933, there was already smoldering resentment among the German people toward the harsh terms imposed on their country in the Versailles Treaty which was signed at the end of World War I. Hitler began to secretly rearm Germany, a violation of the Versailles Treaty. When his autocratic power was secure within Germany, Hitler turned his eyes toward the rest of Europe. He signed a treaty with Japan and Italy against the Soviet Union, and annexed Austria and Czechoslovakia in 1938 and 1939 respectively. Reluctant to fight another war, the British government, led by **Neville Chamberlain**[1], adopted a policy of appeasement toward German expansion, trying to maintain peace in Europe largely by making concessions to Germany when conflicts arose. Ultimately, the invasion of Poland on September 1, 1939 was the final straw for the Allies, with France and Britain declaring war on Germany days later. With this, World War II officially began. The next year, Chamberlain resigned and Winston

---

1   Neville Chamberlain: Neville Chamberlain was the Conservative Prime Minister of the United Kingdom from 1937 to 1940, who tried to appease Hitler and declared war in 1939.

Churchill became Prime Minister. By 1941, a coalition led by Germany, Italy, and Japan (known as the Axis powers) faced an alliance of Britain, the Union of Soviet Socialist Republics (USSR), and the United States (known as the Allied powers). Churchill's wartime leadership was instrumental in bolstering the nation's spirit and determination to resist Nazi aggression. The Royal Air Force (RAF)'s successful defense against the German Luftwaffe during the Battle of Britain marked a turning point in World War II. After six years of fierce fighting with much bloodshed and heavy losses of wealth, fighting in Europe ended in May 1945 with the final defeat of Germany.

The war was an all-consuming experience for every Briton. The country suffered huge casualties and property losses, industry shifted entirely to a war footing, and emergency measures gave the government control over nearly every element of the economy. Even in victory, Britain was sapped of its financial and industrial reserves. It was estimated that the war wiped out more than a quarter of the wealth of the entire nation.

After World War II, it became clear that Britain could no longer afford to maintain its empire, and independence movements were increasing in Britain's colonies. In 1947, India gained its independence from centuries of British colonial rule, which was the first evidence of the fall of the empire. This event inspired other countries across Asia, the Caribbean, and Africa to push for their freedom. As more colonial territories fought for and won their independence, the British colonialism came to its end and the British Empire was dismantled.

2 Britain in Post-war Era

The post war years, by contrast with the first 45 years of the 20th century, were marked by peace and stability. At home, although Great Britain came out of World War II victorious, the country still had to recover. The Labour Party won the 1945 post-war general election in an unexpected landslide and formed their first ever majority government. British policies shifted to a welfare state to protect the health and well-being of all of its citizens. These policies included the establishment of the National Health Service (NHS), educational reform, and relief for unemployment, death, sickness, and retirement. The general consensus between the major political parties' commitment to a welfare estate didn't change until the late 1970s with the rise of Margaret Thatcher. Aiming to reduce inflation, the Thatcher Governments privatized utilities, sold off council housing, and reduced government spending on social services, education, and healthcare to build a free-market Britain, which led to a significant restructuring of the British economy. Although she was the longest-serving British prime minister during the 20th century and the first woman to hold the office, she was considered to be the most unpopular prime minister. This was due to soaring unemployment, recession, higher taxes and increasingly Eurosceptic views on the European Community. The unpopularity brought a serious challenge to Thatcher's leadership of the Conservatives, and she finally resigned in 1990. After the difficult times in the 1970s and 1980s, and the downturn in the early 1990s, the rest of the 1990s welcomed a beginning of the 16 consecutive years of economic growth. In 1997, Tony Blair led Labour to a landslide election victory. Under Blair's premiership, the British constitution underwent extensive changes, such as devolution in Wales and Scotland, **the Human Rights Act 1998**[1], House of Lords reform, etc. Besides, his government implemented several socio-economic reforms to alleviate poverty and bring down unemployment, which brought the UK into a time of continuous growth.

Internationally, Britain had to undergo a worldwide process of decolonization and its gradual adaptation to a new postcolonial and globalized world, which resulted in several economic, political and ideological crises. The Cold War added further complexities, as Britain attempted to insulate former colonies from the potential threats of the Soviet Union. In 1997, Hong Kong was officially handed back to China. Though Britain still maintained overseas territories, the handover marked the end of Britain's empire.

From the mid-twentieth century onwards, the United States and Britain have developed a "special relationship." World War II did much to strengthen that relationship, especially the military partnership between the two nations. During the Korean War from 1950 to 1953, Britain deployed 56,000 soldiers to support Republic of Korea; In the 1960s, Britain supported the US war in Vietnam. During the early 1980s, the Falklands War became a central event in Britain's foreign affairs. Argentina asserted sovereignty over the Falkland Islands, leading to a brief but intense conflict. Although the war didn't involve a great number of losses, it stood as a heavy blow to both two nations. In 1990s, the close relationship with the United States was further strengthened. After Iraqi dictator Saddam Hussein led his troops into Kuwait in 1990, Britain quickly joined a US-led UN coalition in the Persian Gulf to force Iraq to abandon Kuwait. Later in the 1990s, led by President Bill Clinton and Prime Minister Tony Blair, the US and British troops participated with other NATO nations in the intervention in the Kosovo war. The cooperation between the American and British militaries not only damaged Britain's relationship with Europe, but affected the image of the British Government as well.

3 Britain in the 21st Century

The 2001 election gave Labour its predicted landslide victory. The 9/11 attacks led to further military action in Afghanistan and then Iraq. The UK joined the US-led military invasion after both countries jointly accused Saddam Hussein of possessing "weapons of mass destruction." After a month of fighting, Saddam Hussein's regime was overthrown, but it took a further six years before Britain's combat operations came to an end. Over the fierce opposition in the country, Blair's decision to go to war dogged the rest of his political career.

---

1 The Human Rights Act 1998: The Human Rights Act 1998 is a UK law that sets out the fundamental rights and freedoms that everyone in the UK is entitled to.

In 2007, Gordon Brown replaced Tony Blair as Prime Minister and leader of the Labour Party. Brown was noted for his economic management and his support for carbon credits to fight global warming. However, Brown's tenure was troubled by economic crisis, which brought about severe and permanent impact on the size and structure of the UK economy. In the general election in 2010, the Labour Party lost its majority in the House of Commons, resulting in a hung Parliament for the first time since 1974. David Cameron came to power as the head of a Conservative–Liberal Democratic Coalition Government—Britain's first coalition government since World War II.

In 2016, David Cameron instigated a referendum of the British people as to the UK's membership of the European Union. Amid a mass refugee crisis in Europe and furious debate over migration, the UK voted to leave the European Union by 52% to 48%. Therefore, Prime Minister David Cameron resigned and was later succeeded by former home secretary, Theresa May. In 2018, although May survived a vote of no confidence in her leadership, her Withdrawal Agreement was still rejected by Parliament, and the deadline for Brexit was extended several times, which resulted in Theresa May's resignation in mid-2019. May's successor, Boris Johnson, objected to the "soft Brexit." Though he insisted that Britain would leave the EU on October 31st, 2019, with or without a deal, opposition to this plan forced him to seek yet another extension. The UK officially left the EU on January 31st, 2020.

Exercises

Part I. Decide whether the following statements are true (T) or false (F). Write T or F in the brackets.

1. The year 55 BCE, when Julius Caesar launched the first Roman invasions of Britain, is regarded as the beginning of the recorded history of Britain. (   )

2. William the Conqueror, the Duke of Normandy, defeated King Harold II at the Battle of Hastings in 1066, crowning himself King William I. (   )

3. The Glorious Revolution led to the implementation of the Magna Carta, which established Parliament's authority over the Crown. (   )

4. In 1337, the hostility between England and Spain resulted in the Hundred Years' War. (   )

5. "Bloody Mary" was best known for her persecution of Protestant Christians and her attempts to return England to Catholicism. (   )

6. The Victorian Age witnessed the English Renaissance which dated back to the beginning of the

Renaissance in Italy since the 14th century. ( )

7. James Watt improved and developed the steam engine that revolutionized transportation and industry. ( )

8. United Kingdom, Germany, and France joined the Allies in the First World War. ( )

Part II. Fill in the blanks with best answers.

1. The arrival of _____ marked the beginning of the English Language.

   A. Celts

   B. Romans

   C. Angles and Saxons

   D. French

2. The _____ marked the establishment of feudalism in England.

   A. Viking invasions

   B. Norman Conquest

   C. Wars of the Roses

   D. English Civil War

3. In 1265 _____ summoned the Great Council, which has been seen as the earliest parliament.

   A. Henry III

   B. the Pope

   C. the barons

   D. Simon de Montfort

4. After the Wars of the Roses, the House of _____ began its reign in Britain.

   A. Lancaster

   B. York

   C. Stuart

   D. Tudor

5. The English Civil War broke out in 1642 between _____.

   A. the Royalists and the Parliamentarians

   B. the nobles and the peasants

C. the Protestants and the Puritans

D. Roman Catholic Church and the Protestants

6. _____ were some of the inventions from the Industrial Revolution.

   A. Phone and television

   B. Flying shuttle and spinning jenny

   C. Electric light and computer

   D. Automobile and airplane

7. Soon after _____, Britain not only gave up its economic hegemony but also suffered a deep loss of its position of industrial leadership.

   A. Queen Victoria's reign

   B. the First World War

   C. the Second World War

   D. the Great Depression

8. _____ became the first female prime minister of the United Kingdom in 1979.

   A. Margaret Thatcher

   B. Theresa May

   C. Diana Frances Spencer

   D. Elizabeth II

Part III. State your understanding of the following questions.

1. The Magna Carta, officially granted by King John of England in 1215, stands as one of the most influential and pivotal documents in human history. What were the main content and the significance of the Magna Carta?

2. The statement "The sun never sets on the British Empire" was true for many decades. Lasting from the 16th to the 20th century, the mighty British Empire controlled vast territories in Africa, Asia, the Americas, and Australia. But why and how did it decline?

3. Since World War II, the United Kingdom and the United States have enjoyed a unique special relationship grounded in a shared commitment to a world order based on democracy, the rule of law, and free trade. Why do you think these two countries cooperated closely after World War II?

Chapter 3

Government

Preview Questions

1. Who is the head of the British government?
2. How much do you know about the British monarch? Does the monarch hold position in the British government?
3. What are the Commonwealth countries? Can you list some of the Commonwealth countries?

The United Kingdom is a constitutional monarchy—that is, the head of state is a monarch, whose power is often limited by either Parliament or constitutional law. Parliament is the supreme legislative body, consists of the House of Lords, the House of Commons, and the monarch. The British government (His Majesty's Government) is composed of the Prime Minister and a number of ministries led by senior ministers of the Cabinet. The Prime Minister is the leader of the party that wins or holds the most seats in the House of Commons. Fusion of power is a feature of parliamentary democracy. There is no separation of power between the executive and legislative branches of the British government as there is in the US government.

Constitution

The British Constitution comprises multiple documents. The written part consists of the Magna Carta, written in 1215; the Petition of Right, passed by Parliament in 1628; and the Bill of Rights in 1689; and the entire body of laws enacted by Parliament. The unwritten part includes case law (判例法), and common law (普通法), precedents established by decisions made in British courts of law; it also involves various traditions and customs and royal prerogatives. The Constitution continually evolves as new laws are passed and judicial decisions are handed down. All laws passed by Parliament are regarded as constitutional, and changes or amendments to the Constitution occur whenever new legislations override existing laws. Although the Crown gives its royal assent to legislation, this is a mere formality. There is no single body that has the sole responsibility to interpret the provisions of the Constitution, which means that different bodies, such as judges, politicians, and scholars, can all interpret the Constitution.

Chapter 3   Government

The Monarchy

The UK's monarchy is considered the oldest of all modern constitutional monarchies. The British Constitutional monarchy provides the stability and continuity of British politics since the head of the state remains the same while the ministers come and go quite often. Britain has a time-renowned history for its monarchy from Anglo-Saxon times. In 1689, the Parliament of England passed the Bill of Rights, establishing the supremacy of the Parliament. The monarchy serves as a symbol of the state.

Charles III (born on November 14th, 1948) is the king of the United Kingdom of Great Britain and Northern Ireland from September 8th, 2022. He is the eldest child of Queen Elizabeth II and Prince Philip, duke of Edinburgh. After being the longest-serving monarch-in-waiting in British history, Charles ascended the throne at age 73. He was crowned on May 6th, 2023. His complete official royal title is "His Majesty Charles the Third, by the Grace of God, of the United Kingdom of Great Britain and Northern Ireland, and of His other Realms and Territories, King, Head of the Commonwealth, Defender of the Faith," but he is usually referred to as His Majesty or King Charles.

The current heir to the throne is Charles III's eldest son, William, Prince of Wales. According to the Act of Settlement of 1701, only Protestants are eligible to succeed to the throne. A regent may be appointed to rule for the sovereign if he or she is underage or incapacitated.

As the official head of state, the monarch formally summons and dismisses Parliament and the ministers of the Cabinet. The monarch also serves as head of the judiciary, commander in chief of the armed forces, and Supreme Governor of the Church of England. In reality, the government carries out the duties associated with these functions. Upon the advice of the Prime Minister, the monarch appoints all judges, military officers, diplomats, and archbishops, as well as other church officers. The monarch also bestows honors and awards, such as knighthoods and peerages. The monarch has the sole power to declare when the country is at war and when war is over. Today, this power can only be exercised on the advice of ministers. The monarch serves as the ceremonial head of the Commonwealth countries.

The real work of the monarchy consists largely of signing papers. The monarch has the right, however, to be consulted on all aspects of national life and review all important government documents. The monarch may also meet with the Privy Council, a now largely ceremonial body made up of Cabinet members that serves in an advisory capacity to the Crown.

The King, Prince William and the other members of the royal family take part in traditional ceremonies, visit different parts of Britain and many other countries and are closely involved in the work of many charities. So, their duties are largely ceremonial, diplomatic or charitable, helping to strengthen national unity and stability.

Government

In the UK, Prime Minister, who is the Head of Government and the political leader of the United Kingdom, leads the Government with the support of the Cabinet and ministers. The Prime Minister selects the other members of the Government for appointment and dismissal by the King. The Cabinet is made up of the senior members of government. Every week during the session of Parliament, members of the Cabinet (Secretaries of State from all departments and some other ministers) meet to discuss the most important issues for the government. Ministers are chosen by the Prime Minister from the members of the House of Commons and House of Lords. They are responsible for the actions, successes and failures of their departments.

The Government of the United Kingdom contains a number of ministries, which are politically led by senior ministers. The ministers are usually members of one or other of the houses of Parliament. The Prime Minister selects the other members of the Government for appointment and dismissal by the King, but the entire Government must resign if they lose a vote of confidence (信任票) in the House of Commons. Members of the Government are, both individually and collectively, politically accountable to Parliament and the people for advice to the King and all actions carried out in his name by ministers and their Departments of State. A minister may also be supported by a number of junior ministers.

1 The Prime Minister

The Prime Minister of the United Kingdom of Great Britain and Northern Ireland is the political leader of the United Kingdom and the head of the Government. He or she is the leader of the party that holds the most seats in the House of Commons. The monarch goes through the ceremony of appointing the head of the majority party as prime minister. The Prime Minister oversees the operation of the Civil Service and government agencies, appoints members of the Cabinet, and is the principal government figure in the House of Commons. These constitutes the Prime Minister's unique position of authority.

The Prime Minister presides over the Cabinet and selects the other Cabinet members. He or she is responsible for allocating functions among ministers. The Prime Minister should conduct regular meetings with the King, informing him of the general political matters of the government. The Prime Minister's other responsibilities include recommending a number of appointments to the King. The Prime Minister is also the First Lord of the Treasury (第一财政大臣) and the Minister for the Civil Service (公务事务部长).

Sir Keir Starmer became Prime Minister on July 5th, 2024. He is a British politician and lawyer. He was elected a Member of Parliament for Holborn and St. Pancras in May 2015. Starmer was elected leader of the Labour Party in April 2020.

2 The Cabinet

The Cabinet of the United Kingdom is the committee at the center of the British political system and is the supreme decision-making body in the government.

The Cabinet is composed of the Prime Minister and about 23 Cabinet Ministers, all of whom must be members of Parliament (MPs). Members of the Cabinet are leaders of the majority party in the House of Commons. Cabinet Ministers who head a particular government department, such as the Ministry of Defense, are known as secretaries of state.

The Cabinet meets in the Cabinet Room of 10 Downing Street (the Prime Minister's official residence) on a regular basis, usually weekly on Tuesday, to discuss the most important issues of government policy, and to make decisions. Ministers are responsible collectively to Parliament for all cabinet decisions; individual ministers are responsible to Parliament for the work of their departments.

Two key doctrines of cabinet government are collective responsibility and ministerial responsibility. Collective responsibility means that the Cabinet acts unanimously even when Cabinet Ministers do not all agree upon a subject. If an important decision is unacceptable to a particular cabinet member, it is expected that he or she will resign to signify dissent. Ministerial responsibility means that ministers are responsible for the work of their departments and answer to Parliament for the activities of their departments. The policy of departmental ministers must be consistent with that of the government as a whole. The ministers bear the responsibility for any failure of their department in terms of administration or policy.

3 Local Government

Britain has a "unitary" system of government. Parliament is sovereign and decides what the responsibilities of local government are to be.

For local government in the United Kingdom, England, Northern Ireland, Scotland and Wales, each has its own system of administrative demarcation (行政区划). As of May 2024, there are 384 local authorities in the UK. 319 of these are in England, 32 in Scotland, 22 in Wales and 11 in Northern Ireland.

In England, there are five types of local authority: county councils, district councils, unitary authorities, metropolitan districts and London boroughs. County councils cover the whole of the county and provide the majority of public services in their particular area. District councils govern districts in each county. District councils may also be called borough councils or city councils if the district has borough or city status, and cover a much smaller area and provide more local services. Many large towns and cities are unitary authorities; i.e. they have only one tier of local government. Unitary authorities can be city councils, borough councils, county councils, or district councils. Metropolitan districts are unitary authorities, and they can be called metropolitan district councils, metropolitan borough councils, or metropolitan city councils. Each London borough is a unitary authority. However, the Greater London Authority (GLA) provides London-wide government and shares responsibility for certain services.

In Scotland, the local government is organized through 32 unitary authorities designated as councils which consist of councilors, elected every five years by registered voters in each of the council area.

Wales has a uniform system of 22 unitary authorities (also known as county, county councils or county borough councils; city or city and county local authorities). The councils are responsible for the provision of all local government services, including education, social work, environmental protection, and most highways. Below these there are also (in most, but not all, parts of the principal areas) elected community councils to which responsibility for specific aspects of the application of local policy may be devolved.

Northern Ireland has 11 district councils. These local councils do not carry out the same range of functions as those in the rest of the United Kingdom; for example, they have no responsibility for education, road-building or housing (although they do nominate members to the advisory Northern Ireland Housing Council).

Parliament

Parliament is separate from Government in the UK. The role of Parliament is to look at what the Government is doing; debate issues and pass new laws and set taxes.

The British Parliament is the supreme legislative body in the United Kingdom and British overseas territories. The Sovereign, King Charles III, is at its head. The Parliament consists of the King and the two houses, namely, the House of Lords and the House of Commons.

Parliament work include making laws, checking the work of the government, and debating current issues. The House of Commons is also responsible for granting money to the government through approving Bills that raise taxes. Generally, the decisions made in one House have to be approved by the other. In this way the two-chamber system acts as a check and balance for both Houses. But comparatively, the House of Commons is far more influential than the House of Lords, which in effect makes the British system unicameral (单院议会的). The powers of the House of Lords have been limited in the 20th century.

Figure 3.1　The Palace of Westminster

1　The House of Commons

The House of Commons is the lower house of the Parliament of the United Kingdom. The House of Commons is a democratically elected body, consisting of 650 members, who are known as "Members of Parliament" (MPs). Members are elected through the first-past-the-post system (票数领先入选制) by electoral districts known as constituencies. They hold their seats until Parliament is dissolved (a maximum of five years after the preceding election).

The party that wins the largest number of members in the House of Commons forms the government. MPs debate the big political issues of the day and proposals for new laws. It is one of the key working places for government ministers, like the Prime Minister and the Chancellor, and the principal figures of the main political parties.

The government is primarily responsible to the House of Commons. The Prime Minister stays in office only as long as he or she retains its support. The House of Commons holds the real power today. The House of Commons is divided in terms of political parties. The majority party forms the government and the minority parties the opposition.

The members of the House of Commons are elected every 5 years. The last election was held on July 4th, 2024, with Labour Party won and the Conservative Party lost its 14 years' rule. Each MP represents approximately 70,000 people. The presiding officer, head of the House of Commons is the Speaker (议长), who is chosen by a vote of the House. The present Speaker is Sir Lindsay Hoyle, elected since Nov. 4th, 2019. The House of Commons meets in the Palace of Westminster.

2 The House of Lords

The House of Lords is the upper house of the Parliament of the United Kingdom, the United Kingdom's national legislature. It is made up of about 789 Lords. The House of Lords is the oldest part of Parliament, evolving from the Great Council during William I period. Unlike the House of Commons, members of the House of Lords are not elected. Their positions are acquired because of their titles obtained either by themselves from the Queen Elizabeth II, or through family inheritance. Members of the House of Lords are mostly appointed by the late Queen.

The House of Lords is made up of the Lords Spiritual and Lords Temporal. Lords Spiritual refers to Archbishops of Canterbury and York and 23 other senior bishops of the Church of England. The Lords Temporal are either hereditary peers or life peers. However, the House of Lords Act 1999 removed the automatic right of hereditary peers to sit in the Upper House. Only life peerages who are appointed by the Monarch on the advice of the Prime Minister have the right to sit in the House of Lords.

They work with no salary and no personal authority over other people. They only have the right to attend debates, vote, and propose bills, and ask questions of government ministers. No bill of Parliament, except Money Bills, can become law unless the House of Lords has been consulted. It can delay a bill for up to one year, but after that it can be passed whether the Lords agree or not. It can also refuse to accept a bill once, but if it is presented to them a second time, they must pass it. In other words, The Lords acts as a revising chamber for legislation and its work complements the business of the House of Commons.

Traditionally the House of Lords did not elect its own speaker. It is presided over by a Lord Chancellor (上议院大法官). The House of Lords, like the House of Commons, meets in the Palace of Westminster.

Political Parties

Before the mid-19th century, the Whig and the Tory parties dominated the politics in the United Kingdom. By the mid-19th century the Tories had evolved into the Conservative Party, and the Whigs into the Liberal Party. These two parties controlled the political scene of the UK until the 1920s, when the Liberal Party declined in popularity and was replaced as the main left-wing party by the newly emerging Labour Party. Since then the Conservative Party and Labour Party have dominated British politics, and have alternated in government ever since.

There are many other smaller parties in the UK. According to the Electoral Commission, the number of registered political parties was 377 as of December 2023. Just to mention a few of them: the Green Party of England and

Chapter 3　Government

Wales, the Scottish Nationalists and Welsh Nationalists, Sinn Fein, the Ulster Unionist Party, and so on.

1　The Conservative Party

The Conservative Party is no longer the ruling party after the 2024 election, finishing its 14 years' rule starting from David Cameron in 2010 to Rishi Sunak in 2024. After the 2024 General Election, the Conservative Party holds 121 seats in the House of Commons. The Conservative Party has been the most successful political force in Britain and was in power for two thirds of the 20th century, led by such notable leaders as Winston Churchill and Margaret Thatcher. The Conservative Party grew out of the Tory Party, which was formed early in 1678. In 1834, the Tory Party changed its name into the present name. But its members are still called Tories. The membership of the Party consists overwhelmingly of white, middle-class homeowners. Now the Party has a membership of about 172,000 according to the data released by the UK Parliament on August 2022. It is supported by most land-owners and businessmen. This Party believes in "private enterprise" and opposes nationalization and too much government control of industries and businesses.

2　The Labour Party

The Labour Party, a center-left political party, is currently the ruling party of the UK. It has won 404 seats in 2024 General Election, thus becoming the ruling party. It was founded around 1900, and gradually replaced the Liberal Party in the early 1920s as the principal party of the Left to be one of the two major parties in Britain. Under "New Labour", the party's position has moved more towards the center.

The Labour Party surpassed the Liberal Party in general elections during the early 1920s. The Labour Party won the 1997 general election with a landslide majority of 179 seats under the leadership of Tony Blair; it was the largest Labour majority ever, and the largest swing to a political party achieved since 1945. Blair is the Labour Party's longest-serving Prime Minister; the only person to have led the Labour Party to three consecutive general election victories; and the only Labour Prime Minister to serve consecutive terms, more than one of which was at least four years long. The Party's membership peaked at 405,000 in 1997 in the aftermath of Tony Blair election. By far, The Labour Party maintains its position as the party with the largest membership (432,000) as of August, 2022.

The Labour Party's declared purpose is fairness: fair rules, fair chances and a fair say for everyone. The party is also a member of the Socialist International which is the worldwide organization of social democratic, socialist and labour parties.

3 The Scottish National Party

The Scottish National Party (or SNP) is a center-left political party in Scotland. The SNP supports and campaigns for Scotland to leave the United Kingdom and become an independent country. It is the third-largest political party by membership (reaching 104, 000 members as of August 2022) in the United Kingdom. It is the third largest by overall representation in the House of Commons, behind the Conservative Party and the Labour Party. In Scotland, it has the most seats in the Scottish Parliament and 47 out of the 59 Scottish seats in the House of Commons of the Parliament of the United Kingdom.

Combined with the National Party of Scotland and the Scottish Party, the Scottish National Party (SNP) was founded in 1934. The SNP gained power at the 2007 Scottish Parliament election, forming a minority government, before going on to win the 2011 Parliament election. Then it formed the Scottish Parliament's first majority government. It was reduced to a minority government at the 2016 election.

Currently, the SNP holds 9 seats for Westminster MPs. However, the SNP still holds the majority of the Scotland's Westminster parliamentary seats, with 47 MPs and over 400 local councilors. The party does not have any members of the House of Lords as it has always maintained a position of objecting to an unelected upper house.

4 The Liberal Democratic Party

The Liberal Democratic Party, often shortened to Lib Dems or just Liberals, is a centrist political party in the United Kingdom, formed in 1988 by a merger of the Liberal Party and the Social Democratic Party. Founded in 1859, the Liberal Party was one of the two big political parties in the United Kingdom in the 19th and early 20th century. By the end of the 1920s, the Labour Party had replaced the Liberals as the Conservative's major rival. The party went into decline. The Liberal Democrats continue to advocate the traditional Liberal Party positions supporting constitutional and electoral reform, close ties with Europe, environmental issues and individual rights and liberties. They now have a firmer commitment to the free market and support multilateral nuclear disarmament. They also support multilateral foreign policy; they opposed British participation in the War in Iraq. The membership of the Lib Dems was about 74,000 in 2022 and has gained a strong momentum of growth since the coalition government was formed. After the 2024 General Election, the Liberal Democratic Party holds 72 seats in the House of Commons.

Chapter 3　Government

Election

1　General Election

The General Election in the United Kingdom refers to the election of Members of Parliament (MPs) to the House of Commons. It must be held 5 years after the first session of the new parliament, (usually within 5 years and 1 month of the last one, as it allows for parliament to assemble and the election campaign), but are often held before that time as it is up to the parties in government when to call a general election.

The reasons for calling a general election are varied, but generally originate from the desire of governments to obtain a continuing and/or increased majority in the House of Commons for the next five years. Naturally, in such instances, the timing may be determined by the government's view of its chances of victory. But governments may be forced into a position whereby they have no option but to seek a renewal of confidence by the country in their own policies.

When an election is called earlier than expected, it is referred to as snap election (提前选举). The Fixed-term Parliaments Act makes calling a snap election the decision of the House of Commons. So, if two-thirds of members of Parliament vote in favor, a snap election could happen. The 57th Prime Minister Rishi Sunak announced a snap election to be held on July 4th, 2024. The Labour Party won the election, and Keir Starmer became the 58th Prime Minister on July 5th, 2024.

2　By-election

A parliamentary by-election occurs when a seat in the House of Commons becomes vacant during the lifetime of a Parliament. The reasons may be an MP resigns from the House of Commons, or an MP is dead. The law also allows a seat to be declared vacant due to the resignation, expulsion, elevation to the peerage, bankruptcy, lunacy or death of the sitting Member.

Judiciary

The judicial branch of the British government is rather complicated in that England, Wales, Scotland and Northern Ireland all have their own legal systems, with minor differences in law, organization and practice.

Different types of cases are dealt with in specific courts. For example, all criminal cases will start in the magistrates' court (地方法院), but the more serious criminal matters are committed to the Crown Court. Appeals from the Crown Court will go to the High Court, and potentially to the Court of Appeal or even the Supreme Court.

Civil cases will sometimes be dealt with by magistrates, but may well go to a county court (郡法院). Again, appeals will go to the High Court and then to the Court of Appeal.

In British criminal trials, the accused is presumed innocent until proven guilty. Trials are in open court and the accused is represented by a lawyer. Most cases are tried without a jury. More serious cases are tried in higher courts before a jury of 12 (15 in Scotland), which decides whether the accused is innocent or guilty.

Commonwealth Countries

Commonwealth countries (英联邦国家) are the countries who are members of the Commonwealth or the Commonwealth of Nations (英联邦), which is an association of 56 independent sovereign states with 2.5 billion people scattered over all the inhabited continents, most of which were former British colonies, or dependencies of these colonies. After 75 years of its existence, the Commonwealth is a remarkable organization which remains a major force for Change in the world today.

The 1949 London Declaration of the Commonwealth Prime Ministers recognized King George VI as Head of the Commonwealth. Following his death, the Commonwealth leaders recognized Queen Elizabeth II, and then King Charles III in that capacity. The British monarch serves as its symbolic head, and the meeting of the 56 Commonwealth heads of government takes place every two years. The Commonwealth Secretariat was created in 1965 as a central intergovernmental organization to manage the Commonwealth's work.

Exercises

Part I. Decide whether the following statements are true (T) or false (F). Write T or F in the brackets.

1. Since the Glorious Revolution in 1688, there has been no king or Queen in the UK. (   )
2. The House of Lords can delay a bill for up to 10 years. (   )

Chapter 3   Government

3. The House of Commons is far less powerful than the House of Lords. (   )
4. The Prime Minister is the political leader of the United Kingdom and the head of Government. (   )
5. The British Cabinet is composed of the Prime Minister and Cabinet Ministers. (   )
6. The local governments of the UK have wide powers to determine their own laws and levels of taxation. (   )
7. There are two major political parties and many other smaller parties in the UK. (   )
8. The General Election in the UK refers to the election of Members of Parliament to the House of Commons. (   )

Part II. Fill in the blanks with best answers.

1. The British monarchy is known as _____.

   A. constitutional monarchy

   B. congressional monarchy

   C. governmental monarchy

   D. inherited monarchy

2. Which of the following about the House of Commons is true? _____

   A. The House of Commons is the upper house of the Parliament of the United Kingdom.

   B. The House of Commons is far less powerful than the House of Lords.

   C. The House of Commons consists of 650 members, known as MPs.

   D. The Members of the House of Commons are elected every five years.

3. Which of the following about the House of Lords is NOT true? _____

   A. The House of Lords is the upper House of the Parliament of the United Kingdom.

   B. The highest court in England and Wales and Northern Ireland is a committee of the House of Lords.

   C. Members of the House of Lords are mostly appointed by the Queen.

   D. The leader of the House of Lords is called "Speaker."

4. The Cabinet is appointed by the _____.

   A. Parliament

   B. People

55

C. Prime Minister

D. King

5. Which of the following parties can most probably form a government in Britain? _____

   A. The Labour Party

   B. The Greens

   C. The Scottish National Party

   D. Sinn Fein

6. Which is NOT the responsibility of the British government? _____

   A. developing policy

   B. implementing policy

   C. debating current issues

   D. raising taxes

7. How often are general elections held in Britain? _____.

   A. Every three years

   B. Every four years

   C. Every five years

   D. It is up to the parties in government

8. Which of the following statements about the Commonwealth is Not true? _____

   A. The Commonwealth is an association of 56 independent sovereign states.

   B. The Head of the Commonwealth currently is King Charles III.

   C. Most of the Commonwealth countries are former British colonies.

   D. Most of the King's overseas visits are to Commonwealth countries.

Part III. State your understanding of the following questions.

1. What is the relationship between the Government and the Crown in the UK?

2. How powerful can the Prime Minister be in Modern Britain?

3. Compare the similarities and differences of government system between UK and China. Explain why the Chinese political system is a choice in line with China's national conditions?

Chapter 4

Economy

1. What do you know about the UK economic system?
2. How does the UK economy compare to other major economies in the world?
3. How has the UK relationship with the European Union impacted its economy over time?
4. Can you provide an example of a key pillar of the UK economy?

Overview of British Economy

The UK is the sixth largest economy in the world and the second largest economy in Europe. Private enterprises are the mainstay of the British economy, accounting for over 90% of the GDP, with the service sector contributing three-quarters of the GDP and the manufacturing sector only about one-tenth. In 2022, the UK's GDP was £2.55 trillion, with a year-on-year growth of 4.1%, inflation rate of 10.5%, and unemployment rate of 3.7%. The UK has a highly developed and diversified economy. It's one of the world's largest financial centers and home to many multinational corporations. Key sectors include finance, manufacturing, particularly aerospace and automotive, and services, especially healthcare and education.

In the UK, the economy is composed of a private sector, consisting of individuals and businesses that make autonomous decisions based on self-interest, and a public sector, where the state determines the production and distribution of certain goods and services. Any industries—and the jobs created within them—that the central government operates or owns are referred to as the public sector. It's a broad sector, spanning a wide variety of industries and impacting most aspects of public life and livelihood. As its name suggests, the public sector provides a range of public services. They are funded by taxpayers, generally operate on a non-profit basis, and are designed to support people and communities at every level of society. It aims to provide essential services and support to all citizens and uphold individual and collective wellbeing and prosperity. By contrast, the private sector is the segment of the economy under the control of individuals and organizations whose primary goal is to make a profit. Companies operating within this sector are usually free from national ownership, but they can work with the government to form private-public partnerships.

The UK's June 2016 decision to leave the European Union (EU), known as "Brexit" (short for British exit), formally took effect on January 31, 2020. Since the vote, numerous government agencies and nongovernmental organizations reckon Brexit has had a negative impact on the UK economy. Since Brexit officially became effective, there has been a pandemic (COVID-19) and energy crisis, making it difficult to have a clear idea of the exact impact Britain's leaving of the EU will have during normal times.

British Economy Before the Industrial Revolution

Both economists and historians have long recognized that the 16th century marked a significant turning point in Britain's economic history. This period was characterized by various economic revolutions and widely acknowledged as the transitional phase between the decline of the medieval world and the emergence of the modern world. England became a prominent force in commerce and industry in Europe during the latter half of the 16th century due to the combination of its demographic, agricultural, and industrial factors. The British economy before the Industrial Revolution was relatively decentralized, with production and trade centered around small-scale farming, cottage industries, and local markets. The economy was constrained by limited technology, transportation infrastructure and industrialization, which restricted economic growth and development compared to the later period of industrialization.

The population of England and Wales experienced notable growth, leading to an increase in the production of woolen goods through crop cultivation. English agriculture became more efficient and market-oriented compared to other countries on the European Continent. Between 1450 and 1640, grain yield per acre saw a minimum increase of 30%. Larger farms were better suited for commercialized farming, as the growing population drove up demand and prices. Landowners also converted portions of their land into pasture for sheep, aligning with the expanding wool trade.

England's remarkable economic growth was fueled by abundant natural resources such as iron, timber and coal, which were extracted in much larger quantities than in other European countries. The emergence of new industries in and around Birmingham led to the expansion of iron and pewter production.

However, it was the textile industry that had the most transformative impact on the English economy. Woolens, which accounted for 80% of exports, found eager buyers both domestically and abroad. As English merchants began exploring the Americas in the late 16th century, these textiles also became popular there. To lower production costs, cloth manufacturers outsourced work to the villages and farms of the countryside, where poor rural women could spin and prepare fibers for weaving in their homes. The English

textile trade was closely linked to Antwerp in the **Spanish Netherlands**[1] where workers dyed English cloth. Sir Thomas Gresham, an entrepreneur, represented England in Antwerp and greatly enhanced the country's business reputation in the region. This allowed English merchants to operate on credit, a notable achievement in the 16th century.

Three major developments occurred in the financial industry in the 17th century in London. The first was the emergence of equity financing for international trade joint-stock companies. The first joint-stock company, the Muscovy Company, was established in 1551; and in 1599, the East India Company (EIC) was chartered and became the largest among these companies. The second development was the rise of goldsmith-banking. Prior to the Civil War, goldsmith-bankers primarily provided credit to wealthy individuals. During the **Interregnum**[2], these bankers began accepting deposits and lending them to the government. After the Restoration, the scope of goldsmith-bankers' activities significantly expanded as the Crown's demand for credit increased, and they served as intermediaries between individuals and the Crown. The third development was the growth of a secondary market for financial assets. A secondary market for warrants developed during the Interregnum. After the Restoration, a secondary market for shares in joint-stock companies also emerged. In the late 1670s, a secondary market for defaulted royal debts also came into existence.

During this period, Britain established colonies in North America, the Caribbean, and India. These colonies provided valuable resources such as tobacco, sugar, cotton, and spices, which fueled the growth of industries in Britain. The transatlantic slave trade also played a significant role in supplying cheap labor for plantations and industries.

British Economy in the Industrial Revolution

The Industrial Revolution in the UK occurred primarily during the late 18th and early 19th centuries, starting around the mid-1700s and continuing into the mid-1800s.

The 18th-century economy of Britain was characterized by a shift towards a more commercial and

---

1 The city of Antwerp in the Netherlands was under the rule of the Spanish Habsburg dynasty from approximately 1482 to 1585. At that time, Antwerp was one of the most important commercial and financial centers in Europe, especially for the textile trade.

2 The term "Interregnum" in the context of 16th century UK typically refers to a period of transition or discontinuity in governance. It refers to the period between the execution of Charles I in 1649 and the restoration of the monarchy in 1660. This was a time when England was a republic, officially named the Commonwealth of England, and was led by Oliver Cromwell as Lord Protector.

industrialized society, driven by agricultural improvements, overseas trade, financial innovation, and the early stages of industrialization. During this period, Britain was transitioning from an agrarian society to a more commercial and industrialized economy. Agriculture remained a crucial sector of the economy in the 18th century, employing a significant portion of the population. The Agricultural Revolution, which began in the previous century, continued to bring innovations such as crop rotation, selective breeding, and improved agricultural techniques. These advancements led to increased agricultural productivity, allowing for surplus food production and population growth. Trade and commerce flourished in the 18th century in Britain, driven by the expansion of overseas trade routes and the growth of the British Empire. The EIC layed a pivotal role in facilitating trade with Asia, particularly in commodities such as tea, spices, and textiles. The development of the triangular trade route facilitated the exchange of goods between Britain, Africa, and the Americas, with commodities such as sugar, tobacco, and slaves being traded. The rise of the mercantilist economic system in Britain during this period emphasized the accumulation of wealth through exports and the acquisition of colonies. Raw materials from colonies, such as cotton from India and coal from Australia, powered the factories of Manchester and Birmingham. The profits from colonial trade and exploitation financed innovations in technology, infrastructure, and manufacturing, propelling Britain to become the world's leading industrial power. The Navigation Acts were passed to protect British shipping and trade interests, ensuring that goods transported to and from the colonies were carried on British ships. This policy helped to strengthen Britain's naval power and dominance in global trade. The financial sector also saw significant growth and innovation in the 18th-century in Britain. The Bank of England, founded in 1694, played a central role in providing financial stability and facilitating government borrowing. The establishment of stock exchanges in London further promoted investment and the trading of securities, laying the groundwork for modern financial markets. Industrialization began to take root in the 18th century in Britain, with the early stages of mechanization and factory production emerging in sectors such as textiles and mining. Inventions like the spinning jenny and the steam engine paved the way for the Industrial Revolution that would transform the economy in the following century.

Fig. 4.1   Industrial Revolution

The 19th century saw the full flowering of the Industrial Revolution in Britain, with the introduction of new technologies and manufacturing processes leading to unprecedented levels of productivity. The textile industry, which had been the driving force behind the early stages of industrialization, continued to expand rapidly, with innovations such as the power loom and the spinning mule allowing for even greater production of cotton goods. The railway system also played a pivotal role in transforming the economy, revolutionizing transportation and facilitating the movement of goods and people across the country. Railways allowed for faster and cheaper transport of goods than ever before, making it easier to move raw materials and finished products between cities and regions. The growth of new towns and cities led to the development of new industries such as iron and steel production. Advances in metallurgy and engineering made it possible to produce stronger and more durable materials, allowing for the construction of larger buildings and infrastructure projects. The 19th century also saw important developments in finance and banking. The establishment of joint-stock companies and limited liability corporations made it easier for investors to finance large-scale projects, while the growth of the banking sector provided a stable source of capital for those seeking to start or expand businesses. The British Empire continued to expand, acquiring territories in Africa, Asia, and the Pacific. These colonies provided new markets for British goods, sources of cheap labor, and investment opportunities, further enriching the British economy.

British Economy in the 20th Century

1 The Edwardian Era

At the turn of the 20th century, the British economy was one of the most powerful in the world. Its industrial and financial might had helped to make Britain the dominant global superpower during the 19th century. However, by the early 1900s, there were signs that the country's economic dominance was beginning to slip. Britain faced increasing competition from other industrialized nations such as Germany and the USA. This competition put pressure on British manufacturers to become more efficient and productive, which in turn led to a greater emphasis on technological innovation and scientific research.

The Edwardian era, spanning the reign of King Edward VII from 1901 to 1910, was characterized by economic prosperity and social change. Britain maintained its position as a dominant global economic power, with a strong industrial base and extensive overseas trade networks. The country continued to lead in traditional industries such as textiles, coal mining, steel production, and shipbuilding. Urbanization trends continued, with cities expanding and industrial centers growing as the population shifted from rural areas to urban centers in search of employment opportunities.

2 The World War I Period

However, the outbreak of the First World War in 1914 had a profound impact on the British economy. The conflict led to disruptions in trade, increased government intervention, and mounting public debt. One of the most striking changes was the shift in industrial production towards military needs. British factories rapidly converted their operations to produce weapons, ammunition, and military equipment instead of consumer goods. This shift led to a surge in production and employment in industries related to the war effort. However, this shift also created challenges for the civilian population. As resources and manpower were redirected to support the war, shortages emerged in essential goods and services. The government introduced rationing policies to ensure fair distribution of scarce resources, including food, fuel, and clothing. These measures aimed to manage supply and demand, prevent hoarding and maintain social stability. Agriculture faced significant disruptions as many farmers were drafted into the armed forces. This resulted in reduced agricultural production and increased reliance on imports to meet food demands. Additionally, the German naval blockade limited Britain's access to international markets, exacerbating food shortages and driving up prices. To address these challenges, the government encouraged domestic food production through initiatives such as the cultivation of idle land and promoting women's involvement in agricultural work. The labor market also experienced substantial changes during the war. As men enlisted in the military, women entered the workforce in large numbers to fill the vacant positions. Women took on jobs in factories, offices, and other sectors, contributing significantly to the war effort. This increase in female participation in the labor force marked a significant shift in societal norms and paved the way for greater gender equality in the post-war era. To finance the war, the British government borrowed extensively, leading to a sharp increase in public debt. The war also resulted in high inflation due to increased demand and scarcity of resources. To mitigate the effects of inflation, the government implemented measures such as price controls and income tax adjustments.

The period immediately following World War I was marked by post-war reconstruction and economic adjustment. The government focused on rebuilding infrastructure, reestablishing trade relationships, and addressing the high levels of public debt incurred during the war. Efforts were made to revive industries, particularly those related to exports and manufacturing, and to stabilize the currency. The 1920s saw a period of relative economic prosperity, characterized by technological advancements, increased consumer spending, and the rise of new industries such as automobiles, electrical goods, and aviation. However, this period also witnessed social and economic disparities, with high unemployment in certain regions and industries, as well as continued challenges in agriculture. However, the onset of the Great Depression in the late 1920s had a profound impact on the British economy. International trade contracted, industrial production declined, and unemployment soared. The government responded with various measures, including public works programs, monetary policies, and efforts to stimulate domestic demand. These initiatives aimed to alleviate the economic downturn and provide relief to those affected by unemployment and poverty. During this period, the British economy also faced geopolitical challenges, including the impact of the global rise of protectionism and the breakdown of the international gold standard. These factors further contributed to economic instability and uncertainty. In response to these challenges, the government implemented a series of policies aimed at stabilizing the economy and addressing social welfare needs. The introduction of unemployment benefits, housing programs, and other social reforms sought to provide support to those most affected by the economic downturn. Furthermore, the military build-up in the lead-up to World War II resulted in increased government spending and a shift back towards a war economy. This transition brought about changes in industrial production, labor mobilization, and resource allocation, setting the stage for the economic demands of the impending conflict.

3 The World War II Period

During World War II, the British economy faced unprecedented challenges and underwent significant transformations. The war had a profound impact on all aspects of British society and industry, as the country mobilized its resources for the war effort.

At the outbreak of World War II in 1939, the British economy was still recovering from the effects of the Great Depression. The war brought about a massive increase in government spending, as resources were diverted towards military production and defense infrastructure. Industries were retooled to produce weapons, ammunition, aircraft, and other supplies needed for the war. Rationing and price controls were implemented to ensure fair distribution of goods and prevent inflation. The government also introduced policies to regulate wages and working conditions, as well as to provide social welfare support for families of servicemen and those affected by the war. Despite the challenges posed by the war, the British economy experienced a period of industrial expansion and innovation. The demand for military supplies spurred growth in key industries such as aircraft manufacturing, shipbuilding, and engineering. Technological advancements were made in areas such as radar, cryptography, and aviation, which had long-lasting effects on post-war economic development.

The war also had a devastating impact on British cities, as bombing raids caused widespread destruction of homes, factories, and infrastructure. After World War II, the British economy underwent a period of significant transformation and reconstruction. The war had left Britain in a state of financial strain, with considerable damage to infrastructure and industries. However, the post-war years also presented opportunities for economic recovery and growth. One of the key factors that shaped the post-war economy was the implementation of social and economic reforms. The Labour Party, led by Clement Attlee, came into power in 1945 and introduced a series of policies aimed at creating a fairer and more equal society. This included the establishment of the welfare state, which provided universal healthcare, expanded education, and social security benefits. These reforms helped to improve living standards and provide a safety net for the population. The government also pursued an active industrial policy to stimulate economic growth. This involved nationalizing key industries such as coal, steel, and railways, which allowed for greater government control and investment in these sectors. The aim was to rebuild and modernize industries, increase productivity, and create employment opportunities. During this period, there was a push towards international trade and the expansion of exports. The British government actively sought to establish trade relationships and secure markets for British goods. The establishment of the General Agreement on Tariffs and Trade (GATT) in 1947 and later the creation of the European Economic Community (EEC) in 1957 played important roles in facilitating trade and economic integration. Technological advancements also drove economic growth. The post-war years saw the emergence of new industries and innovations, particularly in areas such as electronics, telecommunications, and aerospace. The development of the computer industry, for example, paved the way for the growth of the technology sector in later years.

Fig. 4.2 The Development of Electronic Technology

After World War II, decolonization movements led to the independence of many colonies. The loss of colonial markets, resources, and labor had mixed economic effects on Britain. While some industries suffered from competition and the end of preferential trade agreements, others were able to adapt and find new markets.

4 The Thatcher Era

During the tenure of Margaret Thatcher as Prime Minister from 1979 to 1990, the British economy underwent a period of significant transformation characterized by sweeping neoliberal reforms and a shift towards free-market principles. This era, often referred to as the "Thatcherite revolution," brought about fundamental changes in economic policy, industrial relations, and the role of the state in the economy.

One of the defining features of the Thatcher era was the emphasis on deregulation and privatization. The government aimed to reduce the role of the state in the economy by privatizing state-owned industries such as British Telecom, British Airways, and British Steel. This was accompanied by the liberalization of financial markets and the removal of trade barriers, which aimed to foster competition and efficiency.

Thatcher's government also pursued policies to curb the power of trade unions and overhaul labor relations. This included legislation to restrict union activities, reduce the influence of organized labor, and promote individual employment contracts. These changes were intended to increase flexibility in the labor market and reduce industrial unrest.

Fiscal and monetary policies were also central to the Thatcher government's economic strategy. There was a focus on controlling inflation through tight monetary policy, which at times resulted in high interest rates. Additionally, the government sought to reduce public spending and lower taxes, with the aim of promoting private sector growth and reducing the size of the state.

The Thatcher era also witnessed a reorientation of economic priorities towards services and finance. The City of London emerged as a global financial center, attracting investment and financial services from around the world. The deregulation of financial markets contributed to the growth of the banking and finance sector, while the service industry expanded, becoming a dominant force in the British economy.

The impact of these policies was substantial, leading to both successes and challenges. On the one hand, there were notable achievements in terms of curbing inflation, stimulating entrepreneurship, and fostering economic growth. However, there were also significant social and economic consequences, including rising income inequality, deindustrialization in certain regions, and increased unemployment in traditional industries.

Current British Economy

1 British Economy in the 21th Century

In the 21st century, the British economy has experienced a series of ups and downs, shaped by both domestic and global factors. At the beginning of the 21st century, the British economy enjoyed a period of sustained growth fueled by factors such as low interest rates, increased consumer spending, and a booming housing market. The financial services sector, centered around the City of London, played a key role in driving economic expansion, attracting investment and talent from around the world.

However, the global financial crisis of 2008 had a significant impact on British economy. The collapse of major financial institutions, a sharp decline in housing prices, and a contraction in credit availability led to a severe recession. The government implemented stimulus measures and bailouts to stabilize the economy, but the effects of the crisis were felt for years to come, with high unemployment and slow growth.

Following the financial crisis, the British economy gradually recovered, albeit at a slower pace than before. The government pursued austerity measures to reduce public debt, leading to cuts in public spending and welfare programs. While these measures helped to bring down the deficit, they also sparked debate over their social impact and contribution to income inequality.

One of the defining events of recent years has been the UK's decision to leave the European Union, known as Brexit. The process of negotiating and implementing Brexit has introduced significant uncertainty and complexity into the economy, impacting trade relationships, supply chains, and investment decisions. The full consequences of Brexit are still unfolding, with challenges and opportunities for different sectors of the economy.

2 Main Industries in the UK

Primary Sector—Agriculture

The UK has a strong agricultural industry, with a significant contribution to the country's economy. In 2020, agriculture, forestry, and fishing together accounted for 0.6% of the UK's GDP. Agriculture is particularly important for rural communities and provides employment opportunities for thousands of people.

Agriculture is widespread throughout the UK, with around 217,000 farms located in every region, averaging 87 hectares in size. These farms range in size from modest family-run businesses to huge commercial operations. Farm sizes vary depending on the type of farming being carried out.

Arable farming is an important part of the UK's agricultural industry, and the most common crops grown are wheat, barley, and oilseed rape. Other crops grown in the UK include oats, potatoes, and sugar beet. The UK's mild climate and fertile soils make it well-suited to arable farming.

Livestock farming is a significant part of the UK's agricultural industry, with dairy and sheep farming being the most common. The UK is home to around 10 million cows, producing over 14 billion liters of milk each year. The country is also home to around 20 million sheep, with lamb and mutton being important products.

The UK has a long history of sheep farming and is the largest producer of wool in Europe. The country produces around 28,000 tons of wool each year, with the majority of this being exported to other countries. The wool industry is an important part of the UK's textile industry, with wool used in a variety of products such as clothing, carpets, and upholstery. The UK is a net exporter of agricultural products, with exports exceeding imports. The country is a significant exporter of lamb, beef, and wheat. In 2019, the UK exported around 301,000 tons of lamb, with France and Germany being the largest markets. The UK is also a major exporter of beef, with the Netherlands and Ireland being the largest markets. Wheat is another important export for the UK, with the country exporting around 2 million tons in 2019, mainly to the EU.

The use of technology in farming is increasing, with precision agriculture and robotics being adopted by some farmers. Precision agriculture involves using data and technology to optimize crop yields and reduce waste, while robotics can be used for tasks such as planting and harvesting crops.

The UK government has implemented policies to reduce the use of pesticides and fertilizers in agriculture, with the aim of improving environmental sustainability. In 2018, the use of pesticides in the UK decreased by 18%, and the use of fertilizers decreased by 4% compared to the previous year. This is partly due to the adoption of integrated pest management practices and the use of alternative methods such as crop rotation and cover crops.

Secondary Sector—Manufacturing and Energy Production

(1) Aerospace

The UK aerospace industry excels in research and manufacturing in Europe and worldwide. In 2020, the UK aerospace industry employed over 380,000 people, with a turnover of £79 billion, £45 billion in exports, and an economic value-added of £33 billion.

Fig. 4.3　The Development of Aerospace Industry

(2) Automobile

The UK automobile industry currently employs around 856,000 workers, primarily concentrated in the Midlands and the North. In 2021, the car production in the UK decreased by 6.7% year-on-year, totaling just 859,600 vehicles, the lowest level since 1956 and a 34% decrease from 2019. Electric vehicle production surged by 29.6%, accounting for over a quarter (26.1%) of total car production. Car exports reached 705,800 vehicles, representing 82.1% of total production, with the EU and the US being the top two export markets for UK cars. The UK hosts investments from the world's seven largest car manufacturers, eight sports car manufacturers, eight commercial vehicle manufacturers, and ten large bus manufacturers.

(3) Energy

The UK boasts abundant energy resources, including significant oil and gas reserves. As of the end of 2020, the UK had oil reserves of approximately 300 million tons and natural gas reserves of about 200 billion cubic meters. The UK underwent energy privatization reforms from 1989 to 1999, establishing fully open and competitive electricity and gas markets. Natural gas has replaced coal as the primary energy source, significantly reducing greenhouse gas emissions. Nuclear power has entered the market, while wind and bioenergy, among other renewable energy technologies, have matured, diversifying the energy mix away from sole reliance on fossil fuels. In 2020, UK energy consumption totaled 164 million tons of oil equivalent (6.89 EJ), a decrease of 11% compared to the previous year.

(4) Chemical and Pharmaceutical Industry

The UK is a major player in the global chemical industry, with over 3,700 companies, 70% of which are foreign-owned. In 2020, the industry generated approximately £56 billion in annual sales, over £18 billion in economic value added, and invested more than £5 billion in research and development, creating over 500,000 jobs. The UK is also a key hub for the pharmaceutical industry, with the top 20 global pharmaceutical companies operating in the UK. GlaxoSmithKline and AstraZeneca rank as the fifth and sixth largest pharmaceutical companies worldwide. Foreign companies such as Pfizer and Roche have also invested in manufacturing facilities in the UK.

(5) Food and Beverage

The UK is one of the fastest-growing food and beverage markets globally. Driven by innovation in chemistry and nanotechnology, the UK's food and beverage industry continuously innovates, particularly excelling in high-tech packaging, healthy, and convenient food products. The food and beverage sector is the largest manufacturing industry in the UK, with an annual turnover of around £104 billion, constituting 19% of the total manufacturing output in the UK.

Tertiary Sector—Service Industry

(1) Finance

The financial services industry is one of the key pillars of the British economy. In 2021, the financial services industry contributed £164.8 billion to the British economy. London ranks among the world's top three financial centers, serving as a major hub for foreign exchange trading and the largest over-the-counter derivatives market globally. The London Metal Exchange is the world's largest metal exchange, with non-ferrous metals accounting for over 90% of global trading volume. The London Oil Exchange is a leading energy exchange in Europe. The London Stock Exchange is the most internationally oriented stock exchange globally, and London is also a key center for global gold trading. Edinburgh, Manchester, Cardiff, Liverpool, Leeds, and Glasgow are also significant financial trading centers in the UK.

(2) Tourism

The tourism industry is a vital sector of the British economy. In 2021, the travel and tourism industry in the UK contributed 5.7% to GDP; in terms of GDP contribution, the UK tourism industry ranked ninth globally in 2021, holding a 2.7% share of the global market. Major tourist destinations include London, Edinburgh,

Cardiff, Brighton, Greenwich, Stratford, Oxford, and Cambridge.

(3) Information and Communication

Prior to Brexit, the UK was the largest information and communication industry base in the EU, home to approximately 370,000 businesses. The UK is a global innovation hub in the information and communication industry, renowned for its chip design expertise, accounting for 40% of chip design in Europe and 10% globally. ARM, a UK-based company, is a leading provider of semiconductor intellectual property, with over 95% of smartphones and tablets worldwide utilizing ARM architecture. The UK was among the first countries to adopt wireless local area networks, leading the world in internet proliferation and e-commerce. The UK's telecommunications sector is known for its advanced development, openness, and incorporation of new technologies. The UK was the first country to provide digital television services through artificial satellites, cables, and terrestrial broadcasting, hosting over 200 space and satellite companies and one of the world's largest mobile phone operator. It stands as Europe's most powerful and competitive telecommunications manufacturing and supply base, recognized as a center for telecom technological innovation.

Exercises

Part I. Decide whether the following statements are true (T) or false (F). Write T or F in the brackets.

1. The UK is the fifth largest economy in the world and the second largest economy in Europe. (   )
2. Private enterprises account for over 90% of the GDP in the UK. (   )
3. The manufacturing sector contributes about one-tenth of the UK's GDP. (   )
4. The public sector in the UK provides essential services and support to all citizens. (   )
5. Margaret Thatcher's economic reforms led to a reduction in income inequality. (   )
6. The British economy before the Industrial Revolution was relatively decentralized. (   )
7. The UK's decision to leave the European Union (EU), known as "Brexit," has a negative impact on the British economy. (   )
8. During World War I, agricultural production in Britain significantly increased due to many farmers being drafted into the armed forces. (   )

Chapter 4 Economy

Part II. Fill in the blanks with best answers.

1. _____ sector contributes three-quarters of the UK's GDP.

    A. Manufacturing

    B. Services

    C. Agriculture

    D. Mining

2. The primary focus of the British economy before the Industrial Revolution was _____.

    A. large-scale farming

    B. cottage industries

    C. global trade

    D. financial services

3. World War I had the following impacts on the UK except _____.

    A. disruptions in trade and agriculture

    B. shift in industrial production towards military needs

    C. decrease of female workers in factories

    D. increase of domestic food production

4. The _____ industry had the most transformative impact on the English economy in the pre-Industrial Revolution age.

    A. textile

    B. agriculture

    C. mining

    D. shipbuilding

5. The defining features of the Thatcher era was the emphasis on _____.

    A. deregulation and liberalization

    B. commercialization and privatization

    C. deregulation and privatization

    D. commercialization and liberalization

71

6. _____ sector of the economy is under the control of individuals and organizations whose primary goal is to make a profit.

   A. Non-profit

   B. Public

   C. Government

   D. Private

7. The _____ industry is one of the key pillars of the UK economy and contributed £164.8 billion to the UK economy in 2021.

   A. automobile

   B. financial services

   C. tourism

   D. aerospace

8. The first joint-stock company, the Muscovy Company, was established in _____.

   A. 1559

   B. 1551

   C. 1660

   D. 1670

Part III. State your understanding of the following questions.

1. The UK implemented government intervention during post-war reconstruction, but compared with China, these measures in the UK place more emphasis on the role of market mechanisms and the private sector, with relatively less government intervention. Please find relevant materials to explain how China's macroeconomic policies are forward-looking, scientific, and effective.

2. Colonies had a significant role in the economic development of the UK. Does a country's economic prosperity necessarily have to be based on the seizure of resources from other countries?

3. In the 1980s, the Thatcher government in the UK first extensively auctioned off state-owned enterprises, sparking a wave of privatization worldwide. China has also been exploring the path of reforming state-owned enterprises. Please find information to explain the differences between China's state-owned enterprise reform and that of the UK.

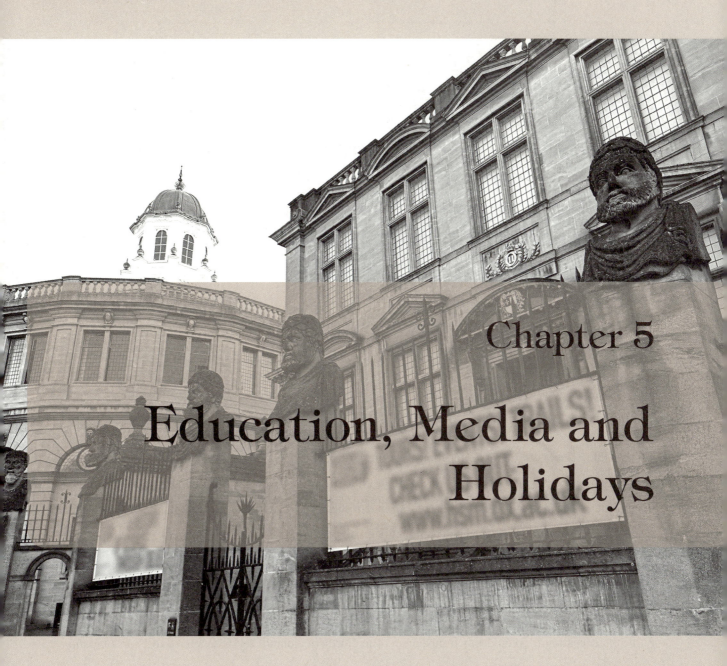

Chapter 5
Education, Media and Holidays

Preview Questions

1. How is the UK education system structured?
2. Can you name some of the famous universities in the UK?
3. What do you know about the main media in the UK?
4. What holidays do people in the UK celebrate?

Education

1 Overview

The ideology of education in the UK emphasizes inclusivity, equality and high standards, ensuring all children have access to quality education regardless of background. It promotes a broad and balanced curriculum, personalized learning and lifelong education, focusing on both academic and holistic development. The system prepares students for modern society by fostering critical thinking, creativity and resilience, and encourages parental and community involvement in the educational process.

Education in the UK is devolved, with separate systems managed by the UK Government for England, the Scottish Government, the Welsh Government and the Northern Ireland Executive. Education in the UK has five stages: early years, primary, secondary, further education (FE) and higher education (HE). Full-time education is compulsory from ages 5 (4 in Northern Ireland) to 16, extended to 18 in England since 2015. Before compulsory schooling, children can attend nursery with universal funding available from age three or younger. Further education, covering advanced education, is non-compulsory and offered at FE colleges and HE institutions. Higher education, beyond A-Levels, typically occurs at universities and colleges.

Chapter 5 Education, Media and Holidays

Table 5.1 UK Compulsory School System in Year Groups

Age	England & Wales	Scotland	Northern Ireland
3	Nursery (Non-compulsory)	Nursery (Non-compulsory)	Nursery (Non-compulsory)
4–5	**Primary-Key Stage 1** Reception Class	Nursery (Non-compulsory)	**Primary-Key Stage 2** Year 1
5–6	Year 1	**Primary** P1	Year 2
6–7	Year 2	P2	Year 3
7–8	**Key Stage 2** Year 3	P3	**Key Stage 2** Year 4
8–9	Year 4	P4	Year 5
9–10	Year 5	P5	Year 6
10–11	Year 6	P6	Year 7
11–12	**Secondary-Key Stage 3** Year 7	P7	**Secondary-Key Stage 3** Year 8
12–13	Year 8	**Secondary** S1	Year 9
13–14	Year 9	S2	Year 10
14–15	**Key Stage 4** Year 10	S3	**Key Stage 4** Year 11
15–16	Year 11 (General Certificate of Secondary Education)	S4	Year 12 **GCSE**
		End of Compulsory Schooling	End of Compulsory Schooling
16–17	Year 12 (Lower Sixth Form)	S5 (Intermediate 1)	Year 13 (Level 2)
17–18	Year 13 (Upper Sixth Form) **A-Levels**	S6 (Intermediate 2) **A-Levels**	Year 14 (Level 3) **A-Levels**
	End of Compulsory Schooling		

2 Early Years Education

In England since September 2010, all three and four-year-olds are entitled to 15 hours of free nursery education for 38 weeks per year. This is offered in state nursery schools, nursery classes, reception classes in primary schools and private or voluntary settings such as pre-schools and childminders.

In Wales, children are entitled to a free part-time place from the term after their third birthday until they begin statutory education. These places can be in maintained schools or approved private or voluntary settings.

In Scotland, local authorities must provide a part-time funded place for every child starting the term after their third birthday. Pre-school education can be in local authority centers or through private and voluntary providers. Children are entitled to a full year of pre-school education before starting primary school.

In Northern Ireland, funded pre-school places are available in statutory nursery schools and units, as well as in voluntary and private settings participating in the Pre-School Education Expansion Programme (PSEEP). Voluntary and private places are part-time, while statutory nursery places can be full-time or part-time.

3 Primary and Secondary Education

The primary stage in the UK includes nursery (under 5), infant (5–7) (Key Stage 1) and junior (up to 11) (Key Stage 2). Scotland and Northern Ireland do not distinguish between infant and junior schools. In Wales, the Foundation Phase combines early years and Key Stage 1 for ages 3–7. English primary schools generally serve ages 4–11, sometimes with attached nurseries. Primary education focuses on basic literacy and numeracy, along with foundations in science and other subjects, with assessments at the end of Key Stages 1 and 2.

Secondary education in England includes various types of schools, often comprehensive, admitting all local children regardless of ability. In Wales, secondary schools cater to ages 11 and up. Scottish secondary schools are comprehensive and offer six years of education, with some remote areas having shorter secondary schooling. The Scottish system emphasizes a broad subject range, while the English, Welsh and Northern Irish systems focus on depth in fewer subjects. Northern Ireland's post-primary education includes five compulsory years and optional further years for advanced courses, with admission based on non-academic criteria, though academic performance can still be considered.

The main goals of primary education are to achieve basic literacy and numeracy and establish foundations in science, mathematics and other subjects. Children in England and Northern Ireland are assessed at the end of Key Stages 1 and 2, while in Wales, assessments occur in the final year of the Foundation Phase and Key Stage 2.

Secondary education in England includes various types of schools, typically comprehensive, admitting all local children regardless of ability. In Wales, secondary schools serve students from age 11 onward. Scottish secondary schools are generally comprehensive and offer six years of education, with shorter options in remote areas. Scotland emphasizes a broad subject range, while England, Wales and Northern Ireland focus on greater depth in fewer subjects. In Northern Ireland, post-primary education includes five compulsory years and two optional years for advanced courses, with admissions primarily based on non-academic criteria, though academic performance can still be considered.

National Curriculum

The National Curriculum in England, established in 1988, provides a framework for education between the ages of 5 and 16. Although the curriculum is compulsory, some private schools, home educators, academies and free schools design their own curricula. Following devolution in 1999, the National Curriculum for Wales was established and is now being succeeded by the Curriculum for Wales. In Scotland, the equivalent is the Curriculum for Excellence. The Northern Ireland Curriculum is a separate system more similar to that in the Republic of Ireland. The national curriculum forms one part of the school curriculum. The school curriculum comprises all learning and other experiences that each school plans for its pupils.

The national curriculum provides pupils with an introduction to the essential knowledge they need to be educated citizens. It introduces pupils to the best that has been thought and said and helps engender an appreciation of human creativity and achievement.

The national curriculum is just one element in the education of every child. There is time and space in the school day and in each week, term and year to range beyond the national curriculum specifications. The national curriculum provides an outline of core knowledge around which teachers can develop exciting and stimulating lessons to promote the development of pupils' knowledge, understanding and skills as part of the wider school curriculum. It is organized on the basis of 4 key stages and 12 subjects, classified in legal terms as 'core' and 'other foundation' subjects.

Table 5.2 Subjects in Compulsory Education in the UK

Subjects		Key Stage 1 Age 5–7 Year 1–2	Key Stage 2 Age 7–11 Year 3–6	Key Stage 3 Age 11–14 Year 7–9	Key Stage 4 Age 14–16 Year 10–11
Core Subjects	English	√	√	√	√
	Mathematics	√	√	√	√
	Science	√	√	√	√
Foundation Subjects	Art and Design	√	√	√	
	Citizenship			√	√
	Computing	√	√	√	√
	Design and Technology	√	√	√	
	Languages*		√	√	

(continued)

Subjects		Key Stage 1 Age 5–7 Year 1–2	Key Stage 2 Age 7–11 Year 3–6	Key Stage 3 Age 11–14 Year 7–9	Key Stage 4 Age 14–16 Year 10–11
Foundation Subjects	Geography	√	√	√	
	History	√	√	√	
	Music	√	√	√	
	Physical Education	√	√	√	√

*At Key Stage 2 the subject title is "foreign language;" at Key Stage 3 it is "modern foreign language."

All state schools are also required to make provision for a daily act of collective worship and must teach religious education to pupils at every key stage. They must also teach relationships education to pupils in primary education, relationships and sex education to pupils in secondary education and health education to all pupils. All schools should make provision for personal, social, health and economic education (PSHE), drawing on good practice. Schools are also free to include other subjects or topics of their choice in planning and designing their own programme of education. All schools must publish their school curriculum by subject and academic year online.

Table 5.3   Statutory Teaching of Religious, Relationship, Sex and Health Education

Education	Key Stage 1 Age 5–7 Year 1–2	Key Stage 2 Age 7–11 Year 3–6	Key Stage 3 Age 11–14 Year 7–9	Key Stage 4 Age 14–16 Year 10–11
Religious Education	√	√	√	√
Relationship Education	√	√	√	√
Sex Education			√	√
Health Education	√	√	√	√

Different Types of Schools

State-funded schools provide education to pupils between the ages of 3 and 18 without charge. Approximately 93% of English schoolchildren attend such 24,000 schools. Since 2008 about 75% of the state-funded schools have attained "academy status," which essentially gives them a higher budget per pupil from the Department for Education. There are a number of categories of English state-funded schools including academy schools, community schools, faith schools, foundation schools, grammar schools, free schools (including studio schools, maths schools and university technical colleges) and a small number of state boarding schools and City Technology Colleges.

Academy schools were introduced by the 1997–2010 Labour Government to replace underperforming community schools in deprived areas. The 2010 Conservative-Liberal Democrat government expanded this to include schools in less deprived areas. Academies are directly funded by the government, monitored by the Department for Education and inspected by Ofsted. Run by an academy trust, they have greater operational control than community schools but must follow the same rules on admissions, special educational needs, exclusions and exams.

About one third of state-funded schools in England are faith schools affiliated with religious groups. Faith schools have to follow the national curriculum, but they can choose what they teach in religious studies. However, evolution instead of creationism should be taught adequately as part of the science curricula. Faith schools may have different admissions criteria and staffing policies to state schools, although anyone can apply for a place. Many faith schools converted to Academy status and are sometimes known as Faith Academies.

Grammar schools are state-funded, academically selective secondary schools with a long history in the UK. Traditionally teaching Latin, they now focus on academic excellence. Pupils are selected based on the "11-plus" exam, with successful candidates attending grammar schools and others going to secondary modern schools. Critics in the 1950s and 1960s argued that this system reinforced class divisions and middle-class privilege, believing that "instead of improving equality, they make it worse." By 1965, the government began phasing out grammar and secondary modern schools in favor of a comprehensive system. Currently, there are 163 grammar schools in 36 English local authorities and 67 in Northern Ireland, but none in Wales or Scotland.

City Technology Colleges and the City College for the Technology of the Arts are free secondary schools in urban areas. Funded by the central government and corporate contributions, City Technology Colleges focus on science and technology, while the City College for the Technology of the Arts integrates technology with performing and creative arts, such as interactive digital design courses. They forge close links with businesses and industry (mainly through their sponsors).

Private schools, also known as "independent schools" or "public schools" in the UK, charge fees to attend instead of being funded by the government. Some private schools have financial endowments while most are governed by a board of governors and are owned by a mixture of corporations, trusts and private individuals. They are independent of many of the regulations and conditions that apply to state-funded schools. For example, the schools do not have to follow the National Curriculum, although many such schools do. Private schools, as compared with state schools, generally have more individual teaching, much lower pupil-teacher ratios at around 9:1, longer teaching hours (sometimes including saturday morning teaching) and homework (known as prep), though they have shorter terms. They also have more time for organized extra-curricular activities. There are around 2,600 private schools in the UK, which educate around 615,000 children, some 7% of all British school-age children and 18% of pupils over the age of 16. Private schools are often criticized for being elitist and seen as lying outside the spirit of the state system. Many of the best-known private schools are extremely expensive.

4 Further Education

Further education may be used in a general sense to cover all non-advanced courses taken after the period of compulsory education. It is post-compulsory education and different from the education offered in universities (higher education). It may be at any level from basic skills training to higher vocational education. It is primarily taught in FE colleges, work-based learning, and adult and community learning institutions.

In England, Further Education (FE) is integrated into a broader learning and skills sector that includes workplace education, prison education, and other forms of non-school and non-university training. In Scotland, FE colleges offer qualifications that can facilitate entry into universities and support apprenticeship programs managed by Skills Development Scotland. In Wales, FE is provided by 15 institutions and various public, private, and voluntary sector training providers like the Workers' Educational Association. Northern Ireland's FE colleges cater to students over 14, offering school-level qualifications, work-based learning, apprenticeships, and some undergraduate and postgraduate courses.

5 Higher education

Overview

Higher education in the UK is regarded as one of the most prestigious and established university systems anywhere in the world. An important principle of higher education provision in the United Kingdom is that higher education providers are autonomous institutions, with a high degree of self-governance and financial and academic independence. But this autonomy must be understood within a wider policy context set at a national level.

The four parts of the UK have a shared history where higher education is concerned. At the same time, the devolution of responsibility for higher education over the last 30 years has allowed England, Wales, Scotland and Northern Ireland to take divergent paths in how they manage their systems. This devolution has led to an increasingly contrasting higher education picture across the UK, with each country responsible for setting policy and the overall regulatory framework for its higher education sector.

Across the UK, higher education is generally understood to mean undergraduate and postgraduate degrees taken by students aged 18 years of age (or in Scotland, 16) and older. Higher education is most commonly pursued in universities and other higher education providers, but may also be offered in colleges alongside further education courses. This is especially true in Scotland. There are around 450 higher education providers across the UK, with over 400 of them in England. The significant difference in the number of providers relates to the respective sizes of each part of the UK, but also how higher education has developed historically, and especially following the devolution of powers in recent decades. There is also a significant difference in the total number of higher education students in each part of the UK.

Government spending on higher education includes direct funding for teaching and research through national funding bodies, as well as student loans to cover tuition fees and help towards living costs. Governments get some of this spending back in the form of loan repayments from graduates. Prior to 2012, most funding for UK universities came from a central Government grant paid through the national funding councils. In 2012, this grant was reduced, and funding for teaching shifted towards increased tuition fees paid by students instead. In Scotland, the fees of eligible students are covered by the Government. Today, tuition fees and grants for teaching and research are the most significant sources of income for most higher education providers among many other ways. The tuition fees share larger portion than the government grant.

Despite being a top destination for international students, only 2% of UK students study abroad, half the EU average and lower than Germany and France (4%). In 2020–2021 shcool year, there were 605,100 overseas students across all types of UK higher education institutions, which meant the UK Government's target of international students numbers by 2030 was met a decade early. Currently, 20% of all UK students studying in higher education are international students—around 15% are undergraduates and 37% are postgraduates.

The top grade possible for undergraduates in the UK is a first-class with honors, and although the second highest grade (an upper second, or 2.1) is still the most common, the share of students graduating with a first has increased from 17% in 2011–2012 to 32% in 2021–2022. In the same year, the most popular subject group for students in the UK was business and management studies, at 530,460 enrollments. Subject allied to medicine and social sciences go to the second and third place.

Gaining entrance to a UK university involves meeting academic requirements, often through A-Levels or equivalent qualifications, writing a personal statement, providing references, and sometimes attending interviews or submitting additional materials. The process is centralized through UCAS (Universities and Colleges Admissions Service), which streamlines applications to multiple universities. The most common qualifications for university entrance are A-Levels. Students usually study three to four A-Level subjects over two years, with exams taken at the end of each year. University offers are typically based on the grades achieved in these exams. For example, an offer might be conditional on achieving AAB or ABB grades. A crucial part of the application process is the personal statement. This is an essay where students explain why they want to study their chosen subject, detail relevant experience and demonstrate their suitability for the course. The personal statement is submitted through the UCAS (Universities and Colleges Admissions Service) application. Applicants must provide an academic reference, usually written by a teacher or tutor, which supports their application and highlights their strengths and suitability for the course. Some courses and universities, particularly for competitive fields like medicine or law, may require an interview. Interviews are used to assess applicants' knowledge, skills and motivation for the subject. For Oxbridge (Oxford and Cambridge), interviews are a standard part of the application process and are often academically rigorous.

Famous Universities

(1) The University of Oxford

Fig. 5.1　The University of Oxford

The University of Oxford, located in Oxford, England, is the oldest university in the English-speaking world, with a history dating back to at least 1096. Oxford is a collegiate university, consisting of 39 self-governing colleges and numerous academic departments organized into four divisions: Humanities, Mathematical, Physical and Life Sciences, Medical Sciences, and Social Sciences. Oxford is known for its excellence in education, research and scholarship. It has produced an array of distinguished alumni, including 28 British Prime Ministers, numerous foreign heads of state, 72 Nobel Prize winners and renowned writers like J.R.R. Tolkien and Oscar Wilde. The Oxford collegiate system provides a supportive and engaging educational experience. Colleges offer a close-knit community, with students receiving personalized attention through the tutorial system. Tutorials are intensive, discussion-based sessions where students work closely with tutors to explore subjects in depth.

(2) The University of Cambridge

The University of Cambridge, established in 1209, is one of the world's oldest and most prestigious universities. Located in Cambridge, England, it consists of 31 autonomous colleges where students live and study, and numerous academic departments organized into six schools: Arts and Humanities, Biological Sciences, Clinical Medicine, Humanities and Social Sciences, Physical Sciences and Technology. Cambridge is renowned for its rigorous academic standards and has produced numerous notable alumni, including scientists like Isaac Newton and Stephen Hawking, writers such as Charles Darwin and Sylvia Plath, and political figures like Oliver Cromwell and Jawaharlal Nehru. The collegiate system at Cambridge offers a unique blend of individualized education and community living. Each college operates independently, managing its own finances and property, but all are part of the university. Students receive personalized tuition through the tutorial system, also known as "supervisions," which are small-group or one-on-one sessions with academic experts.

Fig. 5.2　The University of Cambridge

While both universities share many similarities, including their collegiate structures, rigorous academic environments and global reputations, there are distinct differences. Oxford excels in humanities and social sciences, with a strong emphasis on philosophy, politics and literature. Cambridge is particularly strong in science and engineering, with a significant focus on research in these areas. Both universities offer an unparalleled educational experience, with personalized teaching, vibrant student communities and a commitment to fostering intellectual growth and innovation. Their historic rivalry, known as "Oxbridge," continues to inspire excellence and competition, making them two of the most sought-after institutions in the world.

Media

1　Newspapers

UK newspapers can generally be split into two distinct categories: the more serious and intellectual newspapers, usually referred to as the broadsheets and the quality press; and others generally known as tabloids and popular press, which have tended to focus more on celebrity coverage and human-interest stories rather than political reporting or overseas news. Twelve daily newspapers and eleven Sunday-only weekly newspapers are distributed nationally in the UK. Others circulate in Scotland only and still others serve smaller areas. Most of the newspapers are generally central but with different political orientation. *The Times* is right-wing supported by the Conservative Party and *The Guardian* is more left supported by the Labour Party.

Tabloid newspapers are known for their concise and sensationalist style, and focus on entertainment, celebrity news and human interest stories. They typically use large, bold headlines and a compact format

to attract readers. Prominent examples include *The Sun* and the *Daily Mirror*, which offer a mix of tabloid journalism that includes dramatic stories, sports coverage and scandalous headlines. Often criticized for their sensationalism, tabloid newspapers cater to a broad audience seeking engaging and accessible content. Their impact on public opinion and popular culture makes them a significant part of the UK media landscape.

All the major UK newspapers currently have websites, some of which provide free access. *The Times* and *The Sunday Times* require payment on a per-day or per-month basis by non-subscribers. *The Financial Times* also has limited access for non-subscribers. *The Independent* became available online only upon its last printed edition on 26 March 2016. However, unlike the previously mentioned newspapers, it does not require any payment to access its news content. Instead, the newspaper offers extras for those wishing to sign up to a payment subscription, such as crosswords, Sudoku puzzles, weekend supplements and the ability to automatically download each daily edition to read offline. *The London Economic* is another example of a British digital/online only newspaper; however, unlike *The Independent*, it has never run a print publication.

Most towns and cities in the UK have at least one local newspaper, such as *The Evening Post* in Bristol and *The Echo* in Cardiff. Local newspapers are listed in advertising guides such as *The Mitchell's Press Directories*.

2 Radio and Television

Radio in the UK has been a significant medium since the early 20th century, with the BBC (British Broadcasting Corporation) pioneering public broadcasting in 1922. The BBC renowned for its efficient news and diverse programming, set a high standard for radio content. The 1970s saw the rise of commercial radio, bringing new dynamics to the airwaves with stations like Capital Radio and LBC, which introduced a more varied range of music and talk shows. Today, the UK boasts a rich radio landscape that includes national stations such as Radio 1, Radio 2 and Radio 4, offering everything from music and news to in-depth talk shows. Regional and local stations provide tailored content, reflecting local interests and concerns, while digital and online platforms have further expanded access to diverse genres and on-demand programming. Radio remains a crucial medium for entertainment, information and community engagement across the UK.

Television in the UK, a cornerstone of national culture, began with experimental broadcasts in 1932, followed by regular programming from 1936. Initially a public service without advertising, TV in the UK has since diversified into free-to-air, free-to-view and subscription models, offering over 480 channels and extensive on-demand content. The BBC, established in 1922, is the oldest broadcaster, funded by a TV licence fee and renowned for its broad range of programming, including news, dramas and documentaries. Major commercial broadcasters such as ITV (Independent Television), Channel 4 and Channel 5 provide a variety of entertainment, reality shows and sports. Public service broadcasting remains influential, with channels like BBC Two and BBC Four delivering niche and educational content. The digital era has expanded viewing options through platforms like BBC iPlayer, ITV Hub, and All 4 while streaming services like Netflix and Amazon Prime Video have further diversified how audiences consume television.

3 Internet

The UK has been at the forefront of internet development since its inception. Initially adopting the internet in the 1990s, the UK's telecommunications infrastructure now supports widespread access through fibre, cable, mobile and fixed wireless networks. The longstanding copper network, managed by Openreach, is set to be phased out by December 2025 in favor of more advanced technologies.

Internet penetration in the UK surged from just 9% of households in 1998 to 93% by 2019. The digital divide remains, with nearly universal internet use among adults aged 16 to 44 (99%), compared to only 47% of those aged 75 and over. By 2016, the UK had the seventh-highest internet bandwidth per user globally, and its average and peak connection speeds were in the top quartile in 2017. Usage doubled in 2020, reflecting a surge in digital dependence.

High-speed broadband is extensively available across urban and rural areas, supported by a range of providers offering various packages and speeds. Government initiatives are focused on enhancing connectivity, improving rural broadband access and advancing 5G technology.

Holidays

Holidays in the UK are a vibrant blend of historical and cultural traditions celebrated throughout the year. From national observances to regional festivals, these holidays offer a rich tapestry of festivities and customs.

1 New Year's Day

New Year's Day is celebrated with various festivities. Many people attend parties and gatherings on New Year's Eve, counting down to midnight with fireworks displays and singing "Auld Lang Syne." At midnight, it is common to toast with champagne and exchange kisses and well-wishes for the coming year. On New Year's Day, people often enjoy a day off, participating in parades, such as the famous London New Year's Day Parade, or relaxing at home with family and friends. Some also make New Year's resolutions, setting personal goals for the year ahead.

2 Christmas

Christmas is a joyful time that brings families and communities together through a mix of traditions. The festive season starts with decorating homes and streets with lights, wreaths and Christmas trees covered in ornaments. Many people use advent calendars to count down the days until Christmas. On Christmas Eve, families might attend church services and children hang stockings for Santa Claus. Christmas Day is all about exchanging gifts and enjoying a big meal with roast turkey, stuffing, vegetables and Christmas pudding, along with the fun of pulling Christmas crackers that contain small toys and jokes. Many people go to church for special services with carol singing and nativity plays. The celebrations continue on Boxing Day, December 26th, with big sales in stores, sports events like football matches and visiting friends and family. Special activities like watching pantomimes and going to Christmas markets add to the festive fun, offering a chance to buy gifts and treats.

3 Easter

Easter is another significant holiday. Leading up to Easter, many observe Lent (大斋期), a period of fasting and reflection. On Easter Sunday, families gather for festive meals, often with lamb. Children participate in Easter egg hunts, searching for chocolate eggs hidden around homes and gardens. Decorating eggs and giving chocolate treats are also popular customs. Good Friday, the Friday before Easter, is a public holiday observed with somber reflection, while Easter Monday extends the celebrations, offering a long weekend for family gatherings and leisure activities.

Fig. 5.3 Easter Egg Hunt

4 Others

Additionally, there are bank holidays throughout the year, which are public holidays when banks and many businesses are closed, allowing people to enjoy leisure time with family and friends. These holidays provide an opportunity for extended weekends, often used for travel, relaxation and social activities. The number of

Chapter 5　Education, Media and Holidays

bank holidays varies by region: England and Wales have eight, Scotland has nine and Northern Ireland has ten each year. Additional bank holidays may be added for special events like royal weddings and jubilees. Seven holidays are observed across all regions: New Year's Day, Good Friday, the early May bank holiday, the Spring bank holiday, the Summer bank holiday, Christmas Day and Boxing Day. Easter Monday is a bank holiday in England, Wales and Northern Ireland but not in Scotland. Northern Ireland also observes St Patrick's Day and Orangemen's Day, while Scotland has additional holidays on January 2nd and St Andrew's Day. The Summer bank holiday falls on the first Monday in August in Scotland and on the last Monday in August elsewhere in the UK.

Many other festivals originating out of the UK are also celebrated throughout the year. Chinese Lunar New Year is celebrated in London, Manchester and many other cities with dragon dance, lion dance and other performances. Diwali, the Hindu Festival of Lights from India, is celebrated with fireworks, lighting lamps, prayers and feasts in cities among Indian community. Eid al-Fitr and Eid al-Adha, important Muslim holidays, are celebrated with prayers, feasts, and charitable activities in cities with large Muslim populations. Carnival, inspired by the Brazilian Carnival, is celebrated in the UK with parades, music and dancing, showcasing the rich cultural heritage of the Caribbean community in the UK.

Exercises

Part I. Decide whether the following statements are true (T) or false (F). Write T or F in the brackets.

1. Education in the UK promotes a broad and balanced curriculum, personalized learning and lifelong education, focusing on academic development. (　)

2. Education in the UK is unified and managed by the UK Government. (　)

3. Secondary education in England includes various types of schools, typically comprehensive, admitting all local children regardless of ability. (　)

4. Tuition fees and grants for teaching and research are the most significant sources of income for most higher education providers among many other ways. The tuition fees share smaller portion than the government grant. (　)

5. The University of Oxford, located in Oxford, England, is the oldest university in the English-speaking world, with a history dating back to at least 1096. (　)

6. UK newspapers can generally be split into two distinct categories: the broadsheets and the tabloids. The broadsheets have tended to focus more on celebrity coverage and human-interest stories rather

than political reporting or overseas news. (　)

7. Radio in the UK has been a significant medium since the early 20th century, with the BBC pioneering public broadcasting in 1922. (　)

8. Bank holidays are public holidays when banks and many businesses are closed, allowing people to enjoy leisure time with family and friends, usually with extended weekend. (　)

Part II. Fill in the blanks with best answers.

1. Which of the following is NOT a core subject in compulsory education in the UK?

    A. English

    B. Mathematics

    C. Science

    D. Citizenship

2. Which of the following is a feature of the UK's Further Education (FE) system?

    A. It is compulsory for all students aged 16–18.

    B. It offers only basic skills training.

    C. It integrates workplace education and supports apprenticeship programs.

    D. It is managed solely by the UK Government for all regions.

3. Which of the following statements about the University of Cambridge is NOT true?

    A. It is one of the world's oldest universities, established in 1209.

    B. It consists of 31 autonomous colleges where students live and study.

    C. Its academic departments are organized into six schools, including Clinical Medicine and Technology.

    D. It is located in Wales.

4. What is the highest academic grade achievable by undergraduates in the UK?

    A. Upper Second-Class Honors

    B. Lower Second-Class Honors

    C. First-Class Honors

    D. Pass Degree

5. What is the percentage of international students studying in higher education in UK?

    A. 10%

B. 20%

C. 30%

D. 40%

6. Which of the following media outlets is known for its public service broadcasting and is funded by a TV licence fee?

    A. ITV

    B. Channel 4

    C. BBC

    D. Sky News

7. Which of the following statements about the media landscape in the UK is NOT true?

    A. Most major UK newspapers have websites, some of which provide free access.

    B. The BBC pioneered public broadcasting in the UK in 1922.

    C. *The Independent* ceased printing a physical newspaper in 2016 and moved entirely online.

    D. All local newspapers in the UK require payment for online access.

8. Which of the following holidays is NOT universally recognized across all regions of the UK as a public holiday?

    A. Christmas Day

    B. Good Friday

    C. Easter Monday

    D. St Patrick's Day

Part III. State your understanding of the following questions.

1. Please compare the subjects that students learn in compulsory education in UK and China. Analyze the similarities and differences.

2. Please evaluate the role of political affiliations in shaping the editorial perspectives of newspapers in the UK. How does this influence public opinion?

3. Please do a survey about how Chinese Lunar New Year is celebrated in the UK and try to introduce some more traditional Chinese festivals to foreigners in a way that they could understand.

Chapter 6
Literature

Shakespeare's Birthplace

英美概况
A Guide to the UK and the US

Preview Questions

1. Have you read *Pride and Prejudice*? What is it about?

2. What do you know about Shakespeare and his plays?

3. How do you like the idea of comparing the souls of two lovers to the legs of a pair of twin compasses? How would you interpret this metaphor?

The history of English literature can be roughly divided into several periods: the Old English and Middle English periods, the Renaissance, the period of Revolution and Restoration, the age of Enlightenment, the Romantic period, the Victorian period, and finally the twentieth century, including the period of Modernism and the Post-war period.

The Old English Period and Middle English Period

In the history of English literature, the Old English period (also called the Anglo-Saxon period) covers the time span from the Fall of Western Roman Empire to the Norman Conquest in 1066. In form and content, Old English literature has much in common with other Germanic literature with which it shares an oral tradition and a body of heroic as well as Christian stories. The best existing Old English poem is an epic called *Beowulf*, which is a folk legend brought to England by the Anglo-Saxons from their continental homes. The opening lines of this great epic translated into modern English read like this:

So, The Spear-Danes in days gone by

And the kings who ruled them had courage and greatness.

We have heard of those princes' heroic campaigns.

The poet stands at a distance in time from the events in the story and tells the adventures of the great warriors and courageous kings in the past, when they still lived in the Scandinavian Peninsula and

Denmark. Beowulf, the hero of the epic, is from the southern part of Sweden. When he hears that the mead hall built by Hrothgar, the king of Denmark and a relative of Beowulf's, is attacked by a monster named Grendal and that many warriors have been swallowed by the monster, Beowulf crosses the sea with his warriors to help. He kills Grendel and Grendel's mother and helps to restore peace and joy in the land. Then he sails back to his own country and later becomes the king and reigns for fifty years. In his old age, his own land is ravaged by a fire dragon and he fights and kills it, with himself also mortally wounded. In *Beowulf* there is an emphasis on the ethical principle of loyalty to another—to one's friend, to one's family, to the chieftain and to the tribe. Both Grendel and the fire dragon are symbols of the hostility of the universe to human beings.

The Middle English period roughly refers to the period from the Norman Conquest (1066) to the beginning of the 16th century. After that, the English language entered the modern stage. The Normans brought to England the new language and literature. Metrical romance (tales in verse) is an important form of literature in this period. The finest of such romances is *Sir Gawain and the Green Knight*. It is a story about how Sir Gawain, one of the round-table knights of the legendary king Arthur, accepts the challenge of a knight in green (who has the magical power of being immune to the cut of weapons) to exchange blows from a battle axe on the head, and how he experiences trials and temptations in the process of fulfilling the promise. Sir Gawain's experience is educational and he gains self-knowledge in it.

The greatest writer of the Middle English period is Geoffrey Chaucer (1343–1400). He is called the "father of English poetry." In his masterpiece *The Canterbury Tales*, Chaucer uses an interesting structure "tales within the frame tale." The stories in this long narrative poem are put into the frame tale of a pilgrimage to the shrine of the martyred Saint Thomas à Becket at Canterbury and are supposed to be told by a group of pilgrims on their way there and back. This arrangement enables Chaucer to portray people from all walks of life and to present a cross-section of the English society. Furthermore, he establishes an interesting relationship between the story tellers and the stories they tell. The characters are revealed by the stories. Chaucer's description of spring in the General Prologue to *The Canterbury Tales* shows the traditional view of spring in western culture: spring is usually associated with vitality, new life, and love, both secular love and divine love.

Figure 6.1 Geoffrey Chaucer

The Renaissance

The term Renaissance originally indicated a revival of classical (Greek and Roman) arts and science. It sprang first in Italy in the 14th century and gradually spread all over Europe. Two features are striking of this movement, namely, a thirsting curiosity for the classical literature and a keen interest in the activities of humanity. Renaissance in England refers to the period from 1485, the year when the first Tudor King Henry VII came to the throne, to the first quarter of the seventeenth century, with the Elizabethan Age (1558–1603) being the summit of it. Thomas More (1478–1535) is the greatest of the English humanists and the author of *Utopia* (1516), which is a critical examination of contemporary English institutions and customs. The most important forms of literature during the English Renaissance are the sonnet and the drama.

A sonnet is a fourteen-line lyric poem, traditionally written in iambic pentameter (抑扬格五音步), that is, in lines ten syllables long, with accents falling on every second syllable. The sonnet form first became popular during the Italian Renaissance, when the Italian poet Petrarch (1304–1374) published a sequence of love sonnets addressed to an idealized woman named Laura. Then the sonnet spread throughout Europe and to England. The greatest three poets of sonnets of the Elizabethan Age are Philip Sidney (1554–1586), Edmund Spenser (1552–1590), and William Shakespeare (1564–1616). The sonnet "Shall I compare thee to a summer's day? /Thou art more lovely and more temperate" is the most popular Shakespearean sonnet.

Philip Sidney is also the author of *Defense of Poesy* (or *Apology for Poetry*) (1595), the earliest critical work in English literary history. Sidney argues that poetry has the power to instruct as well as to amuse.

As for the drama in this period, William Shakespeare is undoubtedly the greatest playwright of the Renaissance and in fact he is the greatest writer of all English literature.

Shakespeare's plays include comedies, tragedies, historical plays, and tragicomedies or romances. His greatest comedies, such as *A Midsummer Night's Dream, The Merchant of Venice,* and *Twelfth Night*, were mainly written in the early period of his career, from the year 1590 to 1600. *The Merchant of Venice* gives a brilliant characterization of the Jewish money-lender Shylock, who is also a victim

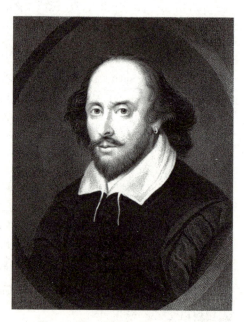

Figure 6.2　William Shakespeare

of the anti-Semitism (反犹主义) of that time. The greatest tragedies of Shakespeare, such as *Hamlet, Othello, King Lear*, and *Macbeth* were all written between 1601 and 1608, which is the most important period in his career. The works in this period are different from those of the early period, not only because he had grown more mature but also because the English society had undergone the fundamental transition from the Elizabethan England to the new regime of James I. So the great tragedies reflect the social and political unrest through the life-and-death struggles between the evil forces and the idealized heroes or heroines.

The most famous of Shakespeare's tragedies is *Hamlet*. Hamlet's soliloquy "to be or not to be" has conveyed the existential dilemma of thousands of people. Because of the delay in executing the revenge on his uncle, the murderer of his father, Hamlet has often been described as being indecisive. Yet, it is in this delay that we see the moral and religious concern of a Renaissance scholar rather than the recklessness of a medieval revenger.

King Lear is also a tragedy familiar to Chinese readers. The play not only discusses the filial duties, but shows the importance of love in general. Love is necessary for the maintenance of order in the world. When love is absent, strife begins to invade. In the play, the storm in nature to which King Lear is exposed is a symbol of this strife. In the process of suffering, King Lear grows mature and compassionate, being aware of other people's harsh living conditions. This moral growth makes him a noble tragic hero rather than a pitiable and foolish old man.

Christopher Marlowe (1564–1593) is a contemporary dramatist of Shakespeare and in his plays he shows the dangers of ambitions going too far. *The Tragical History of Doctor Faustus* tells the story of a scholar who desires infinite power through knowledge. In order to fulfill his strong desire, he agrees to do business with the devil. He gives the devil his soul and then he gets the worldly treasure in return. This pattern of the bond with the devil has a tremendous influence on literature of later generations.

There is also an event that is important for the development of the English language: the completion of the Authorized Version of the Bible in 1611, which is also called the King James Bible.

The Period of Revolution and Restoration

The seventeenth century was mainly a period of revolution and restoration. Although it was an age of political turbulence, this period still produced some great poets. The metaphysical poetry is characterized by the extravagant metaphors, exaggerations and philosophical arguments. John Donne (1572–1631) is

the most famous metaphysical poet. In his poem "A Valediction: Forbidding Mourning", he compares the souls of two lovers to the two feet of a pair of twin compasses, expressing the idea that the souls are united with love and that physical separation does not mean a break of love; instead, it means an expansion and elevation of love. John Donne is also famous for his sermons and meditations. In one of his meditations, he makes the statement that "no one is an island" to show that the fate of all human beings is interconnected. It is from this meditation that Hemingway borrows the title for his novel *For Whom the Bell Tolls*.

John Milton (1608–1674) is the greatest poet of this period. He wrote many pamphlets during the English Revolution, including a defense of divorce and a famous defense of the freedom of the press, *Areopagitica* (1644). In 1649 he was appointed as the Latin secretary for Oliver Cromwell, the leader of the parliamentary army. The Restoration in 1660 put an end to his political career and he produced most of his great works, such as *Paradise Lost* (1667), *Paradise Regained* (1671), and *Samson Agonistes* (1671), after his retirement to private life. Milton became blind in 1652 and his sonnet "On His Blindness" shows his great agony in the "dark world and wide." In his masterpiece *Paradise Lost* (1667), Milton tells the story about "man's first disobedience," that is to say, the story about how Adam and Eve had disobeyed God's command and eaten the fruit from the tree of knowledge of good and evil, and thus lost the privilege of living in the paradise of Eden. *Paradise Lost* is an epic (史 诗) modelled on the classic epics, with the conventional statement of theme and invocation (呼求) to the Muses (缪斯) in the opening lines. Yet Milton has made his own innovations to this epic tradition. He is not invoking the Muses of Greek mythology who are in charge of arts; instead, he invokes the help of the Christian God who had given inspiration to Moses to write the first five books of the Bible. The last lines in *Paradise Lost* about Adam and Eve's leaving the Eden are very touching and show both the solitude of human condition and the admirable courage of human beings.

> The world was all before them, where to choose
>
> Their place of rest, and Providence their guide:
>
> They, hand in hand, with wandering steps and slow,
>
> Through Eden took their solitary way.

As for the prose work in this period, John Bunyan's (1628–1688) *The Pilgrim's Progress* (1678) is the most note-worthy. It is an allegorical (寓言) story about the arduous pilgrimage of the protagonist (named Christian) from the City of Destruction to the Celestial City. Christian's journey takes him to many places, indicating different situations and encounters in life.

The Age of Enlightenment

The 18th century is often called the Age of Enlightenment, or the Age of Reason. Enlightenment is an intellectual movement, aiming to use critical reason to free minds from prejudice and unexamined authority. This emphasis on reason seems natural after a period of political turmoil in the seventeenth century.

Neoclassicism is the major trend in literature of this period. Writers of this trend model themselves after the Greek and Latin authors, trying to guide literary creation by some fixed laws and rules drawn from Greek and Latin works. The neoclassic writings are characterized by the emphasis on the three unities of time, place, and action in plays and the use of heroic couplet (英雄对偶句) in poetry. Heroic couplet refers to the rhyming two lines in iambic pentameter.

Alexander Pope (1688–1744) is the most important poet of neoclassicism. He brings heroic couplet to perfection. Rather than meditative and flowing, Pope's heroic couplets read like mathematical proof, step by step and very logical. His famous works include *An Essay on Criticism* (1711), *An Essay on Man* (1733), and the translation of Homer. According to Pope and his neoclassical theory, the best poets and critics should look to nature as the source of art. He thinks that a good critic needs humility by learning and reading the classics. Pope also believes that everything has a proper place in the chain of being, man being in the middle, between the lower creatures at one end and angels and God at the other. There is a link between Pope's view of the cosmos and his view of art, the order and reason expressed in his works of art being a reflection of his view of a well-ordered universe.

The eighteenth century also witnessed the rise of realistic novels. The English novel appears to have developed in response to a demand for a new kind of literature which emphasizes the significance of private experience. Daniel Defoe (1660–1725), Jonathan Swift (1667–1745), Samuel Richardson (1689–1761), and Henry Fielding (1707–1754) are all important novelists of this period.

Daniel Defoe is most famous for his *Robinson Crusoe* (1719), a novel based on the adventures of a real sailor who was left on an uninhabited island for five years. Defoe is a great realist and a novelist of imagination. He gives his novels the charm of the intense sense of reality, making the adventurous stories seem credible and fascinating by using minute and matter-of-fact details. *Robinson Crusoe* is not merely an adventure story for children. Daniel Defoe puts much emphasis on the moral values in his book. Crusoe is portrayed as an average man struggling against nature and human fate with his indomitable will and hand. His self-reliance, perseverance and resourcefulness have won him the approval of generations of readers.

Jonathan Swift is the author of a lot of powerful satirical essays and books, including *A Tale of a Tub* (1704), *Gulliver's Travels* (1726), and *A Modest Proposal* (1729). *A Modest Proposal* is a very caustic satire on the English oppression of people in Ireland. The author pretends to be giving the English government a proposal as to how to solve the problem of poverty and overpopulation in Ireland. He suggests that the English lords should eat the Irish babies. *Gulliver's Travels* is Swift's best-known work. It is a satire in the form of a travelogue of the protagonist Captain Lemuel Gulliver. The four voyages recorded in the four parts of the book take Gulliver to strange places, such as Lilliput (a land of tiny people), Brobdingnag (a land of giants), Laputa (a flying island), and finally the country of the Houyhnhnms, where the masters are the horses while the servants are the human-like creatures called Yahoos. The book satirizes the state of European governments and the petty differences between religions. Different parts of the book provide the readers with complementing views or perspectives. For example, Gulliver sees the tiny Lilliputians as being vicious and unscrupulous, and then the king of Brobdingnag sees Europe in exactly the same light.

Some literary historians think that Samuel Richardson, with his *Pamela, or Virtue Rewarded* (1740), has established the novel as we know it. Richardson has very serious moral concerns in his work. *Pamela* is an epistolary novel, or a novel written in the form of letters. It is about a virtuous servant girl named Pamela trying hard to resist the seduction of her young master Mr. B. Finally her virtue gets rewarded by respect and marriage and she moves upward along the social ladder. As the book is written in letters, which are very private and immediate, it is convenient for the novelist to reveal the secret thoughts and feelings of the heroine and to make a minute analysis of her emotions and state of mind. This novel is regarded as the first English psycho-analytical novel. Following the success of Pamela, Richardson wrote another novel about a female character, *Clarissa: or the History of a Young Lady* (1747–1748), which is his masterpiece.

Different from Samuel Richardson, who cares more about the psychological aspect of the characters in his novels, Henry Fielding seems to be more concerned with presenting a panorama of the society in his great novels. The major novels by Fielding include *Joseph Andrews* (1742), *The History of Tom Jones, a Foundling* (1749) and *Amelia* (1751). Fielding is a conscious innovator of the art of fiction and in his preface to the novel *Joseph Andrews*, he outlines his idea of the novel as "a comic epic poem in prose". He proposes to take the wide range of characters and incidents from the epic and to remold the material according to "comic" rather than "serious" principles. Fielding believes in the educational function of the novel. His masterpiece *Tom Jones* shows his comic redefinition of the epic hero and is generally regarded as one of the first and the most influential of English novels. It is about the adventures of a foundling named Tom Jones. The novel has a happy ending and the generous Tom forgives all those people who have hurt him. Fielding says that his intention in writing the story is to "recommend goodness and innocence".

In the second half of the eighteenth century, there was still another literary current—sentimentalism, which is the overindulgence in one's emotion because of the bitter discontent with the social reality. Laurence

Sterne (1713–1768) is the most outstanding figure of English sentimentalism. His masterpiece is *Tristram Shandy* (1759–1767), the full title being *The Life and Opinions of Tristram Shandy, Gentleman.* This novel is very modern in its form. The narrative of the book is not organized in a sequential order and there is not a coherent plot. The book is supposed to be an autobiography of Tristram Shandy, the narrator, but by the end of the book, the readers know more about people around Shandy rather than about Shandy himself. For Laurence Sterne, what the story is about is of secondary importance to how it is told. The author is constantly meditating on story-telling itself and keeps interrupting the narration with digressions, which he calls the sunshine and the soul of reading.

As for the sentimentalist poets, Thomas Gray (1716–1771) is the best one and his most famous poem is "Elegy Written in a Country Churchyard" (1751). The poem is a meditation on the obscure destinies of the unknown and undistinguished villagers buried in the village churchyard. The poet imagines that those villagers might have become great people like Milton or Cromwell if they had had the opportunity. The lack of opportunity had "confined" both their talents and their potential crimes. Gray makes a celebrated comment on the unfulfilled greatness.

> Far from the madding crowd's ignoble strife,
>
> Their sober wishes never learned to stray;
>
> Along the cool sequestered vale of life,
>
> They kept the noiseless tenor of their way.

The Romantic Period

The Romantic period roughly refers to the period between 1785 and 1830. It is against the background of Industrial Revolution and the French Revolution, and is a great period in English literature, second only to the Elizabethan Age. In contrast with the emphasis on reason in the eighteenth century, the Romantic writers pay great attention to the spiritual and emotional life of man and the beauty of nature. The major literary achievements of this period are mainly in poetry. There are two generations of Romantic poets. The first generation includes William Wordsworth (1770–1850), Samuel Taylor Coleridge (1772–1834), and Robert Southey (1774–1843). They are called "Lake Poets" as they lived in the Lake District. The younger generation includes George Gordon, Lord Byron (1788–1824), Percy Bysshe Shelley (1792–1822), and John Keats (1795–1821).

Wordsworth collaborated with Coleridge and published *Lyrical Ballads* in 1798. In the "Preface," Wordsworth states some of his ideas on poetry. He puts much emphasis on the imagination and the feelings of man. According to Wordsworth, incidents and situations from common life can be the subject of poetry, and the poetic diction and the coloring of the imagination should enable people to see the incidents in a new light. Perhaps his most famous comment on the source of poetry is "all good poetry is the spontaneous overflow of powerful feeling." Wordsworth is a great lover of nature. In his famous poem "Tintern Abbey" (the full title being: "Lines Composed a Few Miles above Tintern Abbey, on Revisiting the Banks of the Wye during a Tour, July I3, 1798") he expresses his philosophical views on nature. He believes that the memory of the beautiful things in nature has the healing power of "tranquil restoration" and can help a person to become morally better. When immersed in such memories, one may even enjoy the mysterious experience of being in harmony with the universe. Wordsworth sees an interrelationship between a love of nature and a love of humanity. The other major poems of Wordsworth include "Ode: Intimations of Immortality" and *The Prelude*, which is his spiritual autobiography.

Coleridge takes up the more supernatural and exotic subjects, as is shown in his poems *The Rime of the Ancient Mariner* and "Kubla Khan." Coleridge is also a great literary critic. His *Biographia Literaria* (1817), now a classic work of literary criticism, is a collection of writings about his own growth as a poet and his analysis of Wordsworth's poetic diction.

Among the younger generation of Romantic poets, both Byron and Shelley have a rebellious spirit. Byron had achieved an immense European reputation during his life time and through much of the 19th century he continued to be regarded as one of the greatest of English poets and the prototype of literary romanticism. Byron creates in his works a fascinating type of hero— "Byronic hero," who is rebellious, mysterious, gloomy, and passionate. This type first appears in *Childe Harold's Pilgrimage* (1812–1818), a travelogue narrated by a melancholy and well-read protagonist about the tour in some European countries, such as Spain, Portugal, and Greece. The literary descendants of the Byronic hero include Heathcliff in Emily Bronte's *Wuthering Heights* and Mr. Rochester in Charlotte Bronte's *Jane Eyre*. *Don Juan* (1819–1826) is Byron's masterpiece. It is an unfinished satirical poem of 16000 lines. The title character Don Juan is originally a Spanish legendary libertine, with superhuman sexual energy and wickedness. But Byron's version of Don Juan is more acted upon than active, always amiable and well intentioned.

Shelley is best known for his poem "Ode to the West Wind" (1819) to Chinese readers. The west wind is a "spirit" (the Latin word **Spiritus** means the wind, breath and the soul) that destroys in the autumn in order to revive in the spring. In the storm of the natural world, Shelley sees a metaphor for the storm of revolution in human world. The last line of the poem "If Winter comes, can Spring be far behind?" is a prophecy of hope. Shelley's other famous works include poems such as "To a Sky Lark" (1820) and "Ozymandias" (1817), his work of literary theory *A Defense of Poetry* (1821), and his Lyrical drama *Prometheus Unbound*

(1820). *Prometheus Unbound* is based on *Prometheus Bound* of Aeschylus (525 BCE–456BCE.), who is a great tragedian of the ancient Greek. Shelley transforms it into a symbolic drama about the origin of evil and the possibility of overcoming it. His wife Mary Wollstonecraft Shelley (1797–1851) is the author of the very famous gothic story *Frankenstein* or *The Modern Prometheus* (1818).

John Keats is a very talented poet. Constantly disturbed by ill health, he probes the idea of eternity and beauty in his poems. His famous poems include "Ode to a Nightingale" (1819), "Bright Star" (1819), "Ode on a Grecian Urn" (1820), and "The Eve of St. Agnes" (1820). He longs for permanence in a world of change, and what he desires is not the cold and indifferent eternity but the eternity with human love.

There are two important novelists in this period: Walter Scott (1771–1832) and Jane Austen (1775–1817). Walter Scott is a great writer of historical novels, such as *Waverley* (1814) and *Ivanhoe* (1819). Scott's novels cover a period ranging from the Middle Ages to the 18th century, giving a panorama of the feudal society from its early stages to its downfall.

Jane Austen has been regarded as one of the greatest English novelists. Although Jane Austen's life time coincides with the Romantic period, she is realistic in her treatment of life in her novels, which highlight the dependence of women on marriage to secure social standing and economic security. Austen's love stories are among the best such stories in the world. Austen has altogether six finished novels, *Pride and Prejudice* (1813) and *Emma* (1815) being generally considered the most important ones. In *Pride and Prejudice* the young girls live in a world where love and marriage are expected to be based on material considerations. However, Elizabeth, the heroine, puts her moral sense of righteousness ahead of her rational decision making and heroically rejects the proposal made by Mr. Darcy, the richest man in this novel. The story has a happy ending as both Elizabeth and Darcy grow in the process. Elizabeth overcomes her blindness and prejudice while Darcy is humbled by love.

The best essayists of the Romantic period are Charles Lamb (1775–1834) and William Hazlitt (1778–1830). Charles Lamb published with his sister an excellent book *Tales from Shakespeare* (1807), which is a retelling of the plays for children. William Hazlitt, as a literary theorist and a critic of Shakespeare and Elizabethan drama, has a conspicuous influence on his own contemporaries. He is also a literary critic of his contemporary poets. His best essays can be found in such collections as *Characters of Shakespeare's Plays* (1817) and *The Spirit of the Age* (1825).

Figure 6.3　Jane Austen

The Victorian Age

The Victorian Age occupies two thirds of the nineteenth century, from 1830 to 1901, roughly the reign of Queen Victoria. The novel of realism is the major form of literature in this period. Charles Dickens (1812–1870), George Eliot (1819–1880) and Thomas Hardy (1840–1928) are all great victorian novelists. The emphasis on the earnestness and moral responsibility in the victorian society can be seen in the moral sense of the novelists and their works.

Charles Dickens (1812–1870) is generally considered the greatest novelist of the Victorian period. He wants to use the novel as an instrument for reform to make Britain a better place and to throw light on people's hard-heartedness. Dickens is famed for his depiction of the hardships of the working class, his intricate plots, and his sense of humor. But he is perhaps most famed for the characters he creates. The autobiographical elements are noticeable in Dickens' novels, *David Copperfield* being the most autobiographical one. Dickens is a fierce critic of the poverty and social evils of the Victorian society. His novel *Oliver Twist* (1839) shocked readers with its images of poverty and crime and was responsible for the clearing of an actual London slum. Dickens' career can be roughly divided into 2 sub-sections, with the year 1850 as the dividing point. His earlier novels are basically optimistic, being aware of modern ills but still having faith in the charitable spirit of human beings. Works of this period include *Oliver Twist* (1837–1839) and *David Copperfield* (1850). His works of the second period paint a very dismal and agonizing social picture. *Bleak House* (1852–1853), *Hard Times* (1854), and *Great Expectations* (1860-1861) are all works of the second period.

George Eliot and the Bronte sisters are among the best women novelists of this period. George Eliot's novels show Britain's transformation from an agricultural to an industrial nation. In the world of her novels, people feel the manipulation of the forces out of their control, but they still have room for free choice. She has faith in human nature and the goodness of a moral society. Eliot is noted for her masterly psychological descriptions of the characters. Her major works include *The Mill on the Floss* (1860), *Middlemarch* (1871–1872), and *Daniel Deronda* (1874–1876).

The masterpiece of Charlotte Brontë (1816–1855) is *Jane Eyre* (1847), which is a semi-autobiography based on the author's own life experience. It is a typical Bildungsroman (成长小说或教育小说) about the protagonist's pursuit of love and autonomy. A Bildungsroman is a novel of education, or a coming-of-age story. Such novels focus on the psychological and moral growth of the protagonist from youth to adulthood. Dickens' *Great Expectations* also falls into this genre. Charlotte Brontë's other novels include *Villette* (1853),

Shirley (1849), and *The Professor* (1857). Emily Brontë (1818–1848) and Anne Brontë (1820–1849) are also talented writers. The masterpiece of Emily is *Wuthering Heights* (1847).

Thomas Hardy (1840–1928) is the most important novelist of late Victorian Age. Pessimism seems to prevail in his works. In the cold and indifferent world of Hardy's novels, man is insignificant and impotent in face of the overwhelming odds of fate and struggles in vain for survival. The world of Hardy is controlled not by benevolence, but by chance. The major works of Hardy include *The Return of the Native* (1878), *The Mayor of Casterbridge* (1886), *Tess of the d'Urbervilles* (1891) and *Jude the Obscure* (1895), the latter two considered his masterpieces. Tess embodies self-respect and human dignity and she is willing to risk for the sake of her family.

The most important Victorian poets are Alfred, Lord Tennyson (1809–1892), Robert Browning (1812–1889) and Matthew Arnold (1822–1888). The Victorian poetry is characterized by the long narrative, the experiment with perspectives, the dramatic monologue and the representation of mood and psychology. The idea of creating a lyric poem in the voice of a speaker different from the poet is a great achievement of Victorian poetry.

Tennyson became the poet laureate in 1850. He puts emphasis on love, duty, marriage and home. The short poem "Break, Break, Break" is his most often anthologized poem, in which he mourns the untimely death of his friend Hallam. The poem is permeated with a sense of melancholy isolation. The nature seems to be cold and indifferent to human tragedies and the world still goes on, with the speaker himself isolated in his grief. "The Elegies on Hallam" were published as *In Memoriam* (1850), which is a vast poem of 131 sections and reflects the struggle to reconcile traditional religious faith and belief in immortality with the emerging theories of evolution. *The Idylls of the King* (1859) is another masterpiece. It is a series of 12 connected poems surveying the legend of King Arthur from his falling in love with his queen to the ultimate ruin of his kingdom.

Robert Browning is a master of dramatic monologue, which is a form of poetry, with a speaker who is different from the poet. Such a poem presents a situation that seems to be a scene in a drama. The speaker in the poem speaks to an implied listener who never really speaks in the poem. A dramatic monologue does not aim to state the poet's ideas or to express the poet's emotions; instead, it aims to develop the character of the speaker. Browning's "My Last Duchess" (1842) is a very good example to illustrate this point. The speaker reveals himself to be a selfish, possessive, greedy and cruel man who orders to have his wife killed just because he is jealous of his wife's being friendly to others. Browning's greatest poem is *The Ring and the Book* (1868–1869). Browning's wife, Elizabeth Barrett Browning (1806–1861) is also a famous poet, best known for her sonnet sequence *Sonnets from the Portuguese* (1850).

Matthew Arnold (1822–1888) is a poet and a great cultural advocate. His short poem "Dover Beach" (1867) conveys some sadness over the crisis of faith in his age. His other important works include *Culture and*

Anarchy (1868–1869) and *The Function of Criticism at the Present Time* (1864–1865).

There is a new literary trend at the end of the nineteenth century—aestheticism, or the school of "art for art's sake." It is against the traditional assumption that literature should serve a moral function. Oscar Wilde (1854–1900) is the spokesman of aestheticism. His novel *The Picture of Dorian Gray* (1891) portrays the divided personality of a hedonist. Oscar Wilde is well-known for his comedies, such as *An Ideal Husband* (1895) and *The Importance of Being Earnest* (1895).

The Period of Modernism

For convenience of discussion, the twentieth century can be roughly divided into two periods, with WW II being the dividing point. The first part can be regarded as the period of modernism, although the actual high modernism takes place in the 1920s, with T.S. Eliot's *The Waste Land* and James Joyce's *Ulysses* appearing in 1922. Henry James (1843–1916) and Joseph Conrad (1857–1924) can be regarded as the bridge between realism and modernism. William Butler Yeats (1865–1939), T. S. Eliot (1888–1965), James Joyce (1882–1941), Virginia Woolf (1882–1941), and D. H. Lawrence (1885–1930) are all modernist masters.

Henry James is a master of the art of fiction. He presents his novels as works of art. The fundamental theme of Henry James' novels is the innocence and exuberance of the New World in clash with the corruption and wisdom of the Old World of Europe. His major works include *The Portrait of a Lady* (1881), *The Wings of the Dove* (1902), and *The Golden Bowl* (1904). James was born in the US, so he will also be discussed in the chapter about American literature in this book.

Joseph Conrad is an effective transitional figure, with a close affinity in temperament with the rising generation of modernists. His novels put emphasis on the psychology of the characters. Conrad's tales are often concerned with the nature and effects of European imperialism. In Conrad's works, such as *Lord Jim* (1900) and *Heart of Darkness* (1902), colonialism generally emerges as both brutal and brutalizing, alienating the natives and settlers alike. The narrative in *Heart of Darkness* unveils an underlying horror of colonialism, showing how easily the cloak of civilization can be ripped from the white men who happen to enter the jungle.

Modernism is also a kind of realism and it represents a new mode of perception. In the new century, especially with the disillusionment after the First World War, life appears to be fragmentary and chaotic. Against this background, Modernism attaches importance to people's internal reality rather than the external reality of the world. In her essay "Modern Fiction" (1925), Virginia Woolf complains about the over-emphasis on the description of externalities in the representation of life by some realist novelists of early twentieth century. According to Woolf, the internal world of man should take precedence over anything else in novel writing and the purpose of the modernist writings is to reveal the true nature of the modern human condition and its disconcerting absence of meaning, purpose, and order. Stream of consciousness (意识流) is the technique adopted by Woolf and some other modernist novelists in order to reveal the full richness of the mind at work and the fragmentary and disorderly world in which the characters live. When using such a technique, the writer usually incorporates the incoherent thought, ungrammatical constructions, and free association of ideas and images. Virginia Woolf's major works are *Mrs. Dalloway* (1925), *To the Lighthouse* (1927), and the non-fiction work *A Room of One's Own* (1929).

James Joyce, an Irish novelist, is another master of stream of consciousness, which is often used interchangeably with the term "interior monologue." Joyce's masterpiece is *Ulysses* (1922), which describes the experiences of several characters on June 16, 1904. The structure of the novel bears a striking resemblance to Homer's epic *Odyssey*, as the "Ulysses" in the title is the Roman name for Homer's epic hero Odysseus. For Joyce, characterization matters more than the plot. The parallel structure offers an ironic contrast between the heroic, meaningful and noble life of Homer's hero and his petty, ordinary and spiritually poor modern counterpart. *Dubliners* (1914) is a collection of stories, revealing the spiritual paralysis in Dublin and the moments of epiphany (顿悟) of the protagonists. The last story in the collection "The Dead" is considered a world masterpiece.

D. H. Lawrence (1885–1830) is renowned for his novels. For Lawrence, the great and the beautiful come from within the soul, not from the progress of the society and science. The evil of the modern mechanical civilization lies in its ruthless violation of human soul, depriving it of the ability and instinct to love, and thus dehumanizing man. His major novels include *Sons and Lovers* (1913), *The Rainbow* (1915), *Women in Love* (1920), and *Lady Chatterley's Lover* (1928). The novel *Sons and Lovers* deals with the "Oedipus complex" (恋母情结) and its negative impact upon human growth. *Lady Chatterley's Lover* reflects Lawrence's belief that men and women must overcome the deadening restrictions of industrialized society and follow their natural instincts to passionate love.

William Butler Yeats (1865–1939) and T. S. Eliot dominated the poetic scene of the first half of the twentieth century. Yeats, born in Dublin, has a lifelong fascination with mysticism and the occult. He believes that poems and plays would produce a national unity capable of transfiguring the Irish nation. Works in his earlier career, such as *Poems* (1895) and *The Wind Among the Reeds* (1899), have the dreamlike atmosphere and show his interest in Irish folklore and legends. His later works represent the height of his achievement, with the perfect technique that is almost without parallel in the history of English poetry. *The Tower* (1928) is named after the castle he owned and in it the experience of a lifetime is brought to perfection of form. *The Winding Stair* (1929) also contains some of his greatest poems. His short poem

"When You Are Old" is very popular, which is about his love for Maud Gonne, an Irish patriot. Yeats was awarded Nobel Prize in 1923.

T. S. Eliot (1888–1965) was born in the US but later became a naturalized British citizen. He is a poet, a playwright, a literary critic, and a leader of the modernist movement in poetry. His well-known poems include "The Love Song of J. Alfred Prufrock" (1915), *The Waste Land* (1922) and *Four Quartets* (1943). The primary theme of *The Waste Land* is the search for redemption and renewal in a sterile and spiritually empty landscape. It is a poem with fragmentary images and obscure allusions, and requires the reader to take an active role in interpreting the text. *Four Quartets* is Eliot's masterpiece and it is a subtle meditation on the nature of time and its relation to eternity. Eliot is also a distinguished literary critic. In his famous critical work "Tradition and the Individual Talent", he states that a writer should have the historical sense, and that "the poet must develop or procure the consciousness of the past and that he should continue to develop this consciousness throughout his career." He won the Nobel Prize for Literature in 1948.

The most important dramatist in the late Victorian Age and the first half of the twentieth century is George Bernard Shaw (1859–1950). He won the Nobel Prize in 1925. Shaw is a highly prolific writer and his most famous plays include *Mrs. Warren's Profession* (1893), *Major Barbara* (1907), *Pygmalion* (1912), and *Saint Joan* (1923). Shaw draws the attention of his audience to the serious social issues and presents in his plays the conflict of ideas to provoke thinking.

Post-War Literature

The period after the Second World War witnessed many Nobel Prize winning writers, such as Samuel Beckett (1906–1989), William Golding (1911–1993), Doris Lessing (1919–2013) and Seamus Heaney (1939–2013). John Fowles (1926–2005) is also an important writer of this period.

William Golding won the Nobel Prize in 1983. His masterpiece is *Lord of the Flies* (1954), which indicates his concern with moral allegory. It is about a group of English boys who, being stranded on a desert island, fall away from civilization and regress into barbarism and murder. The novel reveals the innate depravity not merely of the boys, but of the whole human race.

Doris Lessing and John Fowles are both very experimental with the form of the novel. Lessing's masterpiece *The Golden Notebook* (1962) is regarded as a metafiction (元小说), which is a postmodernist form of writing about fiction in the form of fiction, telling the readers that fiction is fiction and is not an illusion of reality as the realists have tried to deceive the readers into believing. *The French Lieutenant's*

Woman (1969) is Fowles's best-known work. It is a love story set in 19th-century England that richly documents the social mores of that time. The book combines elements of the Victorian novel with postmodern works and features alternate endings.

Seamus Heaney is regarded as the best Irish poet since Yeats and one of the greatest contemporary English poets. He produces a modern-English translation of the Old English epic *Beowulf* (1999). From the outset of his career, Heaney is determined to speak for the voiceless and the oppressed. And in his works he is concerned with the celebration of the rural people, with their crafts and skills and their contribution to communal life. His famous poems include "The Forge" (1969) and "Digging" (1964). A dominant thematic concern for Heaney is to find "a door into the dark" for the redemption of all humans. He seems to find it in the "displacement" offered by the self-exile in poetry and imagination. He received the Nobel Prize for Literature in 1995.

Samuel Beckett is a monumental figure in postwar English theater. Writing in both French and English, he ushers in the era of the drama of the absurd. Absurdist plays explore the absurd nature of the human condition. Beckett's major thematic focus is to throw in relief modern man's rootlessness, want of identity, and hopelessness. *Waiting for Godot* (1953) is his best-known play and it shows the absurdity and the purposelessness of human life. The two heroes in the play (usually referred to as two tramps) are two human beings in the most basic human situation of being in the world and not knowing what they are there for.

One thing to note is that among the authors we have discussed, Jonathan Swift, George Bernard Shaw, Oscar Wilde, William Butler Yeats, James Joyce, Samuel Becket, and Seamus Heaney are all Anglo-Irish writers, which means that they are Irish either by birth or by residence.

Exercises

Part I. Decide whether the following statements are true (T) or false (F). Write T or F in the brackets.

1. *The Song of Beowulf* is an epic in Middle English. (   )
2. Drama is the most important form of literature in the period of English Renaissance. (   )
3. *Paradise Lost* is a novel written by John Milton. (   )
4. Alexander Pope is the most important poet in the first half of the 18th century. (   )

5. George Eliot is an important woman novelist of the Victorian Age and she is noted for her psychological descriptions of the characters. (   )

6. According to Wordsworth, the memory of the beautiful things in nature has the healing power of "tranquil restoration" and can help a person to become morally better. (   )

7. George Bernard Shaw is a playwright who likes to draw the attention of the audience to the social problems. (   )

8. *The Golden Notebook* is written by the Nobel Prize winning writer Samuel Becket. (   )

Part II. Fill in the blanks with best answers.

1. _____ is regarded as the father of English poetry.

   A. John Milton

   B. William Shakespeare

   C. Geoffrey Chaucer

   D. Alexander Pope

2. *The Tragical History of Dr. Faustus* is a play written by _____.

   A. Oscar Wilde

   B. John Dryden

   C. Christopher Marlowe

   D. William Shakespeare

3. _____ is the most famous metaphysical poet.

   A. John Donne

   B. Philip Sidney

   C. Edmund Spenser

   D. William Butler Yeats

4. *Robinson Crusoe* is the masterpiece of the eighteenth century writer _____.

   A. Jonathan Swift

   B. Daniel Defoe

   C. Henry Fielding

D. Samuel Richardson

5. Jane Austen, the author of _____, is famous for her novels about love and marriage.

   A. *Jane Eyre*

   B. *Wuthering Heights*

   C. *Pride and Prejudice*

   D. *The Portrait of a Lady*

6. Of Dickens' novels, _____ is considered the most autobiographical.

   A. *A Tale of Two Cities*

   B. *David Copperfield*

   C. *Great Expectations*

   D. *Oliver Twist*

7. Of the following books, _____ is not written by Thomas Hardy.

   A. *Jude the Obscure*

   B. *Tess of the d'Urbervilles*

   C. *The Return of the Native*

   D. *The Mill on the Floss*

8. _____ is famous for his stream of consciousness novel *Ulysses*.

   A. James Joyce

   B. Virginia Woolf

   C. D. H. Lawrence

   D. George Eliot

Part III. State your understanding of the following questions.

1. How do you understand Hamlet's delay in taking revenge on his uncle?

2. Do you like the protagonist in the novel *Jane Eyre*? Why do you think she loves Mr. Rochester?

3. What is Virginia Woolf's view of the task of the modern novels?

Part II

The United States of America

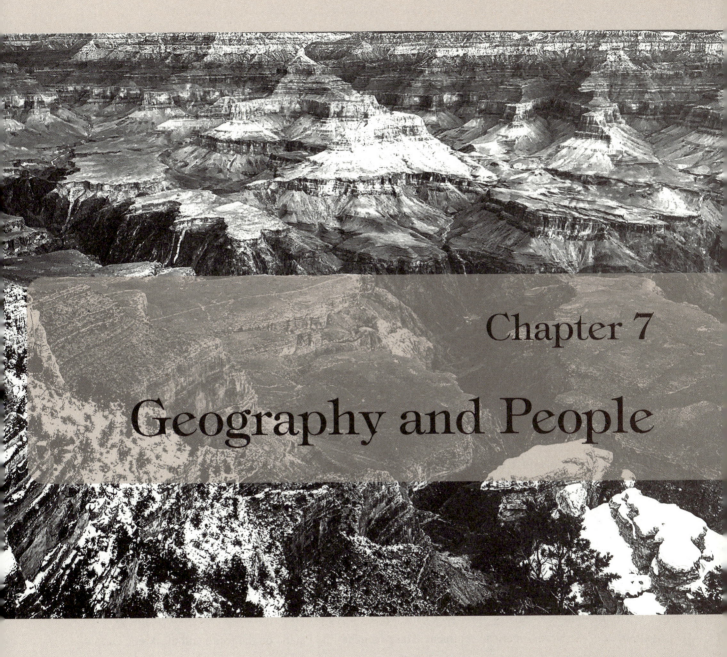

Chapter 7
Geography and People

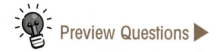

Preview Questions

1. What do you know about New York City and Washington D.C.?
2. What is the general feature of American climate?
3. Do you have any idea of the population distribution of the United States?

Geography

America is a federal constitutional republic comprising 50 states and a federal district. The official name of the country is the United States of America, commonly referred to as the United States, the US, the USA or America.

1 Location and Regions

The country is mostly located in the central part of North America, including 48 contiguous states and 2 non-contiguous states of Alaska and Hawaii, the last two states admitted to the US in 1959. The country stretches from the Atlantic Ocean to the east and the Pacific Ocean to the west (covering 4 time zones), and it is bordered by Canada to the north, and Mexico and the Gulf of Mexico to the south. In addition, the country includes several territories, or insular areas (岛屿), scattered around the Caribbean and the Pacific.

The two youngest states are separated from the continental United States. Situated in the northwest extremity of the North American continent, Alaska touches the Pacific on the south and the Arctic Ocean on the north, with Canada to its east and Russia to the west across the Bering Strait. Hawaii is an archipelago (群岛) located in the central Pacific Ocean southwest of the continental United States.

The 50 states vary widely in size and population. The largest state in area is Alaska, followed by Texas, and California. The smallest state in area is Rhode Island. According to the latest statistics from the US Census Bureau, the state with the largest population is California, followed by Texas, and Florida. Wyoming is the least populous state.

Chapter 7 Geography and People

The United States can be typically divided into six regions: New England, the Mid-Atlantic States, the South, the Midwest, the Southwest and the West. These regions are formed by history and geography and are shaped by the economy, literature and folkways that all the parts of the regions share, and based upon latitude and longitude coordinates.

2 The Terrain of the United States

The US has varied geographical features with large mountains, hills, vast plains, dry deserts, basins, and broad river valleys. It can be divided into three distinct areas according to their geographical features: the eastern part, the western part and the Grand Plains in between.

The eastern part refers to the Atlantic seacoast and west to the Appalachians, consisting of highlands, and is a strip of fairly level area. This area holds one-sixth of the continental American territory. Broad in the south, about 300 kilometers, the coastal plain narrows toward the north and gives way to the rocky coastlines in New England. This broad coastal plain and other islands make up the widest and longest beaches in the United States. In the south, the coastal plain is very low and wide.

The western part consists of high plateaus and mountains. The whole area of this part holds one-third of the country's territory on the continent. The Rocky Mountains, known as "the backbone of the continent," stretch more than 4,830 kilometers with an average altitude of over 4,000 meters above sea level. The large southern portion is known as the Great Basin. The Southwest is predominantly a low-lying desert region. A portion known as the Colorado Plateau, is considered to have some of the most spectacular scenery in the world. It is home to some famous national parks like Grand Canyon.

The Great Plains lie west of the Mississippi River and east of the Rocky Mountains, a more than 290,000-square-mile area. Before their general conversion to farmland, the Great Plains are noted for their extensive grasslands. They stretch from the Great Lakes in the north to the Gulf of Mexico in the south. The early settlers found rich soil on the Great Plains. The Plains are a huge basin sculpted out by glaciers during the Great Ice Age. These large flat areas are untouched by erosion, creating thick sod and productive agriculture. But the Great Plains are semi-arid, experiencing periodic droughts. The Plains became the breadbasket of the world only after irrigation was put into place.

3 Natural Resources

The generosity of nature provides Americans with large and fertile land. The United States has an abundance of natural resources including two expansive coastlines, a wide area of fertile land, abundant fresh water, and huge reserves of oil and coal.

Rivers and Lakes

The United States is rich in water resources. There are many rivers and lakes that can be used to irrigate fields, transport goods and furnish power. Lakes, rivers, and streams provide 87% of the water used in America.

(1) The Mississippi River

The Mississippi River is the most important and longest river in the US, also known as "Old Man River." It can be divided into three sections: the Upper Mississippi, the river from its headwaters to the confluence with the Missouri River; the Middle Mississippi, which is downriver from the Missouri to the Ohio River; and the Lower Mississippi, which flows from the Ohio to the Gulf of Mexico. It flows about 6,400 km from its northwestern source in the Rockies to the Gulf of Mexico, the fourth longest in the world after the Amazon, Nile, and Yangtze rivers. This river is known to some native Americans as "the father of waters."

Nearly all the rivers west of the Appalachians and east of the Rockies flow into each other and empty into the Mississippi River. The chief tributaries are the Missouri River, the Ohio River, the Arkansas, etc. With its hundreds of tributaries, the Mississippi basin drains more than half of the nation, playing an important role in inland navigation, but also the cause of periodic flooding.

(2) The Missouri River

The Missouri River, an important tributary of the Mississippi River, begins in the Rockies and pours into the Mississippi at St. Louis from the west. Since the river runs through the dry west, it carries a large amount of topsoil which turns the river water into deep brown, so the river is sometimes called "the Muddy River".

(3) The Ohio River

The Ohio River, about 1,580 kilometers long, rises in Pennsylvania among the rainy Appalachians and joins the Mississippi at Cairo, Illinois. The area along the river has rich deposits of coking coal and a large heavy industry, so the river is called the American **Ruhr**[1]. The Tennessee River is an important tributary of the Ohio River, and the federal government constructed 33 major dams on the river to control the waters, improve transportation, and generate electricity.

(4) The Great Lakes

The Great Lakes are composed of five lakes: Lake Michigan, Lake Superior, Lake Erie, Lake Huron and Lake Ontario. Among the five lakes, only Lake Michigan belongs to the US completely while the other four are shared by the United States and Canada. Lake Superior (82,414 km2) is the largest fresh water lake (by surface area) in the world.

---

1 Ruhr: The Ruhr (鲁尔河) is a medium river in western Germany. The area where the Ruhr is located originally referred to the mining areas along the Ruhr. Due to the rich coal resources in the area north of the Ruhr, the coal mining industry developed in the Ruhr Valley area.

These five lakes cover an area of about 240,000 square kilometers. They are the largest lake group in the world and contain about half of the world's fresh water. All the five lakes are inter-connected, reaching the Atlantic by way of the St. Lawrence River. They play an extremely important role in the transportation of goods for areas around them. The world-famous Niagara Falls is located between Lake Erie and Lake Ontario.

Forests

In the United States, forests are owned collectively by American people through the federal government and managed by the United States Forest Service, a division of the United States Department of Agriculture. Roughly 36.21% of the land (about one-third of the US) is forested. There are 154 national forests in the United States.

Mountains

The two main mountain ranges in America are the Appalachian Mountains and the Rocky Mountains.

(1) The Appalachians

The Appalachians are a vast system of mountains in eastern North America, mostly located in the United States but extending into southeastern Canada. The mountain range covers about 3,200 kilometers slightly from northeast to southwest. These mountains are now worn low by erosion, usually not over 800 meters in height. The Appalachians have beautiful scenery and many tourist resorts.

(2) The Rocky Mountains

The Rocky Mountains are a major mountain range in western North America. The Rocky Mountains stretch more than 4,800 kilometers from the northern United States to the southwestern United States. There are numerous high peaks, and the tops of them are often capped with snow. There are 38 national parks here, among which the most famous is the Yellowstone National Park, the oldest national park in the world and the largest wildlife preserve in the US.

Mineral Resources

Among the main contributors to the United States' natural resource value are coal, timber, natural gas, gold, lead, copper, silver, petroleum and other resources. The United States has the world's largest coal reserves with 491 billion short tons, accounting for 27% of the world's total. This abundant source of energy helped fuel the US growth during the Industrial Revolution. It fueled steamships and steam-powered railroads. After the Civil War, coke, a derivative of coal, was used to fuel the iron blast furnaces that made steel. Soon after that, coal ran the electricity-generating plants. In 2020, the US accounted for 6.7% of the global coal production, which made the country the fifth largest coal producer in the world.

Coal reserves in the US are widely distributed geographically with Montana, Wyoming, Illinois, West Virginia, Kentucky, and Pennsylvania, hosting more than three fourths of the total reserves. The North

Antelope Rochelle coal mine operated by Peabody Energy in the Powder River Basin of Wyoming is the world's biggest coal mine by reserves.

Climate

The United States is mainly situated in the northern temperate zone. But owing to its large size and varied landform, it has different types of climate in different areas. The climate of New England is relatively cold. The winters are long and hard. In many parts of Maine, there is snow on the ground from early November to late May. The summers are short and warm. The fall, however, is a beautiful time of year. In the fall, the leaves of trees turn different colors, giving the hills and woods a bright look.

The climate of the Middle Atlantic States region is generally pleasant. There are four definite seasons. The winters are cold and snowy; the springs are warm with plenty of rain to help the growth of crops; the summers are short and hot but pleasant, and the falls are cool.

The South enjoys a warm climate and abundant rainfall. Many of its states lie within the band known as the Sun Belt. The climate, however, varies with the geographical position of each state. Virginia and North Carolina have a temperate climate like that of Maryland. In southern Florida, on the other hand, the climate is almost tropical. Georgia, Alabama, Mississippi, and Louisiana all have warm climates. Some states in this region are sometimes harassed by the disaster of hurricanes.

Since the Great Plains stretch from the Canadian border to Texas, the climate in this region varies widely. North Dakota has extreme temperatures, strong winds, and low precipitation. Oklahoma, on the other hand, has a more temperate climate.

The climate of the Midwest is temperate. This region lies in a great valley between the Allegheny Mountains to the east and the Great Plains and Rocky Mountains to the west. This is a largely open area, and the wind blows freely, often bringing sudden and extreme changes in temperature. Midwest summers are sometimes very hot; winters are sometimes extremely cold.

The states west of the Rocky Mountains have sharply different climatic conditions. This is largely due to the effects of the mountain ranges and the Pacific Ocean. Winds from the Pacific bring plenty of rain, and these winds are conditioned by the mountains along the coast. Generally speaking, the western slopes of the Coastal Mountains are cool, rainy, and cloudy. The part of Washington near the Pacific Ocean has the highest portion of rainfall in the country. But after crossing these mountains, very little rain falls and deserts appear.

The United States has experienced a wide variety of extreme weather over the past years. The long coastline with many harbors and inlets not only provides favorable conditions for foreign trade and the fishing industry, but also brings much of the country within the influence of the oceanic air mass (海洋气团). Among the common natural disasters caused by extreme weather are tornadoes, hurricanes, flood, earthquakes and volcanic eruptions.

Major Cities

Among all the cities in the United States, only 10 cities have populations above 1 million and none are above 10 million. 310 cities are considered medium ones with populations of 100,000 or more. According to the official statistics, about 40% of the US population live in cities with 50,000 or more residents. As the population begins to move towards urban areas, the number and size of cities in the United States will continue to grow.

1 New York

New York is the largest city and the commercial and financial center of the US with a population of 8.5 million people. Located at the southern tip of New York State on one of the world's largest natural harbors, it includes three islands: Manhattan Island, Long Island and Staten Island at the mouth of the Hudson River. New York has five boroughs: Manhattan, Bronx, Brooklyn, Queens, and Staten Island. New York is the most populous city in the United States, and also the largest metropolitan area in the world by urban area (4,585 square miles). Anchored by the Wall Street in the Financial District of Lower Manhattan, New York is called the world's leading financial and Fintech center. It is home to the world's two largest stock exchanges by market capitalization of their listed companies: the New York Stock Exchange and Nasdaq. Home to the headquarters of the United Nations, New York is also an important center of international diplomacy. You can find the Times Square, the Statue of Liberty, the Central Park, the Metropolitan Museum and other attractions here. The Statue of Liberty standing at the gate of New York Harbor is the symbol of America, which immigrated to the United States from France in 1886.

2 Washington D.C.

Washinton D.C. (District of Columbia) is the capital city of the United States, located on the east bank of the Potomac River. It was named after George Washington (1732–1799), the first President of the US. The city is not part of any state, governed directly by the federal government. It is an extraordinary city, one with multiple personalities: a working federal city, an international metropolis, a picturesque tourist destination, and an unmatched treasury of the country's history and artifacts. Apart from the government buildings, for example, the White House and the Capitol, it is the location of most US federal government agencies and embassies in the United States, as well as the headquarters of international organizations such as the World Bank, the International Monetary Fund, and the Organization of American States, and has a large number of museums and cultural historical sites.

3 Los Angeles

Los Angeles, known as "the city of Angles," is the most populous city in California and is the second largest city in the country after New York, and it is an important electronic center and the commercial, financial and cultural center. With roughly 3.9 million residents within the city limits, Los Angeles has a diverse economy with a broad range of industries, best known as the home of the Hollywood film industry, the world's largest by revenue. It also has one of the

Figure 7.1   Hollywood

busiest container ports in America. In Los Angeles, major manufacturing sectors include transportation equipment, fabricated metal products, automobiles, aircraft, computers and electronics, according to the Bureau of Labor Statistics. Los Angeles is also home to Beverly Hills, which is featured in many movies, television series and media; and Los Angeles Disneyland, the largest Disney park among the six in the world, is actually the largest amusement park complex in the world.

4 Chicago

Chicago, "the Windy City," is the nation's third largest city. The city is one of the country's leading industrial cities where both heavy and light industries are highly developed. Chicago is an international hub for finance, culture, commerce, industry, education, technology, telecommunications, and transportation. It has the largest and most diverse derivatives market (衍生品市场) in the world. Chicago's economy is diverse, with no single industry employing more than 14% of the workforce. Moreover, Chicago is a major tourist destination and its culture has contributed much to the visual arts, literature, film, theater, comedy (especially improvisational comedy), food, dance, and music (particularly jazz, blues, soul, hip-hop, gospel, and

Figure 7.2   The Art Institute of Chicago

electronic dance music, including house music). Chicago is home to the Chicago Symphony Orchestra and the Lyric Opera of Chicago, while the Art Institute of Chicago provides an influential visual arts museum and art school. The Chicago area also hosts renowned institutions of higher learning like the University of Chicago, Northwestern University, and the University of Illinois Chicago.

5 San Francisco

San Francisco, located on a peninsula between the Pacific Ocean and San Francisco Bay, is a global center of economic activities and the arts and sciences. The well-known Silicon Valley is here, home to many of the world's largest high-tech corporations, including the headquarters of more than 30 businesses in the Fortune 1000, like Wells Fargo, Salesforce, Uber and Airbnb, and thousands of startup companies. It is a cultural and financial center of the western US and one of the country's most cosmopolitan cities. The city is known for its steep rolling hills and eclectic mix of architecture across varied neighborhoods, as well as its cool summers, fog, and famous landmarks like the Golden Gate Bridge. The world-famous university, Stanford University, is located here.

Figure 7.3   The Golden Gate Bridge

6 Seattle

Seattle is a seaport city on the West Coast of the United States, located in the northwest of the state of Washington. It is the northernmost major city in the United States, a major gateway for trade with East Asia. It is a bustling place that thrives with industrial, commercial, and cultural activities. Considered to be an icon of the city, the Space Needle is an observation tower, which has been designated as a Seattle landmark. The famous film *Sleepless in Seattle* and the Chinese film *Finding Mr. Right* were both shot here.

7 Philadelphia

Philadelphia is one of the most historically significant cities in the United States and served as the nation's capital until 1800.

Figure 7.4   The Space Needle

It is known for its extensive contributions to American history, especially the American Revolution, and for its contemporary influence in business and industry, culture, sports, and music. With 18 four-year universities and colleges, Philadelphia is one of the nation's leading centers for higher education and academic research, hosting more outdoor sculptures and murals than any other city in the nation. The city contains 67 national historic landmarks, including the Independence Hall.

Figure 7.5   Independence Hall

8 Boston

Boston, one of the oldest municipalities in the US, is the capital and the most populous city of Massachusetts, and also the cultural and financial center of New England in the Northeastern United States. In the 21st century, Boston has emerged as a global leader in higher education and academic research. Harvard University and MIT, the two highly ranked universities, are both located in neighboring Cambridge, Boston. Founded in 1636, Harvard University is the oldest institution of higher learning in the United States. Boston has become the largest biotechnology hub in the world. The city is also a national leader in scientific research, law, medicine, engineering, and business. With nearly 5,000 startup companies, the city is considered a global pioneer in innovation and entrepreneurship and more recently in artificial intelligence.

Figure 7.6   Harvard University

Chapter 7   Geography and People

People

1 Overview of American People

The United States is the third most populous nation in the world, ranking behind India and China. According to the 2020 US Census, the United States has a population of 331.4 million with an increase of 7.4% compared with the last decade.

The distribution of the population in the US is rather uneven. According to the US Census Bureau, about 80% of the population live in urban areas. The most densely populated region is the northeastern part of the country. California, Texas, Florida, New York and Pennsylvania are the top 5 states with most population in the country, accounting for 37.2% of the total, while the population in Wyoming, Vermont, Alaska, North Dakota and South Dakota together only accounts for 1% of the total. The southern and western part of the country have seen rapid growth in its population. The West is not densely populated, except for some metropolitan centers like Los Angeles and San Francisco.

2 Population Diversity

Throughout the history, the United States has been one of the world's most ethnically diverse and multicultural nations, the product of large-scale immigration from many countries, with one international migrant (net) every 28 seconds.

The German American is the largest ethnic group in over half the states, accounting for roughly 45 million people and approximately 13.6% of the population of the US. Many people came to the US from Germany in the 19th and early 20th centuries. The largest number of Germans are most notably found in the Midwest. The Irish American is the second-largest ethnic group found in the United States, with 31.5 million or 9.5% of the population. Major minorities include Hispanics, African Americans, Asians, Native Americans (American Indians), and Pacific Islanders, etc.

In recent years, the US has seen the white population fall below 60% for the first time, accounting for 58.9%; Hispanic or Latino 19.1%; Black or African American 13.6%; Asian 6.3%.

White Americans

The majority group of people in the US are whites (about 235.4 million in 2022). Among the white people,

123

the most powerful and influential group is White Anglo-Saxon Protestants (WASPs), such as German American, Irish-American and other ancestry groups, who are the mainstream American whites, the descendants of early English and Western European settlers. The other white Americans are immigrants or descendants of immigrants from other European nations (including traditionally Catholic populations of Ireland and Eastern Europe). Over 10 million white people can trace part of their ancestry back to the Pilgrim Fathers who arrived on a ship called the Mayflower in 1620, and over 50 million whites have at least one ancestor who passed through the Ellis Island immigration station in New York City, which processed arriving immigrants from 1892 until 1954.

Hispanics

The Hispanics are Spanish speaking people from Latin America. It is estimated that there are about 62.1 million Hispanics, or constituting 19.1% of the total. Over half of Hispanic Americans are of Mexican descent, and the overwhelming majority of Mexican Americans are concentrated in the Southwest and West, primarily in California, Texas, Arizona, Nevada, and New Mexico.

Hispanic and Latino Americans are the largest ethnic minority in the United States. Mexican Americans, Cuban Americans, Colombian Americans, Dominican Americans, Puerto Rican Americans, Spanish Americans, and Salvadoran Americans are some of the Hispanic and Latino American groups. People of Hispanic or Latino heritage have lived continuously in the territory of the present-day United States since the founding of St. Augustine, Florida by the Spanish in 1565. Hispanics have also lived continuously in the Southwest with settlements in New Mexico that began in 1598.

African Americans

African Americans or Black Americans are citizens or residents of the United States who have origins in any of the black populations of Africa. They make up the second largest minority group in the United States, and the third largest group after White Americans and Hispanic or Latino Americans. The first group of blacks was brought into Virginia colony as slaves in 1619, and from then the slave system developed rapidly because of the urgent demand for cheap slave labors in the southern plantations and farms until 1808 when importing slaves to America became a crime. The slave system was eliminated during the Civil War. From 1954 to 1968 in the United States, the civil rights movement, a social movement and campaign, was introduced to abolish legalized racial segregation, discrimination, and disenfranchisement in the country. Today, no area of human activities in America can be legally closed to blacks, and they can be found in all professions. In 2008, Barack Obama was elected as the first African-origin president in American history. The movies *Green Book* in 2018 and *Black Lives Matter Movement* in 2020 are both about African Americans.

Asian Americans

Asian Americans constitute 6.3%, or 24 million people of its total population and have become the fastest growing ethnic group in the United States. California has the largest population of Asian Americans, with a total of 6 million accounting for 15.5% of California's total population.

The Asian American population is highly urbanized, mostly residing in cities such as Los Angeles, San Francisco and New York City. New York City has a large population of Asian Americans, approximately 1.9 million. And in Hawaii the Asian American population comprises 56% of the island's total population. Although traditionally Asian Americans resided in the northeast and western regions of the US, recent migration studies show that Asian Americans are expanding their footprint by moving to the midwest and the south.

Native Americans (American Indians)

Walking across the Bering Land Bridge to America, the first people came to the continent as early as 12,000 years ago. In the 15th century as Columbus arrived in America, there were perhaps 10 million people called Indians (Native Americans, the indigenous peoples from the regions of North America now encompassed by the continental United States, including parts of Alaska and the island state of Hawaii). Then after the **Westward Movement**[1] started from the end of the 18th century to the end of the 19th century and the beginning of the 20th century, the Indian Citizenship Act of 1924 granted the US Citizenship to all Native Americans. Native Americans today have a special relationship with the United States of America, and today, there are over 5 million Native Americans in the United States who speak more than 300 different languages, 78% of whom live outside **reservations**[2]. They can be found as nations, tribes, or bands of Native Americans who have sovereignty or independence from the government of the United States, and whose society and culture are still kept. The states with the highest percentage of Native Americans in the US are Alaska, Oklahoma, New Mexico, South Dakota, Montana, and North Dakota. Poverty and unemployment are the major problems that Native Americans usually have.

3 A Nation of Immigrants

The United States is a nation of immigrants, and no other country has as many varied ethnic groups as the US does. It is not merely a nation, but a nation of nations (embracing over 100 ethnic groups).

---

1 Westward Movement: the populating of the land by Europeans within the continental boundaries of the mainland United States, a process that began shortly after the first colonial settlements were established along the Atlantic coast.

2 reservation: An American Indian reservation is an area of land held and governed by a US federal government-recognized Native American tribal nation, whose government is autonomous, subject to regulations passed by the United States Congress and administered by the United States Bureau of Indian Affairs, and not to the US state government in which it is located.

There have been three waves of immigrations to the United States during different periods of American history.

The First Wave of Immigration

Before the first wave of immigration, Africans came to the new world, often against their will, in the earliest days of the Age of Exploration. About 12 million people were brought to America from African countries as slaves from the 16th century through the 19th century, working on plantations or large farms of the South.

After the Napoleonic Wars (1803–1815), with the demobilization of large numbers of soldiers, unemployment in European countries was becoming more serious, and the number of immigrants to the United States was increasing year by year. At that time, the United States also changed its policy of restricting immigration because of the need for domestic construction. The first sharp increase in immigrants came mainly in the 1830s to the 1840s from western and northern Europe and particularly Irish craftsmen displaced by the dreadful poverty of **the Great Potato Famine**[1].

The Second Wave of Immigration

After the end of the Civil War, the United States ushered in the peak of industrialization, and the demand for labor was urgent. In the 1890s, another tremendous tide of immigration appeared, largely from Southern and Eastern Europe. Many immigrants settled in cities and worked in factories. Being poor and accustomed to poverty, they were willing to work for very low wages. This made other workers, especially those in labor unions, afraid that the immigrants would lower wage levels and take jobs away from them. This opposition finally led to **the Immigration Act of 1924**[2] that restricted further immigration, particularly from Europe. The first wave of Chinese immigration to the United States occurred during this period. The earliest immigrants were basically from Guangdong Province. They brought Cantonese and Cantonese food to the United States. Chinatown was also mostly formed at this time.

The Third Wave of Immigration

From 1881 to 1920, the number of immigrants soared, which peaked in 1907. But during this period, due to conflicts over employment, religion, and ethnicity, xenophobia (仇外心理) in the United States also reached its peak. The government repeatedly legislated to restrict European immigration and exclude Asian immigrants at that time. Some other groups continued to come and concentrate in different areas. In the 100 years from 1820 to 1920, the United States admitted a total of about 33.5 million immigrants, forming a continuous immigration tide in the United States.

---

1 The Great Potato Famine was a period of starvation and disease in Ireland lasting from 1845 to 1852 that constituted a historical social crisis and subsequently had a major impact on Irish society and history as a whole.

2 The immigration Act of 1924 was a federal law that prevented immigration from Asia and set quotas on the number of immigrants from Eastern and Southern Europe.

4 Cultural Assimilation

Cultural assimilation was a series of efforts in the US to assimilate immigrant cultures into the mainstream American culture. While the white anglo-saxon protestants formed the land's basic cultural values as freedom, equality and desire to work hard for a higher standard of living, American culture has been influenced by many other cultures brought in by immigrants from all over the world.

The United States used to be called a "melting pot," which means that different racial and ethnic groups are assimilated into American culture. However, recently it has been more often called a "salad bowl," which means that immigrants of different backgrounds mix harmoniously, but at the same time keep their distinct cultures and customs.

During the late 19th and 20th centuries, most immigrants came from poverty-stricken nations. For them, assimilation was much harder because of the differences between their culture and language and those of the established Americans. These new immigrants, feeling lost in strange surroundings, clustered together in close-knit communities. Soon, many cities had ethnic neighborhoods such as "Chinatown." Various American agencies, public and private, offered English instruction and citizenship classes to new immigrants to assist in their assimilation and becoming American citizens.

Through new opportunities and new rewards, the immigrants came to accept most of the values of the dominant American culture and were, in turn, accepted by the great majority of Americans. Then the immigrants' attitude toward their old-world background has changed markedly, especially since the mid-20th century. People of various origins have become interested in their foreign past and proud of their cultural heritage. Courses have been organized for them to study their native language and culture that they once tried to forget. Furthermore, they believe that the United States, a land of immigrants, could benefit from retaining its diverse cultural backgrounds. The contributions made by those people have helped America achieve its rapid social and economic development.

Americans have become more positive towards immigrants and immigration, according to public opinion surveys carried out since October of 2018. A majority of Americans think that immigrants have positive attributes such as being diligent and having strong family values and that immigrants have strengthened the country. The United States resembles a colorful quilt stitched together from geographic regions that maintain unique cultural patterns. The Europeans, Africans, Asians, Hispanics and other groups add their own varying cultures to this diversity. Despite these differences, the various regions of the United States mesh together to form a single fabric.

Exercises

Part I. Decide whether the following statements are true (T) or false (F). Write T or F in the brackets.

1. The two non-contiguous states of Alaska and Hawaii were admitted to the US in 1859. (   )

2. The largest state in area is Alaska, followed by California. (   )

3. Washington D.C. is located in the state of Washington. (   )

4. The Great Plains lie west of the Mississippi River and east of the Rocky Mountains. (   )

5. The Mississippi River is the longest river in the US, and it is the third longest river in the world after Nile and Yangtze rivers. (   )

6. The two main mountain ranges in America are the Appalachian Mountains in eastern North America and the Rocky Mountains in western North America. (   )

7. The United States mainly lies in the northern temperate zone. (   )

8. The well-known Silicon Valley is located in Los Angeles, California. (   )

Part II. Fill in the blanks with best answers.

1. The US is located in the _____ part of North America, with the Atlantic Ocean to the _____ and the Pacific Ocean to the _____.

    A. northern, west, east

    B. southern, west, east

    C. central, east, west

    D. eastern, east, west

2. The state with the largest population is _____.

    A. California

    B. New York

    C. Texas

    D. Florida

3. The Great Lakes are composed of five lakes: Lake Michigan, Lake Superior, Lake Erie, Lake Huron and Lake Ontario. Among them, only _____ belongs to the US completely while the other four are shared by the United States and Canada.

   A. Lake Ontario

   B. Lake Michigan

   C. Lake Superior

   D. Lake Erie

4. The United States has the world's largest _____ reserves, accounting for 27% of the world's total.

   A. coal

   B. timber

   C. natural gas

   D. gold petroleum

5. Harvard University and MIT, the two world-famous universities, are both located in _____.

   A. New York

   B. Los Angeles

   C. Boston

   D. San Francisco

6. _____ are the largest minority group in the United States.

   A. African Americans

   B. Hispanics

   C. Asian Americans

   D. German Americans

7. The first sharp increase in immigrants came mainly in the 1830s to the 1840s from _____.

   A. Eastern Europe

   B. Western and Northern Europe

   C. North Africa

   D. Asian countries

8. Asian Americans take up _____ of the total population in the Unites States.

   A. 19.1%

   B. 13.6%

   C. 6.3%

   D. 3.6%

Part III. State your understanding of the following questions.

1. Which term do you think is more suitable to describe the American society, a "melting pot" or a "salad bowl"? Why do you think so?

2. Compare the social positions of African Americans in the past and at present.

3. Discuss the differences between big cities in China and those in the United States.

Chapter 8

History

1. How has British colonialism impacted modern America?
2. How did the Americans struggle for their national unity?
3. How did the United States grow to be a powerful country by the end of World War II?

Pre-Columbian America

When compared with other powerful nations in the western world, such as the UK, the history of the United States is relatively short.

Before the first explorer set foot on American land, famously by Christopher Columbus in 1492, America was a land owned, harvested and cultivated by the Native Americans. Therefore, "Pre-Columbian" (also known as "Pre-Columbian," "Prehistoric," and "Precontact") refers to the period before Christopher Columbus's arrival in America in 1492. Pre-Columbian history spans thousands of years, with evidence of human habitation in the Americas dating back to at least 15,000 years ago. During the last ice age, when a land bridge existed between present-day Siberia and Alaska, the first inhabitants from northeastern Asia migrated across this bridge in search of food. Continually moving southward, these Native Americans eventually populated both North and South America, creating unique cultures that ranged from the highly complex and urban **Aztec**[1] civilization in what is now Mexico City to the woodland tribes of eastern North America.

By the time Europeans were poised to cross the Atlantic, North America was home to a marked diversity of peoples distributed among different tribes. Despite the great diversity, however, North America's indigenous cultures shared some broad traits. Their spiritual practices, social customs, understandings of property, and kinship networks differed markedly from Europeans once they arrived in the "New World."

By 1492, fueled by the quest for wealth and power as well as by religious passions, Europe was anxious to

---

1 Aztec: The Aztec people were certain ethnic groups who in the 15th and early 16th centuries ruled a large empire in what is now central and southern Mexico.

Figure 8.1   Christopher Columbus

improve trade and communications with the rest of the world. Having convinced the King and Queen of Spain to finance his voyage, Christopher Columbus set sail in 1492 in order to find a direct sea route to Asia through the Atlantic Ocean. Instead, he and his crew landed on an island in present-day Bahamas. Between 1493 and 1504, he made three more voyages to the Caribbean and South America, believing until his death that he had found a shorter route to Asia. He referred to the lands he discovered as "the Indies" and the people he encountered as "Indians." Christopher Columbus became the first to discover the "New World" of the Americas. His journeys kicked off centuries of exploration and colonization of North and South America.

Colonial America

In the 16th Century, European colonization of North America expanded through Spanish colonists establishing themselves in present-day Florida. At the start of the 17th century, the English had not established a permanent settlement in the New World. In 1606, Elizabeth's successor, James I, issued charters to the Virginia Company to establish colonies along the eastern coast of North America. Therefore, Jamestown in Virginia became the first permanent English colony in North America. Captain John Smith took control of Jamestown. He enforced a rigorous work schedule, and negotiated with the Indians, which guaranteed Jamestown's initial survival. One of the settlers, John Rolfe, introduced a new strand of tobacco to Virginia. The successful cultivation of tobacco in the colony developed the first profitable export, which provided the economic stability for Virginia. In 1619, the first ship to bring African slaves to North America landed at Jamestown. Initially, they were treated as indentured servants. But gradually, this system evolved into slavery—the treatment of slaves as property, which lasted for 246 years.

In November 1620, seeking freedom from persecution for their Puritan religion, a group of pilgrims sailed to the "New World" and arrived at Plymouth, Massachusetts, establishing the first successful English settlement in the region of New England—the Plymouth Colony. Before anyone left the ship, an agreement called the Mayflower Compact was drafted and signed between the 41 passengers, establishing the form of government of the Plymouth Colony and binding everyone to laws that served the common good. These pilgrims were unprepared for the harsh New England winter. They had very little food, and it was far too late in the season to plant any crops. More than half of the them fell ill and died from the cold and disease that first winter. Those who barely survived were ultimately saved by the Native Americans. The natives taught them how to plant "the three sisters"—corn, beans, and squash, and how to live in the New World. The grateful settlers shared an autumn feast with the natives, which was honored with the establishment of Thanksgiving Day on the last Thursday of November in the United States.

After 1620, British colonization in America grew rapidly in the 17th and 18th centuries. The colonies of New Hampshire, Rhode Island, and Connecticut were founded as extensions of Massachusetts. New York and New Jersey, which used to be Dutch colonies, were captured by Britain in a war, and the rest of the colonies—Pennsylvania, Maryland, Delaware, North Carolina, South Carolina, and Georgia were founded in succession and became considerably prosperous and independent. By 1763 the word "American" was commonly used to designate the people of the 13 colonies.

Instead of being established by royal imperative or government policy, each of the 13 colonies was claimed, explored and settled by British expeditions and companies. The availability of boundless land and abundant resources saw increased emigration and population growth, from just 55,000 in 1650 to over 2 million by the outbreak of the revolution.

The American Revolution

By the end of the **Seven Years' War**[1] in 1763, colonists in the 13 colonies had reaped many benefits from the British imperial system, including the economic growth, religious freedom, and political autonomy. However, the staggering war debt influenced British policies towards the colonies. Britain tried various methods of raising revenue on both sides of the Atlantic, including enforcing tax laws and placing troops in America, which led directly to conflict with colonists.

In December 1773, a group of Massachusetts colonists protested the Tea Act passed that year by boarding three British tea ships docked in Boston Harbor and dumping 342 chests of tea into the water. Outraged by the destruction of the tea, the British Parliament passed the Coercive Acts, also known as the Intolerable Acts, in 1774. The acts closed Boston to merchant shipping, curtailed free elections and instituted martial law in Massachusetts. This political protest, popularly known as the "Boston Tea Party," escalated the crisis between Britain and the 13 colonies, moving the colonies one step closer to war with Britain and eventual independence. In order to discuss a response to the Intolerable Acts, the First Continental Congress assembled in Philadelphia in October of the same year. The Congress formed the Continental Association to enforce a trade boycott against British merchants unless Britain repealed the Coercive Acts.

---

1 Seven Years' War: Seven Years' War was a conflict primarily fought between Britain and France over territory in the Americas, which ended with a British victory.

Throughout late 1774 and into 1775, tensions in New England continued to mount. British forces marched to Lexington, Concord and other towns in Massachusetts with the intention of destroying militia supplies, and they were confronted by the militia men. The first shots of the American Revolution were fired on April 19, 1775, in Lexington, Massachusetts.

Realizing the movement towards independence could not be reversed, the delegates of the Second Continental Congress met in Philadelphia, and discussed the ongoing American Revolution. Serving as the de facto government of the colonies at war, the Congress commissioned Thomas Jefferson to write the Declaration of Independence, which was signed and ratified by Congress on July 4, 1776. This declaration announced the separation of 13 American colonies from Great Britain.

Figure 8.2   Thomas Jefferson

After the Declaration of Independence, the military struggle between Great Britain and its American colonies became a republican revolution. In the following years, a number of battles were fought between American and British forces. Thanks to the leadership of George Washington and the crucial assistance of French forces, the British surrendered in 1781, and the 13 original colonies were granted their independence. Two years later, officials from Great Britain and the United States signed the Treaty of Paris in 1783, and Great Britain formally recognized the independence of the United States of America.

National Expansion and Reform

The Articles of Confederation, ratified several months before the British surrender in 1781, created a loose confederation of sovereign states. As the need for a stronger central government became more apparent after 1783, 55 state delegates met in Philadelphia to compose the Constitution of the United States in 1787, which laid the groundwork for a stronger and more effective federal government. The Judiciary Act of 1789 established a judiciary system with a Supreme Court of six justices, and other courts of different levels. In 1791, the Bill of Rights was taken as the first 10 Amendments to the Constitution, which placed limits on the federal and state governments' power to curtail individual rights and freedoms. In 1788, George Washington was elected as the nation's first president, marking a new era in the history of the United States.

The 19th century was a transformative era marked by significant changes and developments. Especially the period 1830–1850 was labeled by historians as an "age of reform." The abolitionist movement, for example, sought to end slavery and promote equal rights for all individuals. This movement sparked debates and conflicts that ultimately led to the American Civil War. Growing out of the anti-slavery movement, The US women's rights movement first emerged in the 1830s. The movement was characterized by the pursuit of legal equal rights for women, with the emphasis on equality in education, labor and electoral rights.

The 19th century also saw the expansion of the United States from a small republic to a continental nation. The Treaty of Paris, signed in 1783, not only formally recognized the United States as an independent nation, but also established generous boundaries for this new nation, with its territory extending from the Atlantic Ocean to the Mississippi River in the west, and from the Great Lakes in the north to the thirty-one degrees north latitude in the south. In 1803, President Thomas Jefferson purchased the territory of Louisiana from the French government for $15 million. The Louisiana Purchase stretched from the Mississippi River to the Rocky Mountains and from Canada to New Orleans, and it nearly doubled the size of the United States. Through treaties and land purchases, the country acquired more than 1.6 million square kilometers of land west of the Mississippi River, expanding geographically from the Atlantic to the Pacific. This led to a widespread migration west, referred to as Westward Expansion. However, the Westward Expansion took lots of lands away from Native American peoples, which led to frequent wars and other conflicts with Native American tribes. In 1830, the United States Congress passed the Indian Removal Act, beginning the forced removal of Native Americans east of the Mississippi River. As people began moving west, several thousand American settlers in search of economic opportunity established homesteads in the Midwest. This rapid growth helped the economic development, but it also fueled the issue of slavery.

The Civil War

After decades of simmering tensions between northern and southern states over slavery, as well as trade, tariffs, and states' rights, the American Civil War broke out on April 12, 1861, and lasted until May 26, 1865, when the last Confederate army surrendered. As America's bloodiest and most divisive conflict, the war, though brought freedom to 4 million black slaves, claimed more than 600, 000 lives, destroyed property valued at $5 billion, and opened wounds that have not yet completely healed more than 150 years later.

The chief and immediate cause of the war was slavery. The north states were rapidly industrializing, relying heavily on factories and machinery for production; while the agrarian south's economy was based on a system of large-scale farming which depended on enslaved people to grow labor-intensive crops, especially cotton and tobacco. These economic differences increasingly raised political and cultural tensions.

After Abraham Lincoln was elected as President, southern states began to secede from the Union. On February 4, 1861, they established the Confederate States of America in Montgomery, Alabama. The war started on April 12, 1861, when Confederate forces attacked the Union controlled Fort Sumter in Charleston

Bay, South Carolina's harbor. After the first shot of Civil War, over 10,000 battles of various sizes were fought across the United States from the East Coast to as far west as New Mexico during the following four years. One of the most pivotal battles was the Battle of Gettysburg in 1863, which ended in a Union victory and was a major turning point in the Civil War. It inspired Lincoln's "Gettysburg Address," which became one of the most famous speeches of all time. With the Confederate General Robert E. Lee's surrender in 1865, the Civil War resulted in the Union's decisive victory over the Confederacy.

On September 22, 1862, following the Union victory at Antietam, President Lincoln presented the Preliminary Emancipation Proclamation, which declared that as of January 1, 1863, all slaves in the states currently engaged in rebellion against the Union would be "forever free." The proclamation exempted pro-Union border states and parts of the Confederacy already under Union occupation, and it was carefully worded as a measure to assist the North in preserving the Union. But it transformed the Union Army into an army of liberation—fighting to end slavery as well as to preserve the Union. The Emancipation Proclamation paved the way for the permanent abolition of slavery in the United States. Realizing the Emancipation would have no constitutional basis after the war ended, the Congress passed the 13th Amendment in January 1865, and ratified it in December the same year, which outlawed the practice of slavery.

Figure 8.3   Abraham Lincoln

The Civil War was followed by twelve years of reconstruction, during which the north and south debated the future of black Americans and waged bitter political battles. The war also set the south back at least a generation in industry and agriculture. Factories and farms were devastated by the invading armies. The labor system fell into chaos. Not until the 20th century did the south recover fully from the economic effects of the war. In contrast, the north forged ahead with the building of a modern industrial state.

In conclusion, it must be remarked that the Civil War did not raise blacks to a position of equality with whites. Nor did the war bring about the emotional reunion that Lincoln hoped for when he spoke in his first inaugural address of "the bonds of affection" that had formerly held the two sections together.

America in Industrial Age

In the decades following the Civil War, the United States entered a period of unprecedented economic growth

fueled by industrialization. This period marked a shift from hand production to mechanized manufacturing, leading to a stunning explosion in the scale of industry and in the pace of production. The transportation industry saw significant advancements. Railroads, canals, and steamships developed significantly, which stimulated growth in the iron, wood, coal, and other related industries, contributing to the growth of commerce and trade. Moreover, innovations in communication technologies, such as the telegraph, revolutionized long-distance communication, enabling faster and more efficient transmission of information than ever before.

The industrialization of America also brought about significant changes in the labor force and social structure. The industrial growth produced a new class of wealthy industrialists and a prosperous middle class. Besides, with the growth of factories and industries in urban areas, more laborers and skilled workers from rural areas and newcomers from abroad migrated to urban areas in pursuit of opportunity, work, and a better quality of life. This led to the rapid urban growth and a population boom, altering the demographic makeup of the nation. American society became more diverse than ever before.

However, this rapid industrialization was not without its challenges. Workers faced long working hours, low wages, and dangerous working conditions. Disputes between labor and management were rife. As a result, labor movements and trade unions emerged as a response to these issues, advocating for better working conditions, higher wages and improved rights. Meanwhile, farmers also faced hard times as technology and increasing production led to fiercer competition and falling prices for farm products. These social transformations and challenges also extended further out into society. There were many significant reforms aimed to address issues related to labor, women's suffrage, environmental protection, education, health, and social inequality.

America in the 20th Century

1 America in World Wars

Before 1914, the United States, although growing richer and more powerful, opposed any entanglement in international military conflicts. In 1914, when forces of the Austro-Hungarian Empire invaded the tiny Balkan nation of Serbia, World War I broke out in Europe, with the Central Powers led by Germany and Austria-Hungary on one side and the Allied countries led by Britain, France, and Russia on the other. President Woodrow Wilson first adopted a policy of neutrality, but the neutrality was a difficult challenge, which was tested and fiercely debated across the country. In 1917, the United State entered World War I as an ally of Britain. There were several reasons. First, Germany resumed unrestricted submarine warfare and sank three American merchant ships, which would greatly harm the American trade and threaten the freedom and security of American people. Second, British intelligence intercepted and decoded a telegram from German Foreign Secretary to the German ambassador in Mexico. According to the telegram, Germany encouraged Mexico to go to war against America by promising the Mexicans a chance to regain the territory lost in the Mexican-American War. Third, it was a great chance for the United States to influence the outcome of the war. American forces quickly broke the stalemate that had bogged the European forces down in years of inconclusive trench warfare. In the early 1918, President Wilson laid out his **Fourteen Points**[1] for a postwar peace settlement. A few months later, Germany agreed to an armistice and the war shuddered to a close with a victory for the Allies on November 11, 1918. By the end of the war, over 2 million American soldiers had served at the Western Front in Europe, and more than 50,000 of them had lost their lives. America's entry into the war marked the start of American intervention in European affairs. In 1919, Wilson attended the Paris Peace Conference in the hope that the Fourteen Points would form the backbone of the **Treaty of Versailles**[2]. But Wilson's ideas were opposed by the Allies, who were more interested in punishing Germany than pursuing an idealistic blueprint for world peace. The Treaty of Versailles was signed on June 28, 1919. However, the US Congress refused to ratify the treaty.

The decade after World War I witnessed unprecedented economic growth and prosperity in the United States. From 1920 to 1929, the nation's total wealth more than doubled, and Gross National Product (GNP) increased by 40 percent from 1922 to 1929. In this decade, new ideas of liberation, consumerism, and a culture of excess flourished among American citizens. Besides the material affluence, the Roaring Twenties was also marked by drastic changes for women that included the right to vote, symbolizing their increasing influence and role in public life. Women also started to seek employment and education opportunities previously unavailable to them. Another iconic and paradoxical facet of this era was **Prohibition**[3]. Though Prohibition brought the age of speakeasies and bootleggers, which created more conflict than celebration, this era, with profound political, economic and social change, embodied the beginning of modern America.

The economic expansion of the Roaring Twenties came to an end abruptly with the stock market crash in October 1929, plunging many Americans into financial ruin. The Great Depression lasted from 1929 until America's entry into World War II in 1941. During the downturn, industrial production plummeted, unemployment soared, families suffered, and marriage rates fell. At the depths of the depression, over one quarter of the American workforce was out of employment. The Great Depression was the greatest and longest economic recession in the history of the United States, and one of the largest catastrophic economic events of the 20th century.

The American economy plummeted into the Great Depression during Herbert Hoover's presidency. Although

---

1 Fourteen Points: The Fourteen Points were a proposal made by US President Woodrow Wilson in a speech before Congress on January 8, 1918, outlining his vision for ending World War I in a way that would prevent such a conflagration from occurring again.

2 Treaty of Versailles: Treaty of Versailles was a peace agreement between Germany and the Allied Powers after World War I, which imposed harsh penalties on Germany including reparations and territorial losses.

3 Prohibition: Prohibition was a federal ban on the production, transportation and sale of alcohol in the United States from 1920 to 1933.

he repeatedly spoke of optimism, people blamed him for the Great Depression and criticized his efforts to alleviate the crisis. In 1932, Franklin D. Roosevelt won the presidential election in a landslide. As soon as Roosevelt took office, he took strong steps immediately to battle the depression and stimulate the economy. Roosevelt and the Democratic Congress implemented an economic recovery plan, known as the New Deal. Some of these programs were aimed at helping farmers by curtailing farm production, like the Agricultural Adjustment Administration. While other programs, such as the Civilian Conservation Corps and the Works Progress Administration, attempted to help curb unemployment by creating more jobs for people in the construction of roads,

Figure 8.4　Franklin D. Roosevelt

schools, airports, and other public works. Although the New Deal helped ease the hardships of the Great Depression, it did not actually change the economic situation in America. It was not until America turned its attention to the global conflict of World War II that the Great Depression ended in the United States.

After the outbreak of World War II, Roosevelt sought to support the Allies by providing economic support without intervening directly. However, when Japanese warships bombed Pearl Harbor on December 7, 1941, the United States declared war on Japan. A few days later, Germany and Italy declared war on the United States. Roosevelt issued another declaration of war against Germany on December 11. These two declarations meant that the United States, fully engaged in World War II, had to fight on two fronts: Europe and the Pacific. World War II shifted America's focus away from the lingering effects of the Great Depression, which was followed by a massive war mobilization effort. The American people were united in a fervent commitment to war. Millions of men and women served overseas in the armed forces; those who remained at home also did their part to support the war effort. Even women, who used to be homemakers, went to work in military-related industries. American people played a critical role in World War II against the Axis powers. On May 8, 1945, Germany surrendered. After the United States dropped two atomic bombs on the Japanese cities of Hiroshima and Nagasaki in August 1945, the war ended with Japan's surrender.

2　America in Post-war Era

Due to the economic base left after the war, as well as the population growth brought about by the **Baby Boom**[1], and support packages for veterans such as the **GI Bill of Rights**[2] passed in 1944, American society

---

1　Baby Boom: Baby Boom is a term for a temporary marked increase in the birth rate, especially the one following World War II.

2　GI Bill of Rights: GI Bill of Rights was a law passed in 1944 to provide federal aid for World War II veterans to pursue education, employment, housing and health care after the war.

became more affluent in the post-war years. With most European countries severely destroyed after World War II, the United States and the Soviet Union emerged as two global superpowers, and they quickly found themselves locked in a contest for political, economic and ideological supremacy. In 1947, President Harry S. Truman issued what came to be known as the Truman Doctrine, which marked the beginning of the Cold War—the decades-long struggle between these two superpowers along with their respective allies.

To keep the Soviet Union from expanding its influence further into the world, the United States, with a new foreign policy known as containment, helped rebuild the shattered nations of Western Europe with substantial economic aid through the **Marshall Plan**[1]. The United States and Western Europe formed a strong and enduring alliance, **NATO**[2], to defend Europe against possible Soviet advances.

There was no direct military action occurring between the two nations, but many small proxy wars fought in other territories such as Korea and Vietnam were a result of different political viewpoints and ideological struggles. Americans were deployed to Korea to prevent the spread of Communism or regimes backed by the Soviet Union, but the Korean War had other effects on the domestic life of the United States, which hardened American foreign policy into a much more rigidly anticommunist form. After the United States intervened militarily in Vietnam in the mid-1960s, the political consensus concerning the Cold War and anti-Communism began to break down. In 1973, President Richard M. Nixon signed an agreement to stop the American military involvement in the Vietnam War, and the war ended in the unification of Vietnam under a communist government. The Nixon administration marked the end of America's long period of post-war prosperity and the onset of a period of high inflation and unemployment. But his most acclaimed achievements came in his quest for world stability. His trip to China in 1972 ended 25 years of isolation between the two countries and resulted in establishment of diplomatic relations with China in 1979. He also negotiated the first **Strategic Arms Limitation Treaty**[3] with the Soviet Union to reduce Cold War tensions. In addition to the wars, the Marshall Plan, **the Cuban Missile Crisis**[4], and Reagan's "**Star Wars**[5]" all rolled out of the Cold War mentality. Finally, in 1989, with the tearing down of the Berlin Wall, the Cold War ended.

The post-war era also witnessed some of the most fervent social, cultural and political revolutions in the American society. There were problems in poverty, civil rights, etc. Soon after President Johnson proposed the War on Poverty—the Great Society more broadly—in 1964, Congress passed the bipartisan Economic

---

1   Marshall Plan: Marshall Plan was a US-led initiative designed to rehabilitate the economies of 17 western and southern European countries after World War II.

2   NATO: North Atlantic Treaty Organization (NATO) is an association of European and north American countries, formed in 1949 to safeguard their freedom and security through political and military means.

3   Strategic Arms Limitation Treaty: Strategic Arms Limitation Treaty (SALT) was a series of bilateral conferences and treaties between the US and the USSR to reduce strategic arms.

4   The Cuban Missile Crisis: The Cuban Missile Crisis was a 1962 standoff between the US and the Soviet Union over nuclear weapons in Cuba.

5   Star Wars: Star Wars was a US weapons research program begun in 1984 to explore technologies, including ground-based and space-based lasers, for destroying attacking missiles and warheads.

Opportunity Act of 1964, which created the legislative framework to expand economic opportunity through anti-poverty, health, education, and employment policies. However, the poverty rates for the nonelderly population have not decreased, reflecting the increasing labor market difficulties faced by the low-skill population. Besides, the crime rate kept rising in the society. Therefore, the Great Society stopped by 1967.

Figure 8.5   Martin Luther King, Jr.

At the same time, black Americans began mobilizing and demanding the equal rights they were promised by the Constitution and the 13th, 14th, and 15th amendments. They organized peaceful mass protests such as boycotts and sit-ins to pressure governments, especially those in the south, to abolish Jim Crow Laws and guarantee basic equal rights. Martin Luther King, Jr., the leader of the Civil Rights Movement, helped organize the 1963 March in Washington D.C., where he delivered his famous "I Have a Dream" speech. Finally, black Americans succeeded in their goal with the passage of the Civil Rights Act of 1964 by the Kennedy Administration. However, the assassination of Martin Luther King, Jr. in 1968 caused riots in many cities. Racial discrimination, gender biases and social alienation came to the climax in the mid-1960s, which brought cultural, social and political crises. A series of movements challenged the established order of the American society.

Ronald Regan took over as president in 1981 at a time when the United States was suffering a decline. He launched his economic policy, reducing the individual tax burden of millions of people and downsizing government taxation and regulation. He also took a tough stance on crime, launching the controversial "War on Drugs," which was criticized as a mechanism of further oppressing underprivileged blacks. Despite the controversy, he left office when the economy was booming. His successor, George H. W. Bush promised to carry on Reagan's economic legacy after he won the 1988 election, but the problems Bush inherited made it difficult for him to do so. In 1992, Bill Clinton took over the government and he took a series of measures to boost the economy. He even managed to balance the federal budget. In his second term, the United States saw a vigorous economic development. However, Clinton's presidency ended in scandal with a White House intern, Monica Lewinsky, which has diminished the significance of some of his achievements.

America in the 21st Century

The 2000 presidential election turned out to be a turning point in American history. Democrat Al Gore, Clinton's Vice President, won the popular vote, a half million more than his Republican opponent George

W. Bush, but lost the presidency in the electoral college. With a 5–4 majority of the US Supreme Court, George W. Bush, as an embattled president with many questioning his legitimacy, headed the conservative restoration to power. Just a year later came the 9/11 attacks, which involved hijacking and flying airplanes into the World Trade Center in New York City and the Pentagon in Washington, D.C. The attacks killed almost 3,000 Americans and injured over 6,000 more. After September 11th, the Bush administration declared a Global War on Terror. The first front in this war was Afghanistan, where the ruling Taliban regime was providing safe haven to al-Qaeda, and to Iraq, where Saddam Hussein purportedly was harboring weapons of mass destruction. US troops rapidly defeated the Iraqi armed forces, but weapons of mass destruction were never found, and the removal of Hussein's government destabilized the region.

Figure 8.6 The 9/11 Attacks

In 2008, the United States made history by electing Barack Obama, the first African American president in US history. Obama rose to power during the worst economic crisis since the Great Depression. With promises of change, he authorized a massive economic stimulus package that mitigated the worst effects of the crisis and instilled the confidence needed to boost economic growth. Though it helped stave off economic catastrophe, it also substantially increased the federal debt and the federal budget deficit. Other domestic achievements of the Obama administration include the Patient Protection and Affordable Care Act, known colloquially as "**Obamacare**[1]", and the extension of civil rights to the LGBTQ community. He also pressed for a fair pay act for women, financial reform legislation, and efforts for consumer protection. In terms of foreign policy, Obama continued many of the anti-terrorism policies adopted by former President George W. Bush after the 9/11 attacks. In 2011, the Obama administration enjoyed a major success in the War on Terror when US Navy Seals captured and killed Osama bin Laden, a violent terrorist who formed the al Qaeda network and planned the 9/11 attacks against America.

In 2016, Donald Trump managed to win the presidency, which was widely seen as a surprise upset victory. After taking office in 2017, Trump instituted various policies and measures that opposed international trade, limited immigration, and obstructed international cooperation. For example, he began construction of a wall on the Mexico border to increase border security and prevent immigrants from illegally entering the country. Several of Trump's key policies also include his first Supreme Court nomination, the first moves to dismantle the Affordable Care Act, and the US withdrawal from the Paris Climate Agreement.

---

1 Obamacare: Obamacare is the comprehensive health care reform law enacted in 2010. It aims to make health insurance affordable, expand Medicaid, and lower health care costs.

During his administration, the US still had the world's largest economy and the dollar remained supreme, but internal divisions, as well as swelling economic inequality, exposed some of the country's domestic issues. In the 2020 election, the former Vice President Joe Biden, defeating Donald Trump, was elected the 46th president of the United States.

Exercises

Part I. Decide whether the following statements are true (T) or false (F). Write T or F in the brackets.

1. Tobacco became the economic foundation of Virginia's economy in the early 17th century. (   )

2. In 1776, the First Continental Congress in Philadelphia declared the independence of "the United States of America." (   )

3. The Treaty of Paris officially ended the American Revolution and recognized the independence of the United States. (   )

4. The Civil War ended with the Confederacy's decisive victory over the Union. (   )

5. The United States initially declared neutrality at the outbreak of World War I, but ended up entering the war on the side of the Allied powers in 1917. (   )

6. President Herbert Hoover introduced the New Deal to provide immediate economic relief and to bring about reforms to stabilize the US economy during the Great Depression. (   )

7. President Truman declared the "Truman Doctrine" in 1947, symbolizing the beginning of the Cold War. (   )

8. Saddam Hussein, the founder and leader of the terrorist organization al-Qaeda, was the mastermind behind the devastating 9/11 attacks. (   )

Part II. Fill in the blanks with best answers.

1. The first permanent English colony in North America was founded at _____.

   A. Philadelphia, Pennsylvania

   B. Baltimore, Maryland

   C. Plymouth, Massachusetts

D. Jamestown, Virginia

2. _____ was the first military engagement of the Revolutionary War.

   A. Boston Tea Party

   B. Boston Massacre

   C. Battles of Lexington and Concord

   D. Battle of Bunker Hill

3. The National Day of the United States falls on _____ each year.

   A. June 4th

   B. July 4th

   C. June 14th

   D. July 14th

4. _____ led the Continental Army to victory in the Revolutionary War, and was elected as the First President of the United States in 1788.

   A. George Washington

   B. John Adams

   C. Benjamin Franklin

   D. Thomas Jefferson

5. _____, issued by Abraham Lincoln on January 1, 1863, was an important milestone in the long process of ending legal slavery in the United States.

   A. Declaration of Independence

   B. The Articles of Confederation

   C. Emancipation Proclamation

   D. Bill of Rights

6. _____ on December 7, 1941, led to the United States declaring war on Japan and entering World War II.

   A. Hitler's invasion of Poland

   B. The Battle of Stalingrad

C. Italy's declaration of war against France and Britain

D. The Japanese attack on Pearl Harbor

7. _____ was the leader of the Civil Rights Movement and delivered the famous "I Have a Dream" speech during the March on Washington in 1963.

   A. John Lewis

   B. Martin Luther King Jr.

   C. Rosa Parks

   D. Barack Obama

8. _____ was a prolonged military conflict with direct US military involvement ending in 1975.

   A. The Vietnam War

   B. The Korean War

   C. War in Afghanistan

   D. The Gulf War

Part III. State your understanding of the following questions.

1. What were the major causes of the American Civil War (1861–1865)? What were the long-term effects of the Civil War on the United States?

2. How did America's role change in World War I and World War II? What were the reasons behind these changes?

3. What were the key factors that fueled US industrial growth in the late 19th century? Do you see any parallels with 21st century China that might allow China's economy to overtake the United States?

Chapter 9

Government

1. What are the functions of the US Constitution?
2. How much do you know about the "separation of powers" and "checks and balances" in the US politics?
3. Is the US Presidential Election a direct election, i.e. people vote for presidential candidate directly?

The form of the US government is known as Federal Republic, which is based on a constitutional separation of power between the federal government and the state government. The federal government is the central government, established by the US Constitution. The federal government has three branches: the legislative, executive, and judicial branches.

Constitution

The Constitution of the United States is the basis for the machinery and institutions of the US government. Created in 1787 at the Constitutional Convention, and rectified by each state in 1789, it is the world's shortest and oldest written constitution in operation, with 4,300 words and a history of more than 200 years. It consists of 7 articles and a preamble (序言). Twenty-seven amendments have been added to the Constitution since 1789, the first ten known as the Bill of Rights, ratified in 1791. The framers (制宪者) were especially concerned with limiting the power of the government and securing the liberty of citizens. James Madison is hailed as the "Father of the Constitution" for his central role in drafting and promoting the Constitution of the United States and the United States Bill of Rights. The best-known founders of the Constitution also include George Washington, Thomas Jefferson, Benjamin Franklin, Alexander Hamilton, and John Adams.

The Constitution outlines the structure of the national government and specifies its powers and activities, and defines the relationship between the national government and individual state governments. According to US Constitution, neither the national nor the state government receives its powers from each other; both derive them from the Constitution. Each of the 50 states has its own constitution, but all provisions of state constitutions must comply with the US Constitution.

The US Constitution establishes a government based on "federalism." Under the federal system, the national and the state governments have separate and distinct powers laid down in the Constitution. The Constitution says that all powers not specifically granted to the national government are reserved to the states. The Constitution defines exactly what powers are denied to the states. The federal government is responsible for answering questions that affect the whole nation, while the duty of the state governments is to deal with problems that affect the well-being of each state.

"Separation of powers" refers to the constitutional division of powers among the legislative, executive and judicial branches in order to prevent abuse of power. This principle allocates legislative power to Congress, executive power to President and judicial power to the Supreme Court. The Congress is the law-making branch of government. The President and federal government are responsible for enforcing the laws of the land. The Supreme Court decides arguments about the interpretation of laws and how they are applied and decides if laws violate the Constitution. In this system of separation of powers each branch has separate and distinctive powers laid down in the Constitution, and operates independently of the others. "Checks and balances" system prevents a concentration of power in any one branch and protects the rights and liberties of citizens.

To sum up, the Constitution outlines the structure of the federal government; defines the three main branches of the federal government, outlines obligations of each branch, and provides what powers each branch may exercise; reserves numerous rights for the states (According to the Constitution, all powers not specifically granted to the national government are reserved to the states), thereby establishing the federal system of U.S. government.

Government

Under the principles the US Constitution, the federal government has three branches: the legislative, executive, and judicial branches. Through the system of separation of powers and checks and balances, each branch has some authority to act on its own, some authority to regulate the other two branches, and has some of its own authority, in turn, regulated by the other branches.

1 The Legislative Branch

The American Congress is the legislative branch of the federal government, consisting of two houses: the Senate and the House of Representatives. The Congress meets in the US Capitol in Washington, D.C. Article One of the US Constitution states the formation and powers of the Senate and the House of Representatives. The two houses are granted equal powers and all bills have to pass both the Senate and the House of Representatives before going to the President for his signature. The central function of Congress is to make federal laws. Only Congress has the power to collect taxes and levy duties, to pay the country's debts, to regulate foreign commerce, and to raise armies and pay for them. Another important function of Congress is to make investigation. The aim is to prevent corruptions and wrongdoings of high-level officials. The Congress has power to call any American citizens, including federal officials, and usually holds hearings over disputed questions.

The Senate

The Senate has 100 senators. According to the principles of the Constitution, each state, whether big or small, has two senators. One-third of the 100 senators are chosen every two years. A senator serves a six-year term. The presiding officer of the Senate is the Vice President, who serves as chairman when the Senate is in session. A senator must be over 30 years old, a resident in the state which they represent, and must have been a US citizen for at least nine years.

The Senate has several exclusive powers. It has the power to ratify or reject proposed treaties with foreign countries. It has the exclusive power to confirm or reject important nominations proposed by the President. It has the sole power to hear charges filed by the House of Representatives against high-level officials for alleged wrongdoings, and to find them guilty. Some members of Congress may become very influential and powerful in American politics because they may run for re-election for many years. If successful, their increasing experience results in greater influence and Committee chairmanships, which may determine the fate of bills affecting the American daily life. It also results in certain states receiving more federal money for various state needs. The majority and minority parties hold a majority and minority of seats in Congress respectively. The political parties usually vote or act along party lines. Therefore, the majority parties in Congress have the right to choose all the Chairmen for the various major committees in the Senate and House to serve the interests of their political parties or their constituents. There is much power in these chairmanships. After 2024 US elections, the Republican Party controls both the Senate and the House of Representatives.

The House of Representatives

The House of Representatives, commonly referred to as the "House," is the lower house of the bicameral (2-part) United States Congress. Each state receives representation in the House in proportion to its population. The most populous state, California, currently has 52 representatives. The state of Alaska has only 1 representative. The total number of voting representatives is currently fixed at 435. Each representative serves for a two-year term. Congressmen must be at least 25 years old and must have been American citizens for no less than seven years.

The Speaker is the presiding officer of the House, who is elected by the members of the House. The current Speaker is Mike Johnson, a member of the Republican Party, who assumed office on October 25th, 2023. The House was granted its own exclusive powers: the power to initiate revenue bills (收支法案), impeach officials, and elect the president in Electoral College deadlocks. The House meets in the south wing of the United States Capitol.

Legislative Procedure

The most important function of the Congress is to make federal laws. To deal with the large amount of legislative work, both the Senate and the House are divided into a number of committees. The procedure of the law-making process can be summarized as follows.

With the exception of revenue or tax bills, legislation can be introduced in either the House or the Senate. When bills are introduced, they are sent to the appropriate committees by the Speaker of the House or the Senate majority leader.

The chair of the committee sends the bill to a subcommittee, where hearings are held. The subcommittee can summon people to testify, or to attend the hearings and answer questions related to the draft bill.

After the preliminary investigation of the bill, the subcommittee issues a report to the committee chairman. The report is either favorable or unfavorable to the bill. Or, it may report out an amended bill or rewrite the original bill.

After a draft bill is commented on in the Senate or the House, it is then voted upon. If most of the members vote in favor of it, the bill is said to have passed, but a bill passed by one chamber must be sent to the other chamber for deliberation.

A bill passed by Congress must be presented to the President. If the President finds the bill appropriate and necessary, he signs it into law. If the President objects, he vetoes the bill and returns it with his reasons for objection. If the President does not return the bill with 10 days, it automatically becomes a law whether he signs or not.

2 The Executive Branch

The executive branch of the federal government is officially known as the Administration. The Constitution established that the executive branch is headed by the President. In America, the executive branch consists of 14 departments and many independent agencies.

The President

The President of the United States is the head of state and head of government of the United States. The President leads the executive branch of the federal government and is one of only two nationally elected federal officers, the other being the Vice President of the United States. The President is not elected directly by the people but through the Electoral College (elected political officials from each state). The term of office is four years, and the 22nd Amendment limits the President to two terms. By law any natural-born American citizens over 35 years of age, and being a resident within the United States for 14 years can run for the Office of President.

The president-elect takes office on the 20th of January following his election. Outside the capitol, on a temporary platform, he becomes President by taking the oath of office and delivers the inaugural address. Donald Trump who served as the 45th president of the United States form 2017 to 2021, was inaugurated as the 47th president on January 20th, 2025 for his second term.

Among the powers and responsibilities, the President should "faithfully execute" federal law. The President is the commander-in-chief of the US armed forces and has the power to raise, train, supervise, and deploy American troops, provided Congress shows no disagreement. The president is the nation's sole official spokesman with foreign powers. He formulates and implements the American policy, with the authority to make treaties with foreign countries.

The President has the power of appointment. He will nominate, by and with the advice and consent of the Senate, the Secretary of State, other public ministers and consuls, judges of the Supreme Court, and all other officers of the United States. He sends and receives ambassadors, and recognizes new foreign governments and states.

The President has big influence on law-making. He can call Congress into special session and can adjourn Congress if the House and the Senate can't agree on a final date, but he can't dismiss the Congress. He is also authorized to propose legislation. The President can influence the decision of the federal courts. He also has the power to pardon anyone who has broken the federal law.

But the power of President is also limited. Actually, he moves within the limits already drawn for him. His nomination of officials and his foreign treaties must be ratified or confirmed by the Senate. The Supreme Court has the power to declare his policy, unconstitutional and thus abolish it, even if it has already been approved by Congress. If he abuses his power or commits crimes, he may be impeached by Congress.

The Cabinet

There is a central part of leadership under the president in the administrative branch, called the Cabinet, which is the major source of advice and assistance to the President. Every president has had his Cabinet since George Washington, though it is not mentioned by name in the Constitution. The Cabinet is made up of the heads of the major departments (called Secretaries) and other persons chosen by the President. They discuss and advise the President on important issues.

The 15 executive Cabinet departments include the Department of State, the Treasury Department, the Department of Defense, the Department of Justice, the Department of Commerce, the Department of Labor, the Department of Agriculture, the Department of Interior, the Department of Health and Human Services, the Department of Housing and Urban Development, the Department of Transportation and the Department of Energy as well as the Department of Homeland Security, the newest cabinet-level department. The Department of Homeland Security was established soon after the 9/11 terrorist attacks. With more than 240,000 employees, the Department of Homeland Security, the third largest Cabinet department coordinates many of the efforts of the FBI, CIA and NSA in an effort to enhance anti-terrorist activities and safeguard the security of national territory and resources.

The Organization of Executive Branch

The President is assisted by a number of organizations grouped under the general title, the Executive Office of the President. It mainly comprises four agencies: The White House Office; The National Security Council (NSC); The Council of Economic Advisors and The Office of Management and Budget.

The White House Office consists of the President's most intimate friends and personal aides, sometimes called brain-trusters. The President may appoint all of the White House Office staff. The Chief of Staff is the head of the Executive Office of the President. These aides overseas every person, document and communication that goes to the President, as well as the political and policy interests of the President without requiring Senate confirmation for appointment.

The National Security Council (NSC) deals with domestic, foreign, and military policies affecting security issues. By law, the NSC is composed of the President, Vice President, Secretary of Defense, and Secretary of State, the director of the Central Intelligence Agency and the chair of the Joint Chiefs of Staff.

The Council of Economic Advisors provides the President with information on economic policy. It provides much of the empirical research for the White House and prepares the annual Economic Report of the President. The council is composed of a chairman and two members, each of whom is appointed by the President and approved by the Senate.

The Office of Management and Budget is involved in drafting the President's budget proposal to Congress and measuring the quality of agency programs, policies and procedures to see if they comply with the President's policies. It also coordinates inter-agency policy initiatives, and evaluating how effectively federal agencies use their appropriations.

3 The Judicial Branch

The US judicial branch refers to the federal law court that is composed of three levels: the Supreme Court, the courts of appeals, and the district courts. All American courts use the jury system and common law.

The Supreme Court

The Supreme Court, which is the highest court in the federal system, is the only court created by the US Constitution. It has one chief justice and eight associate justices. They are appointed by President with the consent of the Senate. They serve for life, but their powers can be limited by the President and Congress, and can be removed by impeachment.

The Supreme Court has ultimate appellate jurisdiction over all state and federal courts, and original jurisdiction over a small range of cases. The Supreme Court has power to interpret the Constitution and laws, and its decisions are binding upon all lower courts. The Supreme Court also has power to hear appeals from any federal court cases. Under the principle of judicial review, it has the power to examine the bills passed by Congress and policies made by President, and declare them unconstitutional and thus abolish them. It also has power to hear the appeals from the courts of appeals and cases involving original jurisdiction.

The Court of Appeals

The United States courts of appeals (or circuit courts) are the intermediate appellate courts of the United States federal court system. They have been established to share the work of the Supreme Court. Currently, the whole country is divided into 12 appeal regions called "circuits," and each region has a Court of Appeals. Circuit judges are appointed for life by the President with the consent of the Senate. A Court of Appeals hears and decides on appeals from the District Courts located within its Federal Judicial Circuit as well as appeals from decisions of federal administrative agencies and other designated federal courts. There is also a federal court of appeals. The thirteenth court of appeals is the United States Court of Appeals for the Federal Circuit, which has nationwide jurisdiction over certain appeals based on their subject matter, such as those involving patent laws and cases decided by the Court of International Trade and the Court of Federal Claims.

The District Courts

The District Court is the lowest court of the federal judicial system. There are 94 federal judicial districts, of which 89 district courts are located within the 50 states. There is also a district court in the District of Columbia and four territorial district courts in Guam, Puerto Rico, the Virgin Islands, and the Northern Mariana Islands. Each federal judicial district has at least one courthouse, and many districts have more than one. The United States district courts are the trial courts of the federal court system. Within limits set by Congress and the Constitution, the district courts have jurisdiction to hear nearly all categories of federal cases, including both civil and criminal matters. Bankruptcy courts are separate units of the district courts. Federal courts have exclusive jurisdiction over bankruptcy cases, so that they cannot be filed in state courts.

Political Parties

The United States has two major political parties: the Democratic Party and the Republican Party. These two parties have won every US Presidential election since 1852. They have controlled the US Congress to some extent since at least 1856. The rest of the political parties are categorized as the third parties. Major third parties include the Libertarian Party and the Green Party.

Figure 9.1 Emblems of the Two Parties in the US

American cartoonist Thomas Nast drew a political picture with a donkey representing Democrats and an elephant representing Republicans. Later, they became the emblems of the two parties.

The Democratic Party evolved from the party of Thomas Jefferson, formed before 1800. The Republican Party, nicknamed as "Grand Old Party," was established in the 1850s by Abraham Lincoln and others who opposed the expansion of slavery. Since the turn of the 20th century, the Democratic Party is considered to be the more liberal party, and the Republican, the more conservative. The Democratic Party has supported progressive reform, and tends to favor greater government intervention in the economy, education and social welfare. The Republican Party traditionally has supported laissez-faire capitalism, low taxes, and conservative social policies. Republican philosophy is based on a limited influence of government and a dominant foreign policy. During the term of President Obama, the differences between these two major parties widened, and recently they fought for the budget of the United States Government, and the public debt, etc.

The Democratic Party

The Democratic Party evolved from anti-federalist factions that opposed the fiscal policies of Alexander Hamilton in the early 1790s. The party favored states' rights and strict adherence to the Constitution; and the Democratic-Republican Party ascended to power in the election of 1800.

The Democratic Party, once dominant in the southeastern United States, is now strongest in the northeast, Great Lakes region, and the Pacific Coast (including Hawaii). The Democrats are also strongest in major cities. Democrats generally believe that government has an obligation to provide social and economic programs for those who need them.

Historically, the party has favored farmers, laborers, labor unions, and religious and ethnic minorities; it

has opposed unregulated business and finance, and favored progressive income taxes. Today, Democrats advocate more social and economic equality, along with the welfare state. The party seeks to provide government intervention and regulation in the economy.

The Republican Party

The Republican Party, nicknamed "Grand Old Party (GOP)," was founded in 1854 as an anti-slavery party. It was a party of northern capitalists who opposed slavery for their own political and economic interests. In 1856 the party held its first national convention, and the name "Republican" has been used ever since. It first came to power in 1860 with the election of Abraham Lincoln and presided over the American Civil War and Reconstruction.

Politically, the Republican Party inherited some ideas from the Federalist Party that played a major role in promoting the adoption of the US Constitution. Its ideology is American conservatism. It represents the interests of big businesses and prosperous farmers of the West. The Republicans favor an economic system which gives enterprises a greater freedom and fair competition, and demands that the government control inflation. They stress the need for law and order, and favors reduction of public spending as well as taxes. They favor a strong military posture and assertive stand in international relations.

Election

Elections in the United States are held for government officials at three levels: the federal, state and local levels. At the federal level, the nation's head of state, the President, is elected indirectly by the people of each state, through the Electoral College. Today, these electors almost always vote with the popular vote of their state. All members of the federal legislature, Congress, are directly elected by the people of each state. There are many elected offices at state level, each state having at least an elective governor and legislature. There are also elected offices at the local level, in counties, cities, towns, townships, boroughs and villages.

1 Federal Election

Presidential Election

The President and the Vice President are elected together in a presidential election, which take the form of indirect election. In 1971 the 26th Amendment to the Constitution fixed the voting age at 18 years of age.

Voting in America is a two-step process: registering to vote (in advance) and then casting his or her ballot during elections.

Selecting the right candidate for the presidency is extremely important for both parties. From February to June in the election year, the parties choose all their respective candidates for election, except for president, through a process called primary election. All the aspirants for the nomination begin their personal campaigns within the party. These "primaries" choose delegates to represent the state at the national party conventions. The more supporters they have, the greater the chance for them to be nominated for the candidacy. In late summer, the Democratic and Republican parties hold separate national conventions for their state delegates. Both party conventions are responsible for the party's general policy, but its main job is to choose a presidential candidate. The final choice is made when one candidate has received more than half of the votes. After the convention, the whole party will help its candidate run for election all over the country.

Once the presidential candidates of major parties are selected, the general election comes to the campaigning stage. This is a very important stage. By the early fall of the election year, the presidential race is on. The presidential nominees will spend much money, traveling around the country, making countless speeches. They have to face the rival in debates on television, making every effort to win the support from voters.

The general election is always held on the first Tuesday after the first Monday in November, called the Election Day. This stage is to choose a slate of presidential electors in their state who make up the Electoral College. The number of members to the Electoral College of each state is equal to that of its senators and representatives in Congress. There are now 538 presidential electors, 535 from 50 states and 3 from Washington D. C. The candidate with the most votes in a state wins all of that state's electoral votes (选举人票). This is known as the "winner-takes-all" principle. There are 48 states that have a winner-takes-all rule, with the exception of Maine and Nebraska. In these states, whichever candidate receives a majority of the vote takes all of the state's electoral votes.

The Electoral College was created 200 years ago. The framers were not confident that the average citizen knew enough about the candidates and the issues to vote intelligently. Many people argue that with modern media, the average citizen today is much better informed, and that presidential elections should be decided by the direct vote of the people; others disagree. As it stands, the Electoral College is another major reason why the US is not a true democracy, but a republic.

When the presidential electors in each state are chosen, people already know the result of the general election. But, the electors cast their votes for the President in December, and they can only vote for their parties' presidential candidates. The candidate who wins the majority (270) of the Electoral College votes will be the president of the next term. When the new congress assembles on January 6th, the electoral votes are formally counted in a joint session of the two houses, and the President of the Senate announces the result of the vote. The elected president is sworn into office on January 20th. The president's four-year term begins on this date.

Congressional Election

The Congress is divided into two chambers, the Senate and the House of Representatives. Before 1913, senators were chosen by their state legislatures, as the Founding Fathers believed that since the senators represented the state, the state legislature should elect them. The 17th amendment to the Constitution changed this procedure, mandating that senators be elected directly by the voters of their state.

When the first Congress met in 1789, there were 59 members of the House of Representatives. As the number of states increased and the population grew, the number of representatives increased significantly. A law passed in 1911 fixed the size of the House of Representatives at 435 members. Members of the House are up for reelection every two years. The number of representatives in each state depends upon its population as reported in the nation's most recent census. Each state is divided into a corresponding number of congressional districts (国会选区). There is a representative for every congressional district, elected by the voters living in that district.

2　State Election

State Elections, controlled by state legislatures, are regulated by state law and state constitutions. Various officials at state level are elected from state elections. According to the separation of powers, state legislatures and the executive (the governor) are elected separately. Currently, all states in the US directly elect their own governors and representatives to the state legislature. Governors and lieutenant governors are elected in all states, in some states on a joint ticket and in some states separately. The governors of the territories of American Samoa, Guam, the Northern Mariana Islands, Puerto Rico and the United States Virgin Islands are also elected. In some states, executive positions like Attorney General and Secretary of State are also elected offices. All members of state legislatures are elected state senators and state representatives. Nebraska's legislature is unicameral, so only senators are elected. In some states, members of the state supreme court and other members of the state judiciary are elected; but generally these positions are appointed by the governor or legislature.

State Elections are often held at the same time as either the federal presidential or midterm elections, considering convenience and cost-saving. However, there are also quite a number of states holding off-year elections (非大选年选举).

Chapter 9 Government

3 Local Election

At the local level, county and city government positions are usually chosen by election, especially within the legislative branch. The election of offices in the executive or judicial branches varies from county to county or from city to city. Some examples of local elected positions include sheriffs at the county level, city council members, mayors and school board members at the city level. Local representatives are selected by a process of direct election. The candidate wins with a simple majority (the most votes). Same as the state elections, an election for a specific local office may be held at the same time as either the presidential, midterm, or off-year elections.

Exercises

Part I. Decide whether the following statements are true (T) or false (F). Write T or F in the brackets.

1. The national and the state government receive their powers from each other. (   )

2. The Senate is the law-making branch of government. (   )

3. The President is the executive branch of government. (   )

4. The US Senate is considered as the lower house of the bicameral US Congress. (   )

5. The Senate is smaller and its members serve longer terms than those in the House. (   )

6. Each state receives representation in the House of Representatives in proportion to its population. (   )

7. The Democratic Party is considered to be more liberal and the Republican, the more conservative. (   )

8. The winner-takes-all rule means the candidate who receives the most votes takes all of that state's electoral votes, which is applied in all American states. (   )

Part II. Fill in the blanks with best answers.

1. The national or the state government receives its power from _____.

   A. statutes law

   B. treaties

C. largely on common law

D. the Constitution

2. The President and _____ are responsible for enforcing the law of the country.

    A. the federal government

    B. the Congress

    C. the vice-president

    D. the Supreme Court

3. _____ decides arguments about the interpretation of laws.

    A. The President

    B. The Congress

    C. The Supreme Court

    D. The Senate

4. The US Congress consists of two houses, the Senate and _____.

    A. the House of Commons

    B. the House of Lords

    C. the House of Representatives

    D. the Cabinet

5. The power of the President does NOT include _____.

    A. nominating the Secretary of State, and all other officers of the United States

    B. dismissing the Congress if the House and the Senate cannot agree on a final date

    C. proposing legislation

    D. pardoning anyone who has broken the federal law

6. The Cabinet is _____.

    A. the major source of advice and assistance to the President

    B. mentioned by name in the Constitution

    C. made up of the heads of the major departments

    D. made up of persons chosen by the President

7. Who appoints Circuit judges? _____.

   A. The President

   B. The Supreme Court

   C. The Courts of Appeals

   D. The Senate

8. Which of the following statements about the judiciary is Not true? _____

   A. The chief justice of the Supreme Court can be removed by impeachment.

   B. All states in the US have a unified judicial system.

   C. Bankruptcy courts are separate unites of the district courts.

   D. The US district courts are the trial courts of the federal court system.

Part III. State your understanding of the following questions.

1. What serves as the legislative branch in the United States? What about China?

2. What are the relations between the federal government and state governments in the United States?

3. What are the differences between the Democrats and the Republicans in terms of political opinions and state policies?

Chapter 10

Economy

1. What do you know about the American economic system?
2. What do you think of the roles the United States plays in the world economy?
3. In what manufacturing fields does the United States take the leading position in the world?

Overview of American Economy

The United States of America (the US, or America), a giant in economy, is the largest developed country in the world. Its gross domestic product (GDP) was around $25.74 trillion in 2022, ranking first in the world and accounting for about 25% in the global economy, but its GDP per capita ranks sixth. Overall, American economy has maintained a stable growth rate, a low unemployment rate, and high levels of research and capital investments funded by investors at home and abroad. It takes the leading position in such fields as electronics and information technology, computer science, space technology, nuclear energy, and military industry. And it produces a large proportion of machinery, chemicals, automobiles, oil, and electrical energy in the world.

The economic system of the United States is known as free enterprise system, which is largely a market-oriented economy with emphasis on private ownership and free competition. In such a system, individual people and businesses are free to make their own economic decisions. The private sector of American economy is vigorously developed, contributing a lot to the development of the whole country's economic system. According to the US Department of Commerce, in 2022, the private sector accounted for 88.6% of the total GDP with the rest owned by the government. The government is involved in the system by enacting policies and regulations to macro-control the economic system as a whole, such as The New Deal (also called The Roosevelt New Deal), and by adjusting social welfare policies to further regulate the market system.

There is no doubt that the United States, as the world's largest economy, injects major and strong momentum into the world's economic development. Though the world economy is increasingly characterized by multi-polarity, the US is still the strongest economy.

American Economy in the Colonial Period

In 1492, Columbus arrived in America, marking the beginning of the period of European advancement to the New World. Since then, Britain, France, and Spain had all arrived to explore the new land in North America. Among these countries, Britain was a major power in colonial expansion, and established the first British colony in Virginia in North America in 1607.

Since then there occurred the colonization of North America for two centuries, and Britain successively established **13 colonies**[1] in North America. Britain continued to colonize and expand, implementing policies and actions that had a profound impact on the demographic, social and economic development of North America.

The colonial activities were carried out by chartered companies, built by some private sectors for gaining economic growth not only for the companies themselves but for the whole nation. The monarch of Britain empowered the companies some charters to gain legitimacy for all the activities in the colonies, hence the name chartered companies, i.e., companies with privileges. Chartered companies brought far-reaching effects on the colonies, not only on the economic development, but also on politics and religion of the colonies.

The primary factor of colonial expansion was to develop economy. During the British colonial expansion in North America, the main economic development sectors were plantations, trade and others. The British colonists developed the plantation industry mainly in the more populated south, which led to a surge in the need of black slaves, triggering the slave trade; while in the sparsely populated north, they mainly developed manufacturing industries, laying foundations for the future economic development of the United States.

1　The thirteen colonies in North America: Virginia, Massachusetts, New Hampshire, Maryland, Rhode Island, Connecticut, North Carolina, South Carolina, New York, New Jersey, Pennsylvania, Delaware, and Georgia.

American Economy After Independence

After Britain won the Seven Years' War in 1763, it began to impose heavy taxes on the North American colonies, which led to the discontent of the people in the colonies and subsequently the outbreak of the American War of Independence. The United States of America was established by signing the Declaration of Independence in Philadelphia in 1776, and won the War of Independence in 1783 to formally establish the new nation. Meanwhile, in the same year when the independence of the United States of America was proclaimed, **Adam Smith**[1] published ***The Wealth of Nations***[2], a book which established the foundation for economic policies of the United States in the future.

The American War of Independence had a significant impact not only on the political system of the country, but also on its economic framework. After the War of Independence, the United States established a new political system, and the Constitution provided that its core was supremacy and political equality of the people.

Figure 10.1   Adam Smith

The United States also established a system of Separation of Powers to ensure that the power of the government would not be concentrated so as to maintain political stability and democracy; in the economic aspect, the War of Independence also provided the basis for economic evolution and development of the country, which was at that time a sparsely populated nation with abundant natural resources.

After the War of Independence, industrial production became the core of the American economy. The US government strongly encouraged people to use domestic resources for industrial production, while encouraging the construction of factories and railways to promote the development of the country's agriculture and industry. After the

---

1 Adam Smith: Adam Smith is a British economist, philosopher, author, the major founder of economics. He is considered as the father of classical economic theory and the founder of the invisible hand theory that underpins capitalist economic systems.

2 *The Wealth of Nations: The Wealth of Nations* is a clearly written account of economics at the dawn of the Industrial Revolution. The book was a landmark work in the history and economics as it was comprehensive and an accurate characterization of the economic mechanisms at work in modern economics.

Civil War in the 19th century, the second industrial revolution appeared in the United States, ushering in a more advanced industrial and economic system. Thanks to the second industrial revolution, the United States established a more extensive infrastructure system, including railways and the automobile industry; meanwhile, with the development of new technologies, the production efficiency was greatly improved. The industrial production system also gave rise to a lot of employment opportunities, which improved the living standard of people and the economic situation of the whole society.

American Economy in the 20th Century

After its founding, the United States has been pursuing an independent and autonomous free economy, which not only injected a strong impetus to the economic development of the country, but also spawned risks and challenges, including the Great Depression from 1929 to 1933. President Roosevelt launched the New Deal in 1933 to adjust the welfare system and increase social welfare through government intervention in national economy. The government intervention policy was in effect until 1980 when Ronald Wilson Reagan was elected president. It was obvious that the interventionist economic policy led to severe inflation. After Reagan came to power, he released a series of economic recovery plans with good results. After the implementation of the new policies, the US economy continued to grow at a high rate with an increasing GDP share. Yet after Reagan left office, the negative impacts of his policies arose, especially in the form of huge debts. The Clinton Administration led the US economy out of stagnation and inflation with low unemployment rate and high economic growth.

Figure 10.2   Franklin Delano Roosevelt

In the 20th century, the United States experienced two world wars and the Cold War, after which the advent of new technologies and capital influx further promoted the economic development of the country. In the mid-to-late 20th century, the American scientific and technological revolution focused on the development of the service sector and high-tech industries, providing a further innovative power for economic growth.

American Economy in the New Era

The economic development of the United States in the new era has gained unprecedented prosperity, and its primary, secondary and tertiary industries all show positive development trends. Especially with the development of the information industry, the growth of new technologies has promoted the economic development at all levels of industries.

1 Primary Sector—Agriculture

The primary sector mainly refers to agriculture, which is the cornerstone of a country's sustainable development. In 2022, the American primary sector accounted for only about 1.1% of the total GDP, amounting to about $270 billion. The American agricultural population takes up about 2% of the workforce. Of all the 50 states, Texas has the largest population engaged in agriculture, hitting about 270,000 in 2021.

Despite the relatively low share of agriculture, the United States is one of the most agriculturally advanced countries in the world today. This is, first and foremost, due to the abundance of natural resources in the United States, which creates unique conditions for the development of agriculture in the US. Secondly, modern civilization has also created a favorable environment for the development of American agriculture. For example, the fast-growing high-tech industry provides advanced equipment for agriculture so that the agricultural activities can benefit from a high degree of mechanization; and the agricultural biotechnology has been widely used to improve crop genetics, promoting the agricultural development of America.

The development of agriculture in the United States is strongly supported by the government. The American government has introduced a series of policies to advance agriculture, including direct inputs, subsidies, tax incentives, and legislative regulations. With these policies, the government aims to promote the import and export trade of American agricultural products as well as to mitigate the losses caused by natural disasters and guarantee the income of agricultural producers.

Another notable feature of American agriculture is that the US has a lot of large-scale family farms. The **farm typology**[1] focuses primarily on the "family farm," a farm in which the majority of the business is owned by an operator and/or any individual related by blood, marriage, or adoption, including relatives who do not live in the operator's household. According to the Economic Research Service of the US Department

---

1 The development of an internationally coherent classification of agricultural holdings, further called farm typology (FT), with policy relevance has been identified as an important potential component of the long-term framework.

of Agriculture, there were about 2 million farms in the US in 2021, fewer than the peak number in the past. It is reported that farm families earn more than the median household in the nation.

Figure 10.3   Combine Harvester

American agriculture has increasingly become an "agribusiness" (农业企业), a term created to reflect the big, corporate nature of many farm enterprises. Agribusinesses include a variety of farm businesses and structures, from small and one-family businesses to multinational corporations.

Currently, the top five biggest states that own farmlands are Iowa, Kansas, North Dakota, Illinois, and Texas. In terms of the average production, Iowa holds the top position in corn production, Illinois in soybean, Kansas in wheat and Texas in cotton. The United States is the world's largest producer of chicken, and its egg production ranking second in the world. According to the US Department of Agriculture, chicken had the largest share of meat production in the US in 2022, with a high share of 45%, followed by beef and pork, both with production shares of over 25%.

2 Secondary Sector—Manufacturing and Energy Production

The secondary sector mainly refers to manufacturing, energy production, and other processing industries. According to the statistics in 2022, China's manufacturing sector was 1.8 times larger than that of the United States, and China's manufacturing sector accounted for 26.32% of its total GDP, compared with

10.3% in the United States.

Figure 10.4　Auto Manufacturing

In the United States, the three largest manufacturing industries include chemicals; computers and electronic products; food, beverage and tobacco. With the increasing investment in research and development of medicines, the US drug expenditure has increased significantly in recent years and the market size of generics (仿制药) and that of patented drugs have grown remarkably, from which a visible increase in the market demand of the US pharmaceutical industry can be seen.

Important manufacturing industries in the United States also include the automobile industry, aircraft industry and military industry. In the auto-making field, the total number of automobiles manufactured in the United States in 2022 reached about 10 million, witnessing a strong development of the American manufacturing industry. The US also takes the lead in the aircraft manufacturing industry. The Boeing Company is a leading producer of commercial aircraft, military aircraft, space vehicles and missiles. What's more, the military industry in the US takes a large proportion in the world, related to army, navy, air force, marine corps, space force, coast guard and national guard. According to Stockholm International Peace Research Institute (SIPRI, 斯德哥尔摩国际和平研究所), the world's top 5 military companies are all from the United States, with sales totaling approximately $166 billion in 2019.

Manufacturing companies such as Apple, Ford Motor Company, General Motors, and Dell are the giants that hold up the manufacturing industry in the United States. Silicon Valley, the high-tech manufacturing hub of the United States in California, is the cradle of many high-tech manufacturing companies.

Figure 10.5　Mountain Pass in California, the Only Rare Earth Mine (稀土矿) in the US

The mining industry, a traditional energy production industry, is another major industry of the secondary sector. The Gold Rush, one of the famous mining movements, was triggered by the westward migration movement. In 2022, the mining GDP accounted for 1.78% of the total GDP. As of 2021, the total mineral production in the United States was around 2.2 billion metric tons, an increasing scale over the previous years.

3　Tertiary Sector—Service Industry

The tertiary sector is known as the service industry. The tertiary industries of many developed countries account for more than 70% of the total GDP, such as the United States, Japan and Germany. The overall proportion of the primary and secondary industries together in the United States accounts for only about 20% of the total GDP while the tertiary sector accounts for about 80%. It can be seen that the GDP of the United States is mainly supported by the service sector because most industries are related to the service system after industrial upgrading and the adjustment of industrialization.

The fast development of the tertiary sector in the United States provides a lot of employment opportunities for American people. The service sector mainly includes finance, transportation, communication, education, tourism as well as wholesale and retail industry.

Finance

The finance industry covers the banking industry, insurance industry, securities industry, and so on. In 2022, the finance industry in the United States accounted for 20.7% of the total GDP, more than one fifth of its total GDP. The growth of the finance industry is the main driving force of the rapid and high-quality growth of American economy, showing the tendency that the service industry has taken the dominant position in national economy. The American banking industry is one of the most developed and mature banking industries in the world; in 2020, the total assets of the American banking industry reached $22.6 trillion, and the scale of insurance and securities industries also reached more than a trillion dollars. With the development of science and technology, digital finance and other emerging patterns of business are also developing, bringing both opportunities and challenges to the traditional development model.

Figure 10.6　Wall Street Financial Exchange

Transportation

The United States transportation system consists mainly of highways, bridges, railways, aviation, pipelines, waterways and metro transportation. Statistics from the US Department of Transportation show that in 2021, the US highway mileage (including urban and rural street length) reached 6,739,900 kilometers with an increase of 0.36% year-on-year. In 2021, the United States highways reached 108,198 kilometers with an increase of 0.15% year-on-year. With lines of more than 250,000 kilometers under operation, the United States rail network is one of the largest in the world. The United States plans to build a national high-speed rail system of 27,000 kilometers in four phases by 2030. According to the US Department of Transportation, the US airlines carried a total of approximately 940 million passengers in 2022, an increase of 38.7% over the previous year. And there are totally 926 ports in the United States, which provide favorable conditions for foreign trade between the United States and other countries.

Due to the development of transportation routes, the United States transportation and supply chain has developed accordingly, connecting producers and consumers by means of railway, air and water transportation, and contributing to economic development.

Communication

The development of science and technology has also provided a solid foundation for the development of the communication industry. The number of patent applications of the US communications equipment ranks third in the world, and the market size of the US communications equipment industry exceeds $30 billion.

Since 2009, the output of the US communication industry has been increasing year by year, occupying an important position in the world. At the same time, the US has Qualcomm, Apple and other well-known enterprises to promote the development of digitalization, and has established a complete business system with a leading scale of communication manufacturing industry in the world. Since 2018 the United States has been in the leading position in the 6G research.

Education

The United States also ranks first in education in the world. It is home to a large number of the world's leading universities such as Harvard, Yale, MIT, Princeton, Stanford, etc. In 2020, the US education industry accounted for 5.4% of its total GDP. According to the QS World University Rankings, American universities take up a half among the world's top 20 universities, and Massachusetts Institute of Technology (MIT, 麻省理工学院) ranks first in the world. Such world-renowned universities attract large groups of international students every year, contributing a lot to American GDP.

Tourism

Tourism is also a big segment of the service sector that cannot be ignored in the US. In 2022, the US tourism industry contributed about $2 trillion to its total GDP and created 2.7 million jobs. This is not only due to the beautiful natural landscape of the country, but also to the humanity, art and cultural attractions.

Wholesale & Retail Industry

The recent statistics from the US Department of Commerce show that the wholesale and retail industry accounts for about 12.3% of the total GDP in the US, a big proportion in the service industry. And according to the National Retail Federation (NRF, 美国零售联合会), the current top 3 businesses in the wholesale and retail industry are Walmart, Amazon.com and Costco Wholesale. Many enterprises have great achievements in terms of digital transformation, forming the sales pattern of "online plus offline."

Foreign Trade

The US Department of Commerce reports that currently China is the third largest trading partner of the United States, after Canada and Mexico; and the United States is China's third largest trading partner, after **ASEAN**[1] and the European Union.

In 2022, the total growth rate of the US foreign trade, including import and export, was 2.1%, with the total amount of around $5,308 trillion. The US trade has a significant role in promoting both domestic economic development and the global economy.

Figure 10.7   Foreign Trade

According to Global Trade Flow (GTF, 全球贸易观察), a trade flow information system developed by China's National Information Center, the main imported products of the US are crude oil, motor vehicles, automatic data processing equipment, pharmaceuticals, vaccines, integrated circuits, and so on; and the main products exported to the world are refined oil products, motor vehicles, vaccines, motor vehicle parts, liquefied petroleum gas (LPG, 液化石油气), soybeans and others. Hence, America is a giant in both import and export trade. The US export trade has shown a strong growth in the years of 2021 and 2022 after the export downturn in 2020.

The United States has a large number of platforms and institutions to promote the development of its

---

1   ASEAN, an abbreviation for the Association of Southeast Asian Nations, is a political and economic union of 10 states in Southeast Asia. 东南亚国家联盟，简称东盟。

bilateral trade, such as the US International Electric Power Expo, the US Labor and Insurance Expo, etc. Meanwhile, some cross-border e-commerce companies also provide good platforms for the development of US import and export trade, such as Amazon, Ebay, Walmart Marketplace, Rakuten, and so on. The US government has also introduced policies to ensure the smooth running of import and export trade, such as tariff policies.

In 2022, the trade deficit of the United States reached $948.1 billion, a record high. Due to the prevalence of liberalism in the US, most US households emphasize consumption over savings, leading to an increase in the demand for imports of consumer goods. And the decline of the US manufacturing industry has made it necessary to rely on imports for a lot of products, ranging from those needed for manufacturing to household goods. At the same time, the US government has restricted the export of high-tech industries, leading to a weak high-tech export economy. All these factors contribute to the trade deficit of the country.

As the world's largest economy, the growth and decline of the US trade volume is bound to have a direct impact on the world economy.

Exercises

Part I. Decide whether the following statements are true (T) or false (F). Write T or F in the brackets.

1. The total GDP of the United States ranks first in the world. So does its GDP per capita. (   )

2. The American economy is largely a market-oriented economy with emphasis on private ownership and free competition. (   )

3. The economic system of the United States is a system of free enterprise, in which the government cannot get involved. (   )

4. The economic activities during the colonial period were carried out by chartered companies. (   )

5. Roosevelt's New Deal contributed a lot in dealing with the Great Depression during the Cold War. (   )

6. American agribusinesses refer to large-scale farm businesses, not including small and one-family ones. (   )

7. The three largest manufacturing industries in the US are chemicals; computers and electronic products; food, beverage and tobacco. (   )

8. China is the largest trading partner of the United States, and the United States is the largest trading partner of China. (   )

Part II. Fill in the blanks with best answers.

1. The United States takes the leading position in the following fields except _____.

    A. information technology

    B. nuclear energy

    C. textile industry

    D. military industry

2. The United States is a major producer of the following products except _____.

    A. machinery

    B. chemicals

    C. automobiles

    D. furniture

3. _____ published **The Wealth of Nation**, a book which established the foundation for American economic policies.

    A. Alexander Hamilton

    B. Adam Smith

    C. George Washington

    D. Thomas Jefferson

4. Of all the 50 states, _____ has the largest population engaged in agriculture.

    A. Iowa

    B. Kansas

    C. Illinois

    D. Texas

5. The United States has large productions of the following meat products except _____.

    A. chicken

    B. fish

C. pork

D. beef

6. All the following industries belong to the service sector except _____.

   A. finance

   B. transportation

   C. tourism

   D. animal husbandry

7. The main exported products of the United States include the following except _____.

   A. motor vehicles

   B. crude oil

   C. vaccines

   D. soybeans

8. _____ accounts for about 80% of the total GDP in the United States.

   A. The manufacturing industry

   B. The energy production industry

   C. The service industry

   D. The high-tech industry

Part III. State your understanding of the following questions.

1. Some people mistakenly regard the US economic system as a model for other nations to follow. How can you argue against this claim?

2. How can China respond to the harsh restrictions that the United States imposes on China's high-tech companies?

3. In view of the severe trade deficit of the United States, what implications can we have for China's economic policies?

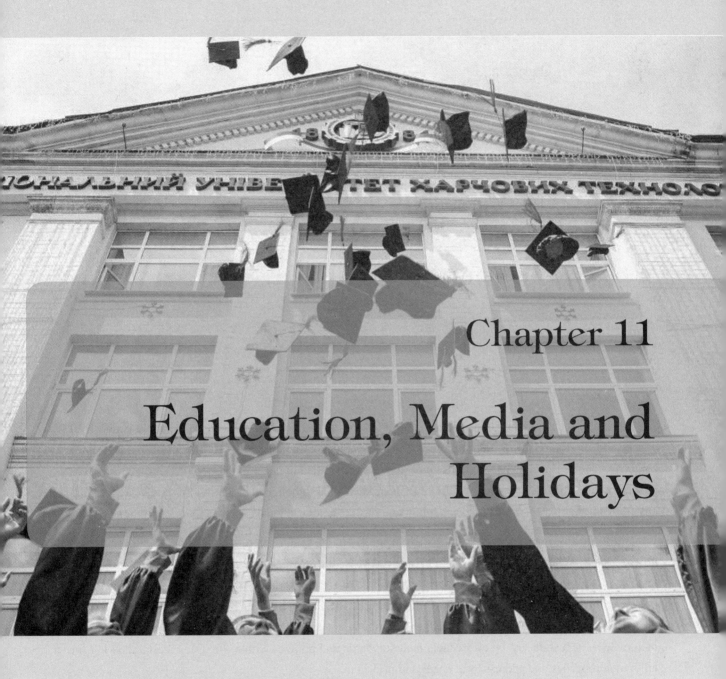

Chapter 11
Education, Media and Holidays

Preview Questions

1. How is the US education system structured?
2. Can you name some of the famous universities in the United States?
3. What do you know about the main media in the United States?
4. What holidays do people in the United States celebrate?

Education

1 Overview

The education system in the United States is built on several distinct ideals. A central principle is universal access and equity, ensuring that everyone in the country has equal access to education regardless of language, income, location or race. This commitment is embodied in the public school system, which strives to serve every child in the nation. Public schools are designed to be inclusive, providing a diverse learning environment that fosters mutual understanding and respect among students from various backgrounds.

Education policy in the US is governed by a multi-tiered system involving federal, state and local governments. While education is primarily the responsibility of individual states and local districts, leading to significant variation in policies, curricula and standards across the country, federal guidelines and programs also play a crucial role. Initiatives like the Every Student Succeeds Act (ESSA) aim to provide a more consistent educational framework across states, ensuring that key educational goals are met nationwide. Each state sets its own educational standards and policies within this framework, allowing for tailored approaches that address local needs and priorities.

The education system values the holistic development of individuals, emphasizing cognitive, social, emotional and physical growth. It promotes critical thinking, problem-solving and knowledge acquisition across a variety of subjects, including STEM (Science, Technology, Engineering and Mathematics), humanities and arts. These subjects are designed to equip students with a broad and versatile skill set, preparing them for a rapidly changing world and a diverse range of careers. Social and emotional learning (SEL) is integrated into curricula to help students develop essential life skills. Additionally, the education system encourages physical health and well-being through comprehensive physical education programs and the promotion of healthy lifestyles.

There are four levels of education: preschool education, compulsory education, continuing education and higher education.

Table 11.1 USA School System in Year Groups

Category	School Grade Level	Ages
Preschool education	Pre-kindergarten	3–5
Compulsory education		
Elementary school	Kindergarten	5–6
	1st grade	6–7
	2nd grade	7–8
	3rd grade	8–9
	4th grade	9–10
	5th grade	10–11
Middle school	6th grade	11–12
	7th grade	12–13
	8th grade	13–14
High school	9th grade / Freshman	14–15
	10th grade / Sophomore	15–16
	11th grade / Junior	16–17
	12th grade / Senior	17–18
Continuing education		
Vocational education		16 and up
Adult education		18 and up
Higher education		
College/University	Freshman	18 and up
	Sophomore	19 and up
	Junior	20 and up
	Senior	21 and up
Graduate school	with various degrees and curricular partitions	22 and up

2   Preschool education and Compulsory Education

Preschool Education

Preschool in the United States refers to non-compulsory classroom-based early-childhood education. In the United States, preschool programs are not required, but they are encouraged by educators. There are state-funded pre-kindergarten (pre-K) programs and the federally funded Head Start program, which targets low-income families. There are also numerous private preschools, which vary in curriculum and cost, and may follow specific educational philosophies.

The primary goals of preschool are to prepare children for the academic and social demands of kindergarten and beyond, promoting a lifelong love of learning and helping to close achievement gaps among diverse populations.

The curriculum often emphasizes play-based learning, fostering creativity and social skills, and also introducing basic literacy and numeracy concepts. Developmentally appropriate practices (DAP) are widely adopted, ensuring activities are suitable for the children's age and developmental stage.

Compulsory Education

Compulsory education in the Unites States is also called K-12 education. K-12 education in the United States includes primary education starting in kindergarten, elementary school, middle or junior high school and high school ending in Grade 12. It is over an age range starting between five and eight and ending somewhere between ages sixteen and eighteen, depending on the state.

Compulsory education is provided in public schools, state-certified private schools and approved home schooling. State governments set overall educational standards, often mandate standardized tests for K-12 public school systems and supervise, usually through a board of regents, state colleges and universities.

The majority of schools in the United States fall into two categories: public or private. A public school is defined as any school that is maintained through public funds to educate children living in that community or district for free. The structure and governance of a public school varies by model but shares the characteristics of being free and open to all applicants within a defined boundary. The majority of public schools operate on two basic enrollment models: boundary or open. Districts with enrollment policies using school boundary lines allow all students within a geographic area to enroll in the school. If a school has an open enrollment policy, then the school will also allow students from other geographic areas within the district to enroll if space permits. School boundary lines are often highly politicized. Schools are publicly rated and this affects everything from property values to the quality of teachers recruited.

A private school is defined as a school that is privately funded and maintained by a private group or organization, not the government, usually charging tuition. Private schools may follow a teaching philosophy different from public schools.

Homeschooling is a type of schooling that would not fall into either the public or private category. Homeschooling is defined as a child not enrolling in a public or private school but receiving an education at home. Each state has its own rules and regulations that families must follow and report on if homeschooling. For example, the Virginia Department of Education (2021) requires that families inform the school division of their decision to homeschool their child, update the school district with the student's annual academic progress and provide evidence that the homeschool instructor (such as a parent) meets specific qualifications to fill the role.

Curriculum and Extracurricular Activities

The curriculum in public education varies significantly by state and school district as it is determined by individual school districts or county school system. The school district selects curriculum guides and textbooks that reflect a state's learning standards and benchmarks for a given grade level. The most recent curriculum that has been adopted by most states is Common Core State Standards Initiative, which provides a clear and consistent framework for what students are expected to learn in language arts and mathematics. These standards have been adopted by most states in the US but not all and outline specific expectations for each grade level. Each state's Department of Education sets specific requirements for curriculum and graduation. These departments provide detailed guidelines for what subjects and courses must be taught at each grade level.

Table 11.2 Subjects in Compulsory Education in the USA

Grade Level	Core Subjects	Additional Subjects
Kindergarten–2nd Grade	Language Arts, Mathematics	Science, Social Studies, Physical Education, Art, Music
3rd–5th Grade	Language Arts, Mathematics, Science, Social Studies	Physical Education, Art, Music
6th–8th Grade	Language Arts, Mathematics, Science, Social Studies	Physical Education, Art, Music, Health, Foreign Language (varies)
9th–12th Grade	English, Mathematics, Science, Social Studies	Physical Education, Art/Music, Foreign Language (varies), Health

Language Arts includes reading, writing, speaking and listening. Mathematics progresses from basic arithmetic to advanced topics like algebra and calculus. Science covers general science, biology, chemistry and physics. Social Studies includes history, geography, civics and economics. Physical Education is required to promote physical fitness. Art and Music aim to foster creativity. Foreign Language requirements vary but are often required in high school. Health Education covers topics like nutrition and personal health.

Social and Emotional Learning (SEL) is a critical component of compulsory education in the United States. SEL is the process through which all young people and adults acquire and apply the knowledge, skills and attitudes to develop healthy identities, manage emotions and achieve personal and collective goals, feel and show empathy for others, establish and maintain supportive relationships and make responsible and caring decisions. SEL focuses on five key components: self-awareness, self-management, social awareness, relationship skills and responsible decision-making.

Table 11.3　Five Key Components of Social and Emotional Education

Component	Description	Key Goals
Self-Awareness	Understanding one's own emotions, values and strengths.	Recognize and label emotions Understand personal strengths and areas for growth Develop self-confidence and self-efficacy
Self-Management	Effectively regulating one's emotions, thoughts and behaviours.	Manage stress and emotions Set and work towards personal and academic goals Develop self-discipline and organizational skills
Social Awareness	Showing empathy and understanding for others from diverse backgrounds.	Recognize and appreciate diversity Understand social and ethical norms for behaviours Demonstrate empathy and compassion
Relationship Skills	Establishing and maintaining healthy and rewarding relationships with others.	Communicate clearly and effectively Listen actively and cooperate Resolve conflicts constructively and seek help when needed
Responsible Decision-Making	Making ethical, constructive choices about personal and social behaviours.	Identify problems and analyse situations Evaluate consequences of actions Make decisions that are respectful and promote collective well-being

SEL is typically integrated into the school curriculum and daily activities through various means. Classroom instruction includes lessons and activities specifically focused on SEL competencies. Schools also aim to create a supportive environment that embodies SEL values, fostering a positive school culture. Extracurricular activities provide additional opportunities for students to practice SEL skills in real-world contexts. Additionally, professional development for teachers ensures they can effectively teach and model SEL skills.

A key characteristic of American schools is the high priority given to extracurricular activities, valued by the community, parents, schools and students. These activities, supervised by the school but outside the regular curriculum, include sports and non-athletic options. Sports programs, particularly football and basketball, are major events and significant funding sources for larger school districts, generating intense community interest. In addition, schools offer a wide range of non-athletic extracurricular activities such as musical groups, marching bands, school newspapers, science fairs, debate teams and clubs focused on academics or community service. For high school students (ages 15–18), extracurriculars are activities that do not require school credit or paid employment and are often pursued for enjoyment or to enhance college applications. These activities foster teamwork, time management, goal setting, self-discovery, self-esteem, relationship building, interest exploration and academic enhancement.

Chapter 11　Education, Media and Holidays

3　Continuing Education

Continuing education in the United States plays a crucial role in personal and professional development, offering adults opportunities to enhance their skills, acquire new qualifications and stay competitive in a rapidly evolving job market.

Programs range from community college courses and professional certifications to online learning platforms and university extension classes, catering to a diverse array of fields such as technology, healthcare, business and the arts. This ongoing learning process supports career advancement, enables individuals to pivot to new industries and fosters lifelong learning habits. Additionally, continuing education often addresses the needs of non-traditional students, including working professionals, veterans and older adults, thereby promoting inclusivity and adaptability in the American educational landscape.

Community colleges in the United States are public institutions that provide affordable and accessible education to a diverse student population. They offer a range of programs, including associate degrees, vocational training and certificate courses, designed to meet the needs of local communities and prepare students for immediate employment or further education. Community colleges serve as a bridge to four-year universities, allowing students to transfer credits and pursue bachelor's degrees. They play a critical role in workforce development, adult education and lifelong learning, making higher education attainable for individuals from various socioeconomic backgrounds and supporting regional economic growth.

Several community colleges in the United States are well-regarded for their academic excellence, innovative programs and successful transfer pathways to four-year institutions. Some of the most famous community colleges include: Santa Monica College (California)—known for its high transfer rates to the University of California and California State University systems; Miami Dade College (Florida)—one of the largest and most diverse community colleges in the country, offering a wide range of programs and degrees; Northern Virginia Community College (NOVA) (Virginia)—renowned for its extensive range of programs and strong partnerships with local universities.

4　Higher Education

Overview

The United States ranks third in the world for the number of universities and leads with the highest number of top-ranked higher education institutions. In 2023, 20 out of the 30 top-ranked universities were American universities. This prominence reflects the increasing educational attainment of the American public, with college graduation rates rising significantly since the 1960s. The United States higher education system is renowned for its diversity and quality, offering a broad range of institutions including universities, liberal arts colleges, community colleges and technical schools. It provides flexibility in choosing majors and customizing educational paths, with prestigious universities like those in the Ivy League known for their rigorous academics, cutting-edge research and distinguished faculty. Beyond academics, United States institutions emphasize extracurricular involvement and support innovation and entrepreneurship through resources and opportunities for research and start-ups.

Funding for American universities has various sources. Public universities also receive significant support from federal and state governments through direct appropriations, research grants and student financial aid programs like Pell Grants and federal loans. Private universities, often rely heavily on private donations and endowments, which provide a steady income stream for operations and initiatives. Additional revenue comes from research grants and contracts awarded by federal agencies, private foundations and corporations. Universities also generate income through auxiliary enterprises such as campus bookstores, dining services and athletic events. Investment income from endowment funds further contributes to their financial resources. This diverse funding mix helps universities support their academic programs, research and student services.

Unites States is a top destination for international students. In 2022–2023 school year, international students make up 5.6% of the total US student population. In 2022–2023, China remained the largest source country for international students with a grand total of 289,526 enrolled in undergraduate, graduate, non-degree and optional practicing training programs. This number has been decreasing for years. India came second with 268,923 students—a count that has been increasing, most recently by a whopping 35 percent. Republic of Korea is in rank 3 with 43,847 international students in the past academic year, followed by Canada and Vietnam. In 2021–2022 school year, 5.9% of US students studied abroad for weeks or one year with Europe, Latin America and Caribbean and Asia as top destinations.

College entrance requirements in the USA generally include a high school diploma or equivalent and academic transcripts showing courses taken and grades received, with a strong GPA (Grade Point Average) being important. Many colleges require standardized test scores, such as SAT (Scholastic Assessment Test) or ACT (American College Test), though some have adopted test-optional policies. Applicants must typically submit a personal statement or essay showcasing their writing skills, personality and experiences, along with letters of recommendation from teachers or counselors. Extracurricular activities, such as sports, clubs, volunteer work and leadership roles are also considered. Some colleges may require or offer optional interviews to provide a personal context to the application.

Major Universities

The Unites States is home to some of the world's most prestigious universities, known for their academic excellence, research contributions and influential alumni.

Chapter 11　Education, Media and Holidays

(1) Harvard University

Harvard University, established in 1636 in Cambridge, Massachusetts, is the oldest and one of the most prestigious universities in the United States. As a private Ivy League institution, Harvard boasts the largest endowment of any university globally and offers a wide range of undergraduate, graduate and professional programs through its various schools, including Harvard College, Harvard Law School and Harvard Business School. Known for its rigorous academic standards and influential faculty, which

Fig. 11.1　Harvard University

includes numerous Nobel laureates and Pulitzer Prize winners. Harvard emphasizes research and innovation across disciplines. The historic campus features iconic landmarks like the Widener Library and Harvard Yard. Harvard's extensive and influential alumni network includes US Presidents, Supreme Court justices and leaders in various fields. Additionally, the university offers a vibrant student life with numerous extracurricular activities, supporting a well-rounded educational experience.

(2) Massachusetts Institute of Technology (MIT)

Massachusetts Institute of Technology, established in 1861 in Cambridge, Massachusetts, is a renowned institution known for its focus on science, engineering and technology. Offering undergraduate, graduate and doctoral programs across five schools, MIT boasts a faculty of Nobel laureates and other distinguished scholars driving groundbreaking research. The campus hosts cutting-edge facilities like the MIT Media

Fig. 11.2　Massachusetts Institute of Technology

Fig. 11.3 Stanford University

Lab, fostering innovation in fields such as artificial intelligence and robotics. Known for its hands-on approach to learning and entrepreneurial culture, MIT continues to lead in science and technology education and research.

(3) Stanford University

Stanford University, founded in 1885 and located in Stanford, California, is a top-tier research institution known for its strong emphasis on innovation and entrepreneurship. Situated in Silicon Valley, it offers diverse undergraduate, graduate and professional programs across seven schools, including engineering, business and humanities. Renowned for its influential faculty and cutting-edge research, Stanford has produced numerous Nobel laureates and leaders in various fields. The expansive campus features iconic landmarks like Hoover Tower and advanced research facilities. Stanford alumni have founded major tech companies like Google and Instagram, highlighting the university's impact on the tech industry and global leadership.

Media

1 Newspapers

Newspapers in the United States have long been a cornerstone of the country's media landscape, playing a critical role in informing the public and shaping discourse. Historically, newspapers have served as a vital source of news, analysis and opinion, covering a wide array of topics from local community events to national and international affairs. Major newspapers are renowned for their in-depth reporting and investigative journalism, often setting the agenda for public conversation.

Newspapers in the United States often have distinct political affiliations, which influence their editorial perspectives. For example, *The New York Times, The Washington Post*, and the *Los Angeles Times* are generally considered to lean towards the Democratic side, often supporting progressive policies and viewpoints. On the other hand, *The Wall Street Journal* and the *Chicago Tribune* have Republican-leaning editorial stances, frequently advocating for conservative policies. *USA Today* is known for its centrist position, striving to provide balanced coverage without a strong ideological tilt.

Chapter 11 Education, Media and Holidays

Despite the rise of digital media, traditional newspapers remain influential though they face significant challenges, including declining print readership and advertising revenue. The advent of the internet and the proliferation of digital news sources have disrupted the traditional newspaper business model. In response, many newspapers have adapted by transitioning to digital platforms, offering online subscriptions and utilizing social media to reach broader audiences. This digital shift allows newspapers to engage with readers in real-time and provide multimedia content, including videos and interactive graphics, enhancing the storytelling experience.

Local newspapers continue to serve crucial functions in communities, providing coverage of local events and issues that might otherwise be overlooked. These publications are essential for maintaining informed citizenry, holding local governments accountable and fostering community engagement. However, local newspapers have been particularly hard-hit by financial difficulties, leading to closures and consolidations, which in turn has created "news deserts" —areas with limited access to local news.

2 Radio and Television

Radio in the United States has been a vital medium for entertainment, news and information since the early 20th century. It began with AM broadcasting and later expanded to FM, offering higher quality sound and a clearer listening experience. Today, the United States boasts a diverse array of radio stations, including commercial, public and community stations, each serving unique audiences and interests. Major networks like NPR (National Public Radio) provide in-depth news, cultural programs and educational content that appeal to a broad audience, while commercial stations offer a wide variety of music genres, talk shows and sports coverage, catering to diverse tastes and preferences. Satellite radio, exemplified by services like SiriusXM, has further broadened the range of available content, offering specialized channels and programs without geographical limitations. Platforms such as Spotify, Apple Podcasts and Pandora have revolutionized how listeners consume audio content, offering personalized experiences and vast libraries of options. Traditional radio remains a significant part of American life and a trusted source for unbiased news, reaching millions of listeners daily.

Television in the United States is a dominant force in entertainment, news and cultural influence. Since its rise in the mid-20th century, TV has evolved from a handful of networks to a vast array of channels and platforms. Major broadcast networks like ABC (American Broadcasting Cooperation), CBS (Columbia Broadcasting System), NBC (National Broadcasting Company) and FOX (Fox Broadcasting Company) provide a mix of news, drama, comedy and reality programming, reaching millions of households. Cable and satellite TV expanded choices further, introducing specialized channels such as CNN (Cable News Network) for news, ESPN (Entertainment Sports Programming Network) for sports and HBO (Home Box Office) for premium content. The advent of digital streaming has transformed the industry with platforms

like Netflix, Hulu, Amazon Prime and Disney+ offering on-demand viewing and original programming. This shift has led to a new golden age of television with high-quality series and movies attracting global audiences. Despite the rise of streaming, traditional TV remains significant, especially for live events like sports, award shows and news broadcasts. Local TV stations continue to provide crucial community news and programming. The US television landscape is characterized by its diversity and innovation, continually adapting to technological advances and changing viewer habits.

3 Internet

Federal initiatives and private sector investments aim to expand broadband access and ensure that all Americans can benefit from the opportunities provided by the digital age. With widespread broadband availability, most Americans have access to high-speed internet through various providers, including cable, fiber optic and mobile networks.

The United States is home to major tech giants such as Facebook, Amazon and Microsoft, which lead global digital innovation and services. The internet has transformed how Americans work, learn, shop and socialize, with significant growth in e-commerce, online education and social media platforms. Streaming services like Netflix, Hulu and Disney+ have revolutionized entertainment, allowing on-demand access to a vast array of content. Additionally, online gaming and digital news consumption have become integral to many people's lives. While urban areas generally enjoy robust connectivity, rural regions still face challenges in access and speed, prompting ongoing efforts to bridge this digital divide and enhance nationwide internet infrastructure.

Holidays

The United States, like other nations, sets aside a number of days each year to commemorate events, people or public occasions. Technically, the United States does not celebrate national holidays, but Congress has designated 10 "legal public holidays," during which most federal institutions are closed and most federal employees are excused from work. Although the individual states and private businesses are not required to observe these holidays, in practice all states and nearly all employers, observe the majority of them. Since 1971, a number of these holidays have been fixed on Mondays rather than on a particular calendar date so as to afford workers a long holiday weekend.

1 New Year's Day

Americans celebrate New Year's Day with festive traditions that start on New Year's Eve, December 31st. Major events include the iconic Times Square ball drop in New York City, where a large ball descends as midnight strikes, accompanied by fireworks and confetti. People often attend parties, watch live broadcasts and enjoy countdowns to the new year. On New Year's Day itself, the mood is generally more relaxed. Many people use the day to recover from the previous night's festivities, reflect on the past year and make resolutions for the coming year. Traditional foods, such as black-eyed peas and collard greens, are enjoyed in some regions for their symbolic association with good luck.

2 Independence Day

Independence Day on July 4th is one of the most widely celebrated holidays in the USA. It commemorates the adoption of the Declaration of Independence in 1776. Throughout the country, fireworks displays are popular, ranging from the spectacular exhibition on the National Mall to more modest shows in city parks across the country. In New York City, Macy's department store sponsors the nation's largest July 4th fireworks display. It is also a family celebration when picnics and barbeques are common. Construction of important public works sometimes begins on July 4th. The Erie Canal, Washington Monument, Baltimore and Ohio Railroad (the nation's first) all broke ground on Independence Day. The date reflects a desire symbolically to stamp these projects as true civic improvements.

3 Thanksgiving Day

Thanksgiving Day falls on the last Thursday in November. It started from a harvest festival with roots in the 1621 feast shared by the English pilgrims and the Wampanoag tribe in Plymouth Colony (now Massachusetts), and evolved into a major US holiday. In 1863, President Abraham Lincoln declared the last Thursday in November as a day of Thanksgiving during the Civil War, and in 1941, Congress made it a federal holiday. Today, Thanksgiving is celebrated with family gatherings and a traditional feast that includes roast turkey, stuffing, mashed potatoes, gravy, cranberry sauce, sweet potatoes and pumpkin pie. The holiday features watching the Macy's Thanksgiving Day Parade, famous for its giant balloons and performances and NFL (National Football League) football games. Thanksgiving marks the beginning of the holiday shopping season, with Black Friday following immediately.

Fig. 11.4 Thanksgiving Dinner

4 Others

Throughout the year, many other holidays are also celebrated, such as Easter, Christmas, Hanukkah, Ramadan, Diwali, Lunar New Year and many more, reflecting the diversity of the American population.

Additionally, there are holidays that honor historical figures and events, such as Martin Luther King Jr. Day (the third Monday in January), Presidents' Day (third Monday in February), Memorial Day (last Monday in May), Labor Day (first Monday in September) and Veterans Day (November 11th), which pay tribute to the contributions of individuals and groups who have shaped the nation's history.

State and local holidays are also abound, ranging from Mardi Gras in Louisiana to the Cherry Blossom Festival in Washington, D.C., highlighting the unique cultural heritage and traditions of different regions across the country.

Exercises

Part I. Decide whether the following statements are true (T) or false (F). Write T or F in the brackets.

1. A central principle of American education system is universal access and equity, ensuring that everyone in the country has equal access to education regardless of language, income, location or race. (   )

2. Education policy in the US is solely governed by federal laws without state or local government involvement. (   )

3. The US education system does not encourage physical health and well-being through physical education programs. (   )

4. Social and Emotional Learning (SEL) is not a part of the compulsory education curriculum in the US. (   )

5. The major media in the US include both traditional outlets like newspapers and television, as well as digital platforms. (   )

6. Newspapers in the US often have distinct political affiliations that influence their editorial perspectives. (   )

7. Cultural holidays originating from other countries are not recognized or celebrated in the US. (   )

8. A number of holidays in US have been fixed on Mondays rather than on a particular calendar date so as to afford workers a long holiday weekend. (   )

Part II. Fill in the blanks with best answers.

1. Which act aims to provide a more consistent educational framework across states in the US?

    A. No Child Left Behind Act

    B. Every Student Succeeds Act

    C. Higher Education Act

    D. Education Reform Act

2. How many levels of education are there in the US?

    A. Three

    B. Four

    C. Five

    D. Six

3. Which of the following is emphasized in the US education system for holistic development?

    A. Only cognitive development

    B. Social and emotional learning

    C. Only physical development

    D. Sports and recreation only

4. Which of the following best describes the role of federal guidelines in the US education system?

    A. They dictate the exact curriculum for all schools.

    B. They provide a framework while states set their own standards.

    C. They have no influence on state education policies.

    D. They only apply to private schools.

5. Which newspaper is generally considered to have a centrist position in the US?

    A. *The New York Times*

    B. *The Washington Post*

    C. *USA Today*

D. *The Wall Street Journal*

6. What has been a significant challenge for traditional newspapers in the US?

    A. Increasing print readership

    B. Declining print readership and advertising revenue

    C. Excessive digital revenue

    D. Lack of news topics

7. What is a traditional food associated with New Year's Day in some regions of the US?

    A. Roast turkey

    B. Black-eyed peas

    C. Mashed potatoes

    D. Pumpkin pie

8. When is the Independence Day celebrated in the US?

    A. January 1

    B. July 4

    C. June 4

    D. July 14

Part III. State your understanding of the following questions.

1. Please analyze the multi-tiered governance of the education system in the US. How do federal, state and local governments interact? What are the benefits and drawbacks of this structure?

2. Please evaluate the role of social media in the US. How does this influence public opinion?

3. Please examine national holidays in the US, such as the Independence Day and Thanksgiving, and major holidays in China, like the Lunar New Year and the National Day. How do these holidays reflect the cultural values and historical narratives of each country?

Chapter 12

Literature

1. Do you know Hawthorne's novel *The Scarlet Letter*? What is it about?
2. Have you read any stories written by Mark Twain? How do you like them?
3. What do you know about Hemingway and his major works?

The history of American literature can be roughly divided into several periods: the Colonial and Revolutionary periods, the period of American Romanticism, American Realism, American Modernism, and American Literature after 1945.

The Colonial and the Revolutionary Periods

The Colonial and the Revolutionary periods cover the time span from about 1607 to 1800. The era from the founding of the first settlement at Jamestown in 1607 to the outbreak of the American Revolution in 1775 is often called the Colonial Period. Most of the writings in this period are produced by the Puritan writers, with the "original sin" and "grace" being the two most important themes. Puritanism was a religious reform movement in the late 16th and 17th centuries that sought to "purify" the Church of England of remnants of the Roman Catholicism. Being noted for a spirit of moral and religious earnestness, these Puritan writers believe that God chose the Puritans to create in America a New Jerusalem, as He had once chosen the Israelites and led them to the Promised Land in ancient times. They have a deep-seated belief in America's unique role in history. The American dream for the Puritans is to build a "city on a hill", which is expected to be a model of God's ultimate plan for humanity.

The writings in this period mainly include history, sermons, and diary. William Bradford (1590–1657) was the leader of the group of pilgrims who came to the New World on board the ship *May Flower* in 1620 and established the colony of Plymouth. Bradford's best-known work is *Of Plymouth Plantation*, which he began in 1630 and was first published in 1856. His concern is mainly with the spiritual pursuit in America and the work is to record God's providential work among the colonists.

The group of Puritans under John Winthrop (1588–1649) came and established the Massachusetts Bay Colony in 1630. Winthrop preached the famous sermon "Model of Christian Charity" on board the ship, which is about the ideal of taking the Christian charity as the basis for governing all affairs in the colony. Winthrop served as governor or deputy governor of the colony for nearly 20 years and he upheld the standards set in this sermon.

Anne Bradstreet (1612–1672) is a woman poet of the colonial period. Her poems were published in *The Tenth Muse Lately Sprung Up in America* (1650). Bradstreet's domestic poems and the "Contemplations" (1678) are very moving and the personal feelings expressed in those poems help the readers to understand the Puritan culture. Her famous poems include "To My Dear and Loving Husband," "The Author to Her Book" and "Upon the Burning of Our House."

Edward Taylor (1642–1729) is the best of the Puritan poets. Taylor is a meditative poet and in his series of meditations there is often the contemplation on the self and the search for God. In "Meditation 8" (1684), the poet tries to find in astronomy the link between heaven and man.

Jonathan Edwards (1703–1758) is a pioneering philosopher and the greatest thinker of the colonial period. He represents the spiritual side of the Puritan thought that emphasizes the inner life and the pursuit of personal redemption. Jonathan Edwards plays an important role in the Great Awakening, which is an evangelical movement meant for the revival of faith and for addressing the new "sins". The revivalists call on sinners to repent. The masterpiece of Edwards is *Of Freedom of the Will* (1754). His best known sermon is "Sinners in the Hands of an Angry God" (1741), in which he persuades the sinners to correct the sins by invoking the fear of hell.

Benjamin Franklin (1706–1790) represents the tendency in Puritanism that stresses hard work, good conduct and the freedom of the individual will. He is an exemplary self-made man, and his life experience is a typical American success story that has become part of American popular culture. His achievements as a statesman, a diplomat, an inventor, and an author are all remarkable. He is the inventor of the lightning rod. With his optimism and innovative spirit, Franklin exemplifies the Age of Enlightenment, which emphasizes reason and science. He marks a historical shift in emphasis from Providence (上帝，天意) to the individual, from the afterlife to this life. Benjamin Franklin's achievements as an author mainly include his *Poor Richard's Almanacs* (1732–1757) and his famous *Autobiography*, which he worked on at different times and remained unfinished. The margins of the *Poor Richard's Almanacs* are full of axioms, including the familiar saying "Early to bed and early to rise, makes a man healthy, wealthy and wise."

Puritanism is not the only concern of literature in this period. Literature of the South is non-puritan and the dream for the settlers in the South is to find the "vale (valley) of plenty," that is to say, the good life of a fertile valley.

The greatest work of the Revolutionary period is the Declaration of Independence (1776), mainly drafted by Thomas Jefferson (1743–1826). It is a national symbol of liberty and a monument to Jefferson as a statesman and author. The statement that "all men are created equal, that they are endowed by their Creator with certain unalienable Rights, that among these are Life, Liberty, and the pursuit of Happiness" describes the ideal of the nation.

Another author should also be mentioned here for his great influence on the American Revolution and the Declaration of Independence. Thomas Paine (1737–1809) was born in England and he arrived in Philadelphia with letters of introduction from Benjamin Franklin when he was 37. Some of Paine's works are among the most influential and controversial works of the 18th Century, including *Common Sense* (1776), *The American Crisis* (1776), and *Rights of Man* (1791–1792). He urges the colonies to be independent from Britain.

The most important poet of this period is Philip Freneau (1752–1832). He is regarded as a forerunner of American Romanticism. Before Whitman no other poet celebrated America as passionately as Freneau did. His famous poems include "The Beauties of Santa Cruz" (1776) and "The Wild Honey Suckle" (1786), which is a lyrical lament for the transience of nature and also an expression of faith in man's ability to learn universal truths from nature.

American Romanticism Period (1800–1865)

The half century before the Civil War was a period of rapid growth and rapid expansion. There was a huge population expansion as a result of the immigration, which brought about a mingling of races and gave American literature a variety of subject matters. The spread of industrialization and the Westward Movement filled people with optimism and hope. American romanticism emerged against this background and this period is regarded as a period of Renaissance in art and literature in the United States.

Romanticism refers to a literary and philosophical theory that tends to see the individual at the very center of all life and experience. Romanticism places the individual at the center of art and makes literature an expression of unique feelings and particular attitudes. Romanticism is partly an escape from the modern industrialization by turning inside. Romantic writers generally emphasize the importance of imagination and emotion over logic and reason. As for American romanticism, it has some uniqueness because of the Puritan moral values and the hope and optimism brought by the Westward Movement. Many writers tend to moralize more than their English counterparts. American romanticism is both imitative and innovative. The true American literature was born in this period.

Washington Irving (1783–1859) and James Fenimore Cooper (1789–1851) are two important writers of early American romanticism. Washington Irving is the first American writer to have achieved an international literary reputation. And he is also the first to make use of the Old Dutch traditions around Hudson and to reveal to his countrymen the literary possibilities of their early history. His best known stories include "Rip Van Winkle" (1819–1820) and "The Legend of Sleepy Hollow" (1819–1820), which are called the first American short stories. The experience of Rip Van Winkle shows people's confusion about their new identity and situation after the American Revolution.

James Fenimore Cooper is more American than Irving. And he is one of the earliest writers to deal with the American subject matter—the Westward Movement. Cooper originates the novel of the wilderness and he creates the Indians in literature. He is mainly known for his Leather-Stocking Novels, including *The Pioneers* (1823), *The Last of the Mohicans* (1826), *The Prairie* (1827), *The Pathfinder* (1840), and *The Deerslayer* (1841).

New England Transcendentalism (超验主义) is the summit of American romanticism and it is romanticism on the Puritan soil. The American Puritanism represented by Jonathan Edwards and Benjamin Franklin argues that the knowledge of God and truth can be obtained only through meditation or spiritual insight. Transcendentalism means that knowledge can be obtained through mental process apart from experiences. Its doctrines mainly include the concept of the Oversoul, the importance of the individual and the view that nature is the garment of the Oversoul. "Oversoul" refers to an omnipotent and all-pervading power that exists in nature and man alike. The transcendentalists believe that the regeneration of the society can be achieved through the perfection of the self-reliant individuals. As for their view of nature, the physical world is regarded as the symbol of the spiritual. This adds to the tradition of literary symbolism. The most important representative writers of transcendentalism are Ralph Waldo Emerson (1803–1882) and Henry David Thoreau (1817–1862).

Emerson's importance in the intellectual history of America lies in the fact that he embodies a new nation's desire and struggle to assert its own identity in its formative period. He calls for an independent culture and he advocates that American writers should write about America here and now. America itself is a long poem that is worth celebrating. Emerson also possesses a cheerful optimism. His best-known essays include *Nature* (1836), "The American Scholar" (1837), and "Self-Reliance" (1841). *Nature* is regarded as the Bible of Transcendentalism and "The American Scholar" is regarded as the "Declaration of Intellectual Independence". "Self-Reliance" shows the importance of the intellectual self-reliance or independence. Emerson advocates people to trust their own intuition and not to be a conformist. Emerson plays an important role in shaping the American individualism.

Thoreau is the man who puts into practice many of Emerson's theories. In 1845 he began a two-year residence at Walden Pond in a hut built by his own hands. The result of this experience is his masterpiece *Walden* (1854), which probes into the question whether man can live more meaningfully by living simply. For Thoreau, as for Emerson, self-reliance and independence of mind are very important. "Civil Disobedience" (1849) is a famous essay by Thoreau, which states his belief that no man should violate his conscience at the command of a government.

Not all writers in this period agree with Emerson in his optimistic view of the nature and the individual. Nathaniel Hawthorne (1804-1864) and Herman Melville (1819–1891) take a critical distance from transcendentalism.

Hawthorne is interested in the Puritan past of New England and is concerned with the sinful nature of man. Hawthorne often complains about "the poverty of materials" and he tries to create "a neutral territory, somewhat between the real world and fairy-land where the actual and the imaginary may meet". In order to have more freedom to deal with this "neutral territory," he calls his novels "romance," which he believes to be the predestined form of American narrative. In writing a romance, the writer may be freer to create a certain atmosphere or to add something marvelous to bring out the full effect. His most famous work is *The Scarlet Letter* (1850), in which he investigates the nature of evil and the consequences of sin. Literary historians believe that *The Scarlet Letter* is the first great American novel. Hawthorne is also the author of many excellent short stories, such as "Young Goodman Brown" and "The Minister's Black Veil."

Melville is a writer with little formal education. He has famously said that a whaling ship was his Yale College and Harvard. Melville owes a lot to his reading. In his masterpiece *Moby Dick* (1851), before the main body of the novel, he inserts a part called "Extracts", in which he lists the major sources of reading material for the preparation of the novel. The list includes such classic works as John Milton's *Paradise Lost* and Shakespeare's plays. The novel shows the influence of these works in many aspects, including the characterization and the form. *Moby Dick* examines the danger of extreme egotism and the importance of friendship and cooperation. Ahab, the protagonist, is the kind of individualist advocated by Emerson. He trusts his own intuition and goes to extremes in asserting his own dignity, saying that he would strike back if the sun insulted him. In order to take revenge on a white whale named Moby Dick who has chewed off one of his legs, he leads the crew of the whaling ship around the world to search for it, and finally the whole ship gets destroyed in the battle with Moby Dick, with only one survivor left. The novel is narrated by this survivor named Ishmael. In Ahab's view, Moby Dick embodies all the evil in universe. Melville also writes wonderful short stories, such as *Bartleby the Scrivener: A Story of Wall Street*, which deals with the sense of isolation in a world that expects people to be conformists or copyists. It is worth noting that the writing of *Moby Dick*, which is vastly different from his previous successful novels, also shows Melville's refusal to copy what he wrote before.

Edgar Allan Poe (1809–1849) is a writer of his own type. He is regarded as the father of detective stories.

He is especially famous for his horror tales and in-depth probing of people's psychology. He has exerted an important influence on many writers, such as Arthur Conan Doyle (1859–1930), a British writer and the author of "Sherlock Holmes Series", and Fyodor Dostoyevsky (1821–1881), a great Russian novelist and the author of *Crime and Punishment* (1866). Poe's horror stories—which include, among others, "The Cask of Amontillado," "The Fall of the House of Usher," and "The Tell-Tale Heart"—are often told by a first-person narrator. Through the narrator's voice, Poe shows the workings of a character's psyche. In "The Cask of Amontillado," the narrator takes his enemy-friend to the catacombs of his house in order to fulfill his plan of revenge. This journey to the vault is also a psychological journey into the mind of the murderer. The narrators in Poe's stories are often unreliable, either for self-defense or due to the unstable state of mind, as his characters are often afflicted with various forms of insanity and melancholy. As a poet and a critic, Poe is the principal forerunner of the "art for art's sake" movement in nineteenth-century European literature. For him the sole purpose of art is to create beauty, and the most beautiful thing is the death of a beautiful woman.

Walt Whitman (1819–1892) and Emily Dickinson (1830–1886) are two major poets in the 19th century. They are of different styles and personalities.

Walt Whitman is a fervent advocate of equality and democracy, and he sees himself as the poet of American individualism and liberty. He celebrates everyone and everything in the universe, men and women, body and soul, life and death, stars and grass. The image of "grass" in the title of his collection of poems *Leaves of Grass* shows his idea of democracy and equality. For Whitman, every free citizen is a unique leaf of grass. Yet all the individual citizens together can form a rolling grass land. *Leaves of Grass* was first published in 1855 and then he devoted himself to the revision of it. His best poems include "Song of Myself" (1855), "When Lilacs Last in the Dooryard Bloom'd" (1865), and "O Captain! My Captain" (1865). In "Song of Myself" he identifies himself with everything in the world and therefore the song that celebrates the self is a song that celebrates everyone and everything in the world, especially the things in the growing nation of America. The poem is also intended to be a bridge between the poet and the readers. Whitman shows his eagerness to be read and understood in the closing lines of the poem: "I bequeath myself to the dirt to grow from the grass I love, / If you want me again look for me under your boot-soles. /…/ Failing to fetch me at first keep encouraged, / Missing me one place search another, / I stop somewhere waiting for you." Whitman's poems are mostly written in free verse, a kind of poetry that does not follow a regular meter or rhyme and does not have a regular line length. He creates a rhythm that corresponds to the vibrancy and flow of his emotions and sensory perceptions and he uses long lists to give free rein to his poetic imagination. "When Lilacs Last in the Dooryard Bloom'd" (1865) is a very touching elegy paying tribute to the passing of Abraham Lincoln.

Emily Dickinson is a woman poet with nearly two thousand poems and few of them got published

Fig. 12.1 Emily Dickinson

during her life time. She lived as a recluse for most of the time. Dickinson is an individualist and a nonconformist as advocated by Emerson in his "Self-Reliance." Her nonconformity shows itself in both the form and the ideas of her poems. She likes to use the punctuation marks, especially the dashes, in an unconventional way. Her poems often cover such themes as death, immortality, religion, and nature. Dickinson uses very rich metaphors and images, not merely to make the poems beautiful or interesting, but to express her ideas with more subtlety. She says that a poet should "Tell all the Truth but tell it slant", that is to say, not to tell the truth directly, but in a roundabout way, with images and metaphors. For example, she does not simply say that death is irresistible, instead, she says "Because I / could not stop for Death— / He kindly stopped for me—". Dickinson is obsessed with the themes of death and immortality, which appear in almost one third of her poems. Her views on nature are not as optimistic as those of Emerson and Thoreau. For Dickinson, nature is complex and ambiguous, hard to grasp, and maybe hostile. In "A narrow Fellow in the Grass," she presents nature as a slippery snake that is elusive and inclined to attack.

There are also writings against slavery in this period, the most famous ones being *Uncle Tom's Cabin* (1851–1852) written by Harriet Beecher Stowe (1811–1896) and *Narrative of the Life of Fredrick Douglass, an American Slave* (1845), which is the autobiography of Frederick Douglass (1818–1895), a former slave. *Uncle Tom's Cabin* was a best-seller after its publication and it boosted the abolitionist sentiments. Lincoln once met Harriet Beecher Stowe and said to her: "So this is the little lady who made this big war!"

American Realism (1865–1914)

The period of American realism is from 1865 to 1914, between the end of the Civil War and the beginning of the First World War. The American Civil War marks a tremendous change in American moral values, with the society gradually becoming a materialistic one based on mass labor and mass consumption. The gulf between the rich and the poor was widened as a result of the growth of industry, and the sense of disillusionment and frustration was widespread. This is a period described as the "Gilded Age" by Mark Twain. In the literary scene, realism becomes the dominating trend in literary writing of this period.

Reacting against romanticism's emphasis on intuition, imagination, and the general optimistic belief in the goodness of things, realist writers believe that literature imitates reality. They try to portray American life as it really is, insisting that the ordinary and the local are as suitable for artistic portrayal as the magnificent and the remote. They are generally interested in the details rather than the "story," and prefer a straightforward and matter-of-fact manner of narration, attempting to reflect reality faithfully. Yet, realism does not mean giving a camera picture of life. It aims to give form to experience by using the techniques of selection, deletion and concentration. American realism also includes naturalism, regionalism and local color writing.

There are three great masters of realism: Mark Twain (1835–1910), William Dean Howells (1837–1920), and Henry James (1843–1916).

Regional and local color writing is considered the early stage of literary realism. A regional work relies on the cultural, social and historical settings of a region. Local color writings also depend on a specific geographical location and emphasize the local details by tapping into its folklore, history, customs, beliefs and speech. Mark Twain is a novelist of this kind. He is a writer of great importance in American literature. Ernest Hemingway once remarked: "All modern literature comes from one book by Mark Twain called *Huckleberry Finn*." Mark Twain shows to the world that one's childhood experience can be transformed into classic novels. In his novels, he sees the adult through the eyes of a child and sees the child from an adult's perspective. *The Adventures of Tom Sawyer* (1876) and *The Adventures of Huckleberry Finn* (1885) are both very popular books for children now. His other works include *The Gilded-Age: A Tale of Today* (1873), *The Prince and the Pauper* (1882) and many short stories, such as "The Celebrated Jumping Frog of Calaveras County" (1865) and "The Man That Corrupted Hadleyburg" (1900). Mark Twain is a master of showing his hatred for hypocrisy and pretentiousness through the use of humor.

William Dean Howells is concerned with a faithful representation of reality as he knows it. He defines realism as "nothing more and nothing less than the truthful treatment of material." Howells commands enormous respect in his life time, yet he is out of favor after his death. Now, he is mainly regarded as an important critic and editor. He is the first to celebrate Emily Dickinson's poetry. His best-known novel *is The Rise of Silas Lapham* (1885). The title character Silas Lapham refuses to make an unethical choice in the business competition and then falls in his fortune, but rises in the moral sense.

Henry James is a powerful example of realism and he is also regarded as a modernist. As is mentioned in the chapter about English literature, Henry James is a transitional figure between realism and modernism. The central reality to James is more an intellectual or psychological one than a social one. He cares about the predicament of the sensitive mind in a special era. His major concern is American innocence in contrast with European sophistication and decadence. In fact, he observes the American culture by placing it in the space between cultures. The protagonists of many of his novels are Americans who are ignorant of the conventions and social sophistication of Europe. Their ignorance leads to unhappy experiences, sometimes even death. Henry James usually probes deeply into the individual psychology of his characters. His major novels include *Daisy Miller* (1879), *The Portrait of a Lady* (1881), *The Wings of the Dove* (1902), and *The Golden Bowl* (1904). Henry James also writes some Gothic stories, the most famous one being *The Turn of the Screw* (1898), which is psychologically very complex.

Literary naturalism is also a kind of realism, striving for objectivity. It draws upon scientific or socio-economic determinisms (such as Darwinism). The naturalistic works are usually pessimistic, expressing the belief that humans react to things that they cannot control, such as the biological need for sex and self-preservation, internal stresses, and environmental forces. The major writers of naturalism are Stephen Crane (1871–1900), Jack London (1876–1916) and Theodore Dreiser (1871–1945). Crane is the author of *Maggie: A Girl of the Streets* (1893) and *The Red Badge of Courage* (1895). Crane's world is governed by a God who is indifferent to human affairs. The characters are involved in the struggles in life and the author observes them with pessimistic detachment and psychological insights.

In Jack London's stories, there is a determinist overtone. Man's behavior is determined by laws of nature and the fittest survive. Besides, the life of an individual is subjected to the survival of a community or the human species. *The Call of the Wild* (1903) is Jack London's masterpiece. It is about how Buck, a dog kidnapped from California and taken to Alaska, manages to survive and finally answers the call of the wild and becomes the head of a pack of wolves. His other works include *The Sea Wolf* (1904) and *White Fang* (1906).

Determinism is also a key word in the novels of Theodore Dreiser. His novels have details selected and arranged to suggest causation and motivation. A major theme of his works is that men and women will, according to their place in society, talent and temperament, seek to achieve the fulfillment of such desires as sexual gratification, power and materialism. Human tragedy comes as a result of the collision between man's biological needs and ruthless manipulation by the society. His masterpieces are *Sister Carrie* (1900) and *American Tragedy* (1925).

American Modernism (1914–1945)

Modernism is also a kind of realism except that its sense of reality is more complex. In a broad sense, the term "modernism" refers to any kind of literary production in the interwar period that deals with the modern world. More narrowly, it refers to the works that represent the breakdown of traditional values and conventions in the modern world, which critics now call "high modernism." Modernist literature of this sort is largely anti-modern, interpreting modernity as an experience of loss. T. S. Eliot's *The Waste Land* (1922), which represents the modern world as a scene of ruin, is a good example to show this. At the heart of the modernist aesthetic lies the conviction that the previously sustaining structures of human life, either social, political, religious, or artistic, have been either destroyed or revealed as being false. To show this falsehood, the techniques adopted in the works of art have to be innovated. Order, sequence, and unity in works of art would only be expressions of a desire for coherence rather than actual reflections of reality. The traditional form of a story, with its beginning, complications, and resolutions, may fail to reflect the flux and fragmentation of the modern experience. Thus a key formal characteristic of the modernist work is its construction out of fragments. The modernist work often omits the explanations, interpretations, and summaries that provide coherence in traditional literature, only consisting of vivid segments juxtaposed without integrating transitions. Shifts in perspective and the use of irony and symbols are also the characteristics of modernist writing.

William Faulkner (1897–1962), F. Scott Fitzgerald (1896–1940), and Ernest Hemingway (1899–1961) are all modernist novelists.

William Faulkner is a writer of American South. He said "I discovered that my own little postage stamp of native soil was worth writing about." In fact, what Faulkner talks about in his novels concerns not only the American South but the human situation in general. An important message of Faulkner's stories is that the spiritual deterioration which characterizes modern life stems directly from the loss of love and want of emotional response. Faulkner is a great master of the techniques of "stream of consciousness" and the multiple points of view. His major novels include *The Sound and the Fury* (1929), *As I Lay Dying* (1930), *Light in August* (1932), and *Absalom, Absalom!* (1936). *The Sound and the Fury* is a very experimental novel. It is divided into four parts and each part is narrated through the mind of a different character. The "sound and the fury" in the title is taken from a soliloquy in Shakespeare's tragedy *Macbeth*, in which Macbeth reflects on time and the meaninglessness of life: "Life's but a walking shadow, a poor player /That struts and frets his hour upon the stage/And then is heard no more: it is a tale/Told by an idiot, full of sound and fury,/Signifying nothing."

Fig. 12.2   Ernest Hemingway

Ernest Hemingway is the spokesman of the "Lost Generation," a term given by the expatriate American writer Gertrude Stein (1874–1946), mainly referring to the American writers and artists living in Paris after the First World War. For Hemingway, the essential condition of life is solitary, and the only serious business is the management of that solitude. "Grace under pressure" is a central Hemingway theme, as is shown by the often quoted statement: "A man is not born to be defeated." Hemingway's style is noted for its simplicity, which is described as the principle of iceberg, with seven-eighths of the iceberg being under the water. His major novels include *The Sun Also Rises* (1926), *A Farewell to Arms* (1929), *For Whom the Bell Tolls* (1940), and *The Old Man and the Sea* (1952), for which he won the Nobel Prize in 1954. *The Sun Also Rises* depicts the search of values of a group of lost-generation characters and the spiritual pilgrimage of Jake Barnes, the protagonist, to search for meaning in life.

F. Scott Fitzgerald is also a member of the "Lost Generation" and his works portray the wealth and materialism of the 1920s, which is also called the "Jazz Age." Fitzgerald's most important work is *The Great Gatsby* (1925), which tells the story of Jay Gatsby, a self-made millionaire, and his pursuit of Daisy, a wealthy young woman whom he loved in his youth. This novel is a complex study of the beauty and illusion of the American dream, which is embodied by the title character Gatsby. The first person narrator of the novel is both involved in and critically distanced from the events of the story, thus enabling the readers to look upon Gatsby with both sympathy and criticism. Fitzgerald's other major works include *This Side of Paradise* (1920) and *Tender Is the Night* (1934).

As for the poetry of this period, the important poets include Ezra Pound (1885–1972), T. S. Eliot (1888–1965), Robert Frost (1874–1963), and Wallace Stevens (1879–1955).

Ezra Pound (1885–1972) is the founder of imagism. An imagist poem often contains a dominant image or a quick succession of related images. The image represents a moment of revealed truth. Pound defines "image" as something that "presents an intellectual and emotional complex in an instant of time." His famous poem "In a Station of the Metro" consists only of two lines "The apparition of these faces in the crowd: / Petals on a wet, black bough", presenting the faces of a few pretty women and children he saw in a crowd hurrying out of a dim and damp subway station as the flower petals on a wet and black bough. Chinese poetry, with its conciseness and rich images, has an important influence on Pound and on the imagist movement. His major poetic works include the collection *Personae* (1926), and the poetry collection *The Cantos*, which he began writing from about 1915 and the last part of which was published in 1968.

T. S. Eliot is the first to sense the futility and fragmentation of modern life and to see modern society at its most disgusting. He won the Nobel Prize for literature in 1948. According to T. S. Eliot, the only way the modern writer has of "giving shape and significance to the immense panorama of futility and anarchy which is contemporaneous history" is by indicating or "manipulating a continuous parallel" between contemporaneity and antiquity. His major poems include *The Waste Land* (1922) and *The Love Song of J. Alfred Prufrock* (1917). *The Love Song of J. Alfred Prufrock* is very interesting. Its title is ironic, considering the absence of love in the poem. The poem is to portray the frustration, the emotional conflict, and the physical and spiritual impotence of a modern man. *The Waste Land* is one of the most influential works of the 20th century. It expresses the disillusionment of the period after World War I. A series of fragmentary descriptions are loosely linked by the legend of the search for the Holy Grail to portray a sterile world and human beings waiting for some sign or promise of redemption.

Robert Frost is the most popular modern poet. His poetry addresses familiar subjects and uses an accessible language. There is a deceptive simplicity on the surface of his poetry and a profound understanding of life can often be found beneath that surface. "The Road Not Taken" is a good example to illustrate this point. On the surface, the poem is about the choice between the forked roads in the wood. But a careful reading reveals that it is about the decision-making in life. Robert Frost is concerned with constructing, through poetry, "a momentary stay against confusion and chaos." In his poem "Birches," through a boy's game of swinging on the birch branch, the poet expresses the idea that when life is becoming too tough for him, he would like to "get away from earth awhile/ And then come back to it and begin over." His other well-known poems include "Stopping by Woods on a Snowy Evening" (1923) and "Mowing" (1913).

Wallace Stevens (1879–1955) embodies an affirmative spirit. His poetry affirms the vitality of living that bursts through the stale and the tedious. According to Wallace Stevens, a poet should find beauty, pleasure, excitement, and meaning in the sordidness of reality. He attaches much importance to imagination, which helps to create meaning out of the otherwise nothingness. His best-known poems include "Sunday Morning" and "Anecdote of the Jar." "Anecdote of the Jar" shows that reality is an integration of imagination and the external world. "Sunday Morning" is the poet's meditation on life, divinity and death.

American Literature Since 1945

American literature after 1945 is characterized by the ethnic diversity. There are African-American writers like Tony Morrison (1931–2019) and Alice Walker (1944–); Jewish-American writers like Saul Bellow (1915–2005) and J. D. Salinger (1919–2010); and Asian-American writers like Maxine Hong Kingston (1940–) and Amy Tan (1952–).

Toni Morrison is a Nobel Prize winning novelist (in 1993). Her important works include *The Bluest Eye* (1970), *Song of Solomon* (1977), and *Beloved* (1987). *Song of Solomon* tells the story of an African American trying to recover his family roots. The story covers the one hundred years of African American history from the Civil War to the 1960s. Morrison's best-known novel is *Beloved*, which is based on the true story of a slave mother killing her own children to avoid slavery for them.

Alice Walker is a feminist black writer. Her works are often concerned with the black woman's struggling towards self-realization in a hostile environment. She creates strong women characters with heroic achievements as the new image of African American women. Alice Walker's best-known novel is *The Color Purple* (1982). It is an epistolary novel, that is to say, it is written in the form of letters. The novel is about the growth of the protagonist against the social and familial oppression.

Saul Bellow writes in the mainstream intellectual tradition of the novel and he modifies the tradition by the use of Jewish fables and romance. He is culturally Jewish, but he has cultivated his Jewishness for his parables of the human condition in the contemporary world. His important works include *Seize the Day* (1956), *Herzog* (1964), and *Mr. Sammler's Planet* (1970). In *Herzog*, he reveals the intellectual inner life of the title character Moses Herzog. Much of the action in the novel takes place within Herzog's disturbed consciousness, including a series of flashbacks about his marriage in the past. Bellow won the Nobel Prize in 1976.

J. D. Salinger is the author of the famous novel *The Catcher in the Rye* (1951). The novel is about two days in the life of the 16-year-old protagonist Holden Caulfield after he has been expelled from school. Holden wants to remain true and innocent in a world full of "phonies" (falseness) and he wants to be the "catcher in the rye"—someone who saves children from falling off a cliff, which can be seen as a metaphor for the loss of innocence. Confused and disillusioned, he ends up emotionally unstable. It is from a sanatorium that Holden is telling the story.

As for the Asian American writers, two Chinese-American women writers are worth mentioning. Maxine Hong Kingston (her Chinese name being Tang Ting-ting) is the author of *The Woman Warrior* (1976). Its publication is a signal to show that the Asian American writers have broken into the mainstream of literature. The book is a fictionalized autobiography and it outlines a young Chinese American girl's growing up, with the ambition to become a woman warrior like Hua Mulan. Kingston also writes two other novels about the experience of Chinese Americans, *China Men* (1980) and *Tripmaster Monkey: His Fake Book* (1989).

Amy Tan, or Tan En-mei in Chinese, is the author of *The Joy Luck Club* (1989), which has been adapted to a successful movie. Her stories mainly depict the relationship between a Chinese American daughter and her Chinese mother. The relationship is full of tension when the girl is a teenager resenting the mother's advice rich in Chinese heritage. Then in the daughter's adult life, in a moment of epiphany, the past tension would take on some new meaning and the daughter would finally realize the value of her cultural heritage.

The important poets in the postwar period include Robert Lowell (1911–1977), Adrienne Rich (1929–), and Allen Ginsberg (1926–1997).

Robert Lowell is the foremost of the "confessional" poets. "Confessional" poets refer to the poets in the 1950s and 1960s who intensely explore their dark selves by closing the gap between the poet and the speaker of the poem. Such a gap or distance is favored by the modernist poetics for the effect of impersonality and irony. Lowell's *Life Studies* (1959) won the National Book Award for poetry and it contains an autobiographical essay and a series of 15 confessional poems. "Waking in Blue", which tells of his confinement in a mental hospital, and "Skunk Hour," which conveys his mental turmoil, are two major poems in the book.

Adrienne Rich's famous poem "Aunt Jennifer's Tigers" (1951) shows her feminist concern. Aunt Jennifer in the poem is a woman who seems to be crushed beneath patriarchal authority. However, the tigers that she has embroidered prance and "do not fear the men." This shows her indomitable spirit.

Allen Ginsberg is the greatest poet of the Beat movement, which is an American social and literary movement originating in the 1950s. A group of American poets and artists in the 1950s and 1960s waged a rebellion against American mainstream cultural values and middle-class tastes in poetry. Both the poetry and the life style of Ginsberg are meant to challenge social values and to give spiritual instruction to the young in the counterculture. Ginsberg's best and most influential poem is "Howl" (1956). As a denunciation of the weaknesses and failings of American society, it is the most representative poetic expression of the Beat movement. Ginsberg and other major figures of the movement, such as the novelist Jack Kerouac (1922–1969), advocate a kind of free, unstructured composition in which the writer puts down his thoughts and feelings without plan or revision in order to convey the immediacy of experience. The masterpiece of Jack Kerouac is *On the Road* (1957), which had a broad cultural influence before it was recognized for its literary merits.

The great achievements of American drama in the 20th century are reflected in the works of the three major playwrights: Eugene O'Neill (1888–1953), Tennessee Williams (1911–1983), and Arthur Miller (1915–2005).

O'Neill's plays are highly experimental in form and style. He has great influence on later American playwrights. His major plays include *Beyond the Horizon* (1920), *The Hairy Ape* (1922), *Desire under the Elms* (1924), and *Long Day's Journey into Night* (written in 1939 to 1941 and produced and published posthumously in 1956). He won the Nobel Prize in 1936. O'Neill's plays show a profound understanding of human existence and cover a wide range of themes, such as the destructive consequences of drug and alcohol abuse, the desire to ally oneself with some larger purpose and the tragic predicament of humanity. His plays rely heavily on distorting appearance to convey the essence of reality as perceived by the characters.

Tennessee Williams is the most important dramatist after World War II. His major plays include *The Glass Menagerie* (1945) and *A Streetcar Named Desire* (1947). Williams often portrays the marginalized and isolated individuals who represent the values that are no longer possible. The characters often have some memories of the past, maybe glorious and beautiful. Because of the memories, they become paralyzed and dysfunctional, and try to escape from the present. There is an air of fantasy in his seemingly realistic plays. He explains in the preface to *The Glass Menagerie* that "truth, life, or reality is an organic thing which the poetic imagination can represent or suggest, in essence, only through transformation, through changing into other forms than those which were merely present in appearance."

Arthur Miller is mainly concerned with the conflict in the American middle-class families, often with the tension between the father and the son. Miller is interested in the theme of the American dream of achieving material success. The dream becomes neurotic obsession that destroys the characters. His masterpiece *Death of a Salesman* (1949) is familiar to the Chinese audience. It is a tragedy about an ordinary salesman Willy Loman. In his youth, Willy was a successful salesman. But when he gets old, he becomes ineffectual and later gets fired by a company for which he has worked for thirty-six years. Finally, he kills himself in order to get a large amount of insurance for his family. The play offers a psychological and emotional landscape of Willy and enables the audience to understand the sense of failure deep inside him. Arthur Miller's other works include *All My Sons* (1947) and *The Crucible* (1953).

Exercises

Part I. Decide whether the following statements are true (T) or false (F). Write T or F in the brackets.

1. "Original sin" and "grace" are the important themes of the Puritan writing of the Colonial period. ( )

2. Romantic writers generally emphasize the importance of logic and reason over imagination and emotion. ( )

3. Thoreau's "Self-Reliance" shows the importance of the intellectual self-reliance or independence. ( )

4. In his masterpiece *Moby Dick*, Herman Melville examines the danger of extreme egotism and the importance of friendship and cooperation. ( )

5. The woman poet Emily Dickinson is very unconventional in the use of punctuation marks and images in her poems. ( )

6. Henry James usually probes deeply into the individual psychology of his characters and his masterpiece is *The Rise of Silas Lapham*. ( )

7. Theodore Dreiser is a naturalist writer and his novels show that human tragedy comes as a result of the collision between man's biological needs and ruthless manipulation by the society. (   )

8. "Man is not born to be defeated" is a statement made by Ernest Hemingway. (   )

Part II. Fill in the blanks with best answers.

1. Of the following writers, _____ are from the Colonial and Revolutionary Periods.

   A. Benjamin Franklin and Edgar Allan Poe

   B. Edgar Allan Poe and Jonathan Edwards

   C. Benjamin Franklin and Jonathan Edwards

   D. Edgar Allan Poe and Washington Irving

2. Ralph Waldo Emerson and Henry David Thoreau are representatives of _____.

   A. New England Transcendentalism

   B. American Realism

   C. American Modernism

   D. American Naturalism

3. *The Scarlet Letter* is a novel written by _____.

   A. Herman Melville

   B. Nathaniel Hawthorne

   C. Henry James

   D. Thomas Hardy

4. *Leaves of Grass* is a collection of poems by the great American poet _____.

   A. Walt Whitman

   B. Emily Dickinson

   C. Robert Frost

   D. Wallace Stevens

5. William Dean Howells, Henry James, and Mark Twain are all masters of _____.

   A. American Romanticism

   B. American Modernism

C. American Realism

D. American Naturalism

6. *The Great Gatsby* is the masterpiece of _____, a writer of the Jazz age.

    A. F. Scott Fitzgerald

    B. William Faulkner

    C. Mark Twain

    D. Herman Melville

7. *The Joy Luck Club* is a novel written by the Chinese-American writer_____.

    A. Amy Tan

    B. Maxine Hong Kingston

    C. Alice Walker

    D. Saul Bellow

8. Tony Morrison is a Novel Prize winning African-American writer and she is the author of _____.

    A. *Sound and the Fury*

    B. *Tender is the Night*

    C. *Sister Carrie*

    D. *Beloved*

Part III. State your understanding of the following questions.

1. What are the main doctrines of New England Transcendentalism?

2. What do you know about American Realism?

3. What are the characteristics of American modernist writing?

References

GREENBLATT S, ABLOW R. EISNFR E, et al., eds. Norton Anthology of English Literature [M]. 8th ed. New York: W.W. Norton & Company, 2006.

ANDREW S. The Short Oxford History of English Literature[M]. Oxford: Clarendon Press, 1994.

常耀信. 英国文学简史 [M]. 天津：南开大学出版社，2008.

常耀信. 美国文学简史 [M]. 天津：南开大学出版社, 2008.

范存忠. 英国文学史纲 [M]. 南京：译林出版社，2015.

来安方. 新编英美概况 [M]. 郑州：河南人民出版社，2005.

童明. 美国文学史 [M]. 南京：译林出版社，2002.

王九萍, 张锦萍. 英美概况 [M]. 西安：西安交通大学出版社，2009.

王俊生, 刘沛富. 最新英美概况 [M]. 北京：外语教学与研究出版社，2012.

王守仁. 新编美国文学史 [M]. 上海：上海外语教育出版社，2019

王佐良. 英国文学史 [M]. 北京：外语教学与研究出版社，2018.

吴伟仁. 英国文学史及选读 [M]. 北京：外语教学与研究出版社, 2013.

谢福之. 英语国家概况 [M]. 北京：外语教学与研究出版社，2013.

谢世坚. 英语国家概况 [M]. 北京：中国人民大学出版社，2016.

张富生, 曹德春. 英美概况导读 [M] 郑州：河南人民出版社，2006.

https://parliament.uk

https://uk.usembassy.gov

https://www.britannica.com/

https://www.eia.gov/

https://www.history.com/

https://www.gov.uk/government/organisations/department-for-environment-food-rural-affairs

https://www.migrationpolicy.org/

http://www.mofcom.gov.cn/

https://www.gov.uk/government/how-government-works

https://www.gov.uk/government/ministers#cabinet-ministers

https://www.transportation.gov/

https://www.usa.gov

https://www.usda.gov/

www.house.gov

www.senate.gov

www.whitehouse.gov

https://tse2-mm.cn.bing.net/th/id/OIP-C.fyf31vljwfjM5id5bID2sgHaHa?rs=1&pid=ImgDetMain

https://www.margaretbrazearbooks.com/images/TudorRose.jpg

https://image.geo.de/30084716/t/wX/v3/w960/r0/-/heinrich-pop-jpg--40575-.jpg

https://www.thefamouspeople.com/profiles/images/elizabeth-i-of-england-1.jpg

https://www.meisterdrucke.uk/kunstwerke/1200w/Dutch_School_-_The_Beheading_of_King_Charles_I_(1600-49)_1649_(engraving)_(bw_photo)_-_(MeisterDrucke-36975).jpg

https://ts1.cn.mm.bing.net/th/id/R-C.d3636f40e1f1b00d4386dda9f6495568?rik=iHhA7gcQ1bJ00w&riu=http%3a%2f%2fvictorian-era.org%2fimages%2fglorious-revol.jpg&ehk=CdeKq2dyuoe6vlPEiBud3UBe%2fNP4oe%2b6FyRH4xEjqhw%3d&risl=&pid=ImgRaw&r=0

https://tse1-mm.cn.bing.net/th/id/OIP-C.OnDkR-NA_ji0I6fVMhOwWgAAAA?rs=1&pid=ImgDetMain

https://www.thefamouspeople.com/profiles/images/queen-victoria-7.jpg

https://www.parliament.uk/business/news/2024/july/parliament-returns-tuesday-9-july/

https://tse4-mm.cn.bing.net/th/id/OIP-C.flKKMRJ7DBJ217Ww-XRvYQHaEK?rs=1&pid=ImgDetMain

https://tse3-mm.cn.bing.net/th/id/OIP-C.ZPluu12-eGHia4W5DnlbMwHaE8?rs=1&pid=ImgDetMain

https://tse1-mm.cn.bing.net/th/id/OIP-C.BAvUjn6u5MTwp4eauRPPLQHaHa?rs=1&pid=ImgDetMain

https://tse1-mm.cn.bing.net/th/id/OIP-C.aQ3AbdaiULOQb5xeSENjTgHaHP?rs=1&pid=ImgDetMain

https://cdn.britannica.com/18/1918-050-0166D6BB/Martin-Luther-King-Jr.jpg

https://baike.baidu.com/pic/9%C2%B711%E4%BA%8B%E4%BB%B6/5536910/5399879011/91ef76c6a7efce1b9d16e43af409e4deb48f8d54cfb1?fr=newalbum&fromModule=album#aid=5399879011&p

ic=91ef76c6a7efce1b9d16e43af409e4deb48f8d54cfb1

https://www.laurelpetersongregory.com/blog/history-of-democratic-donkey-republican-elephant/

https://unsplash.com/photos/a-large-building-with-columns-and-steps-leading-up-to-it-0bJGEJellrs

https://unsplash.com/photos/a-view-of-a-building-from-across-the-street-uVqbETXiDqg

https://unsplash.com/photos/a-large-building-with-a-clock-tower-in-the-background-_ge2fkbfR6U

https://www.pexels.com/zh-cn/search/thanksgiving%20dinner/

https://www.thoughtco.com/emily-dickinson-4772610

https://literariness.org/2021/05/25/analysis-of-ernest-hemingways-in-another-country/

https://www.britannica.com/biography/Geoffrey-Chaucer